# WINGS TO THE WORLD

# WINGS TO THE WORLD

## The Story of Qantas 1945-1966

HUDSON FYSH

ANGUS AND ROBERTSON

*First published in 1970 by*
ANGUS & ROBERTSON LTD
221 George Street, Sydney
54 Bartholomew Close, London
107 Elizabeth Street, Melbourne
89 Anson Road, Singapore

National Library of Australia card number and
ISBN 0 207 95378 3

Registered in Australia for transmission by post as a book
PRINTED IN AUSTRALIA BY HALSTEAD PRESS, SYDNEY

# Contents

## APPENDIXES

# Illustrations

# MOST COMMONLY USED ABBREVIATIONS

| | |
|---|---|
| ANAC | Australian National Airways Commission |
| ANA<br>Ansett-ANA | } Australian National Airways Pty Ltd |
| AOA | American Overseas Airlines |
| BCAS | British Commonwealth Air Services |
| BCPA | British Commonwealth Pacific Airlines |
| BOAC | British Overseas Airways Corporation |
| CAB | Civil Aviation Board (U.S.A.) |
| CATC | Commonwealth Air Transport Council |
| IATA | International Air Transport Association |
| JAL | Japan Air Lines |
| KLM | Royal Dutch Airlines |
| Lufthansa | Lufthansa German Airlines |
| NZNAC | New Zealand National Airways Corporation |
| PAA | Pan American Airways |
| PAWA | Pan American World Airways |
| PICAO | Provisional International Civil Aviation Organization |
| Qantas | Queensland and Northern Territory Aerial Services |
| QEA | Qantas Empire Airways (since 1967 Qantas Airways) |
| SAA | South African Airways |
| SAS | Scandinavian Airlines System |
| SPATC | South Pacific Air Transport Council |
| TAA | Trans-Australia Airlines |
| TCA | Trans-Canada Airlines |
| TEAL | Tasman Empire Airways Ltd |
| TOA | Trans Oceanic Airways |
| TWA | Trans-World Airlines |

# Introduction

THIS BOOK, the third of a trilogy, *Qantas Rising, Qantas at War,* and *Wings to the World,* brings the reader to the time I was retired on 30th June 1966. The three books range over the whole life of air transport in Australia from its beginnings in 1920. They trace the rise of the original Qantas, and then Qantas Empire Airways which became one of the great international airlines of the world.

Some difference in treatment of subject matter, or rather a developed treatment, will be noted in this book. The very size of the Qantas organization now prevents my giving the close attention to personalities and their doings which I was able to give in the earlier books. I have, to some extent at least, been unable to express the warm feelings for the rank and file of staff which I would have liked to record. Also I could not write about recent events and personalities with the same freedom with which I wrote of those of earlier years. To quote details of a business deal of forty years ago is a very different matter from doing the same about one just concluded, and I have no wish to embarrass Qantas Airways. Much has had to be omitted, and the original MS. has been shortened.

Another change in treatment resulted from the passing of novelty and adventure in our business. To see a Boeing 707 fly over, or to take a trip in a jet, is now an everyday matter, though the joy of travel is still there. How different though from the adventurous propeller pulse beats of an Empire Flying Boat when, thirty years ago, it touched down on some fascinating unknown island! The old romance has departed, and we must look for new thrills in supersonic flight and, for some perhaps, a trip to the moon.

The major change I record in this book is how Qantas advanced from local State interest to Australian national interest, and thence into the international arena. It is because of this last and most important phase that I have given so much attention to the formation of international air transport controls and to the work of the International Air Transport Association, the operators' forum, which has been the instrument over twenty years that has, with the support of the nations of the world, kept international air transport, in all its intricacies, functioning, and if not always on an even keel, at least without capsizing.

Qantas is still building, still rising. Even the golden years of the first big jets will fade and be forgotten before what the future holds. It is for that future that I have endeavoured in these books to record the great formative periods of Qantas. Of the three historical eras, first came what I call the "Founders' Years", which marked the formation of the original Queensland and Northern Territory Aerial Services Limited (Qantas), the early struggles and then the successful establishment. Secondly, came the formation of Qantas Empire Airways and the commencement of overseas operations. This was followed after the last war with QEA becoming owned by the Commonwealth of Australia. Of these three events, the most critical occurred when the competitive tender of QEA was, in 1934, accepted for Australia's overseas operations.

I do not emphasize the great years of latter day expansion for these were never critical for QEA, which had become a protected, firmly established business, a Federal government instrumentality, not subject to failure, take-over or similar catastrophe. The problems of Qantas Airways Limited today might be considered to be those of maintaining wise business direction and management, and understanding government support. In the words of Sir Robert Menzies when speaking of Qantas: "Governments cannot pioneer, they take over."

In this record of history I have been aware that it must of necessity be also autobiography, and I am conscious of the problems when the two are mingled. But I may be excused if I say that I also realize the dangers of history written to order long after the principal actors in the piece have gone. I have in the narrative frequently gone out of my way to write myself down, to record weaknesses I saw in myself, and if, to balance, I have included some of the pleasant things said to myself, much has also been omitted. One thing I would ask the reader to believe is that though mistakes there must inevitably be, I have in these books made a continuous effort to state what I sincerely and searchingly feel is the truth.

During the preparation of this book, my old secretary, Miss Ida Isaacs, the acme of Qantas as it was, has looked in and helped; but my main assistant has been Miss Alwyn Tassell of Qantas Airways, a knowledgable young "old-hand" of QEA who has, indeed, done a dedicated job and to whom I am grateful. A number of Qantas Airways friends have been helpful in supplying or checking information, and Sir Donald Anderson, as always, has been most helpful.

*Sydney*
*November, 1968*                                          HUDSON FYSH

# I

*Out of the rubble of war was born international air transport—it had to be organized or chaos loomed—so the nations went to work.*

*Then the Qantas organization, battered and war-weakened, was refashioned, and rose in a memorable period for the further great things which lay ahead.*

# ✦ 1 ✦

## Rebuilding International Air Transport

THE ROLE of civil air transport in Australia and the United Kingdom during the war was to assist where possible the Allied war effort. It was a minor role when compared with those of the other Services, and, indeed, threatened with extinction at times, civil air transport had a hard struggle to survive.

Not until late 1944 and early 1945, when ultimate Allied victory was in sight, were plans made for the resumption of international air transport services after the war. On 2nd August 1944, after an important visit to Melbourne, I summed up the Australian situation:

> The general picture one got was of weak direction, monkeying and dithering about without any conception of what the word *Civil Aviation* is going to mean to this country in the next 25 years, and how necessary is the formation of a strong foundation.
>
> The Civil Aviation Department is starved, underpaid, and generally holds a low status, and it is impossible to pitchfork a man of McVey's calibre into it without something of a clean up at the same time.

In this comment I foreshadowed the appointment of Dan McVey (later Sir Daniel) as Director General of Civil Aviation, and the creative work he shared in the reconstruction of Australia's civil aviation and in ensuring Australia's place in world aviation.

In London, the Air Ministry whose instrument was BOAC, also existed in a weakened position. Little else could be expected while the Doodlebugs and V2s were still falling on London. But there was much truth in the savage satire of the time entitled "Alice on board H.M.S. Air Ministry". The satirist told of the Director of Public Relations whose function was to prevent people from learning anything of the work of the Ministry, of the Director of Plans whose work was so secret that no one was allowed to know anything about it.

> "And who are those?" said Alice, pointing to the Walrus guard of honour. "Oh, those are the Directors of Organization," replied the Mock Turtle. "I suppose they organize everything that goes on?" "Well," said the Mock Turtle, "as a matter of fact they are so busy organizing and reorganizing themselves that they have very little time to organize anything else."
>
> There were the Directors of Policy, chameleons whose colour changed every ten seconds and their tune every twenty-five seconds, the imposing

but unintelligent Directors of Intelligence, peacocks sitting on deck-chairs with their feet on the after-rail, the secretary-birds, each looking over the shoulder of the one in front and writing busily on slates.

"What are they writing?" asked Alice. The Mock Turtle, looking rather proud, said, "They are re-drafting the notes written by the ones in front of them."

There was the Finance Branch, a group of ostriches, their heads buried in buckets of sand, whose duty was to see that no one spent any money.

"Where are the people who do all the work?" asked Alice. As they descended the nearest companion to the lower deck, there came into view a great crowd of ants and red-tapeworms, engaged in taking files off an endless travelling belt and putting them on again.

Alice, once again on the bridge, gazed at the clouds of battling aircraft receding farther and farther towards the horizon. "What an extraordinary ship," she said to herself.

Early in 1944, on 19th February, at a time when eventual victory could be foreseen and preparation to deal with the coming peace was urgently needed, I prepared a 7,000 word paper entitled "Post War Overseas Air Transport as affecting Australia." The concluding paragraph of this read:

> The history of mankind is written in communications from the day some savage gleefully invented the first wheel, and sent up the first smoke signal, and now it seems that in our times and the near future, we are destined to see the effect on the peoples of the world, and their affairs, of the crescendo development of air transport which will throw us together in a way that challenges our civilization to cope with the new conditions so imposed. The secret of success lies only in increased co-operation.

It was then ten years since Australia was first connected with the outside world by Qantas Empire Airways which began to operate out of Brisbane, Queensland, with DH86 aircraft. This service operated successfully for four years until, in 1938, the Empire Flying Boat Service commenced. It ran for only one year before World War II broke out. Then for seven years Australia's civil air connections ceased with other countries. The flying boats had hardly a fair trial. At the beginning of the war, neither they nor the land planes possessed the range and payload to fly economically the world's great oceans. The time had not arrived for round-the-world services which were first developed by the Lockheed Constellation and DC6 aircraft. During the war the U.S.A. was able to operate these long range transport types, but England was forced to concentrate on fighters and bombers. The U.S.A., while building up vast military overseas transport services, continued to operate domestic services on a peacetime basis, so that by the end of 1944 the country had the aircraft available for world-wide civil transport services.

4

From this position of advantage the United States called the International Civil Aviation Conference which met at Chicago from the 1st November 1944 until the 7th December, and was attended by fifty-four nations, Russia being the only absentee among the Allies. In the pioneering days of civil aviation it was the private operator who had been the dominant force in development. The government's status in Australia, and the knowledge of its ministers of the fundamentals of the business, were not impressive. But at Chicago the operators were content to remain in the background, suggest what they could, and anxiously await the outcome. The Australian overseas operator took no part in the long and historical marathon, though BOAC, Pan American Airways and KLM were well represented by advisers, and BOAC, as our partner, held a watching brief for QEA.

Australia was represented at the Conference by Arthur S. Drakeford, Minister for Air and Civil Aviation and Chairman of the Delegation, Daniel McVey, Director-General of Civil Aviation, Lieutenant-Colonel W. R. Hodgson, Secretary, Department of External Affairs, and Captain E. C. Johnston, Assistant Director-General of Civil Aviation and a practical airman.

At this time Labour was in office in Australia and New Zealand and nationalization was a prominent feature of Labour policy both here and in Great Britain where Labour took office in 1945. Before Arthur Drakeford left Australia for Chicago, Cabinet declared its policy to be the "International Ownership and Operation of International Airlines". The Australian and New Zealand delegations, with the support of the U.K. Labour Party, were saddled at the Conference with what may be described as a utopian but impractical policy. The phrasing is as follows:

> Believing that the unregulated development of air transport can only lead to misunderstanding and rivalries between Nations,
> Being convinced that air transport can and should be utilised as a powerful instrument in the cause of international security and in the attainment of "Freedom from Fear" as embodied in the Atlantic Charter,
> Believing that the interests of all Nations, both large and small, can best be advanced by the joint utilisation of the material, technical and operational resources of all countries for the development of air transport,
> Believing that the creation of an effective economic and non-discriminatory instrument responsible for the ownership and operation of air transport services between Nations of the world is in the best interests of orderly world progress,
> AGREE that these objectives can best be achieved by the establishment of an international air transport authority which would be responsible for the operation of air services on prescribed international trunk routes and which would own the aircraft and ancillary equipment employed on these

5

B

routes; it being understood that each Nation would retain the right to conduct all air services within its own national jurisdiction, including its own contiguous territories subject only to agreed international requirements regarding landing and transit rights, safety facilities, etc. to which end it is desirable that this Committee of the Conference should consider the organisation and machinery necessary for the implementation of this resolution.

Australia and New Zealand submitted these ideas in a motion but were unable to support them with practical reasoning. Under the adroit handling of Lord Swinton, leader of the United Kingdom delegation, the motion was allowed to lapse. In this Dan McVey assuredly played an important part. My own comment at the time on the policy of the Australian Government was to quote Earl Grey, "What is wanted in politics is an idealist who can estimate rightly the limits of what is possible in his generation." To the Royal Aeronautical Association on the 13th November 1945 I promised, "We shall play our part in attempting to secure ordered international co-operation and peace in the air *by our membership of PICAO and IATA.*"

There was sharp conflict at Chicago when PICAO (Provisional International Civil Aviation Organization) was formed, with the U.S.A. and the U.K. as the chief opponents. However, after days of debate and drafting, the Conference agreed on the famous Freedoms of the Air which formed the basis for the conduct of international air transport in the years ahead and which stand as a monument to the work of the Conference. The five Freedoms are:

> *First*—The right of the aircraft of one State to fly across the territory of another State without landing.
>
> *Second*—The right of an aircraft of one State to land in the territory of another State for non-traffic purposes (e.g., refuelling, maintenance).
>
> *Third*—The right of an aircraft of one State to set down in the territory of another State *traffic* (passengers, cargo and mail) which originated in the country of nationality of the aircraft.
>
> *Fourth*—The right of an aircraft of one State to pick up in the territory of another State *traffic* (passengers, cargo and mail) destined for the country of nationality of the aircraft.
>
> *Fifth*—The right of an aircraft of one State to pick up and set down in the territory of another State *traffic* (passengers, cargo and mail) which neither originates in or is destined for the country of nationality of the aircraft.

This Charter of the Air, however, did not resolve the problems of competition, free or otherwise, rates and conditions of carriage. The English and American concepts caused a head-on collision of opposing views. While the Americans stood for unrestricted free competition for world traffic, the British demanded a degree of international control. The conflict remained unsolved during 1945 and it was not until January 1946 that a fresh and successful attempt was made at Bermuda, where a meeting took place between the two governmental departments actually concerned with the regulation of air traffic.

> The effective, if empiric compromise reached at Bermuda delegated the determination of equitable rates to the Traffic Conference of IATA (International Air Transport Association) with the stipulation that they could not become effective until both governments had approved them—if necessary, after review of the economic data on which the rates were based. By this means, both governments obtained what they desired: control great enough to assure that, on the one hand, rates would not become involved in cut-throat competition and, on the other, that they could be kept as low as possible in the interests of the travelling public.
>
> *IATA, the First Three Decades.*

Among the delegates at Chicago were men who were later responsible for the successful conduct of the new world set-up of civil aviation and air transport. Edward Warner from the U.S.A. Aeronautics Board, an efficient, practical man beloved by all who knew him, became Secretary-General of the International Civil Aviation Organization (ICAO). W. P. Hildred (later Sir William), Director-General of Civil Aviation at the Air Ministry in London, became Director-General of International Air Transport Association and steered this often contentious and difficult organization to success. He was aided by his impartial outlook on world affairs and the gracious support of his wife at IATA gatherings. John C. Cooper, a vice president of Pan American Airways, carried out invaluable work on the legal side. Our own Dan McVey was in these early years a wise counsellor and our leading official representative. Many others helped.

After the conference at Chicago there was on 7th December a meeting of operators to consider and draft articles of association for the world-wide organization. H. J. Symington, chairman of Trans-Canada Airlines, was in the chair and became first president of the International Air Transport Association (IATA). At Havana, in April 1945, the representatives of airlines covering thirty-one nations met, and the present articles of association were enacted. The first executive committee was appointed, the members being:

Major J. R. McCrindle of BOAC, Dr J. Bento Ribeiro Dantas of Servicos Aereos Cruzeiro Do Sul, Per A. Norlin of Swedish Intercontinental Airlines, Rene Briend of Air France, J. C. Cooper of Pan American Airways, John Slater of American Overseas Airlines, A. F. T. Cambridge of Indian National Airlines, Albert Plesman of KLM and Hudson Fysh of Qantas Empire Airways.

At the first annual general meeting of IATA at Montreal in October 1945 there were added to the committee: Dr Hassan Sadek Pasha of Misr, T. B. Wilson of TWA and T. H. Shen of China National Aviation Corporation. John C. Cooper was named first chairman of the executive committee and acting director general until a permanent director general could be appointed.

The Chicago conference had taken place a few months before Germany capitulated, and the meeting at Bermuda a few months after the Japanese surrender. The year 1946 saw international air transport all set to spread its peacetime wings over the world. No country was more likely to benefit than Australia because of her geographical position, her distance from the world's great centres of culture and business. As always, out of the ashes of the past had sprung some new and wondrous instrument for the use of mankind.

At the two gatherings, Chicago and Bermuda, were laid the foundations for future international civil aviation and air transport. The unique capability of the U.S.A. to have swept all before it as the only nation to benefit from the war had been reasonably limited. The United Kingdom, in a war-weakened position, was handicapped by the lack of up-to-date civil air transport aircraft. In addition, there was no agreement between the home country and the self-governing Dominions in the contemplated operation of trunk world routes.

For Australia, there followed a period of six and a half difficult years of evolutionary growth. A sound workable pattern was only resolved when QEA began to operate from Sydney to London in December 1947 and took over the trans-South Pacific Service from Sydney to San Francisco and Vancouver in May 1954.

At the end of 1944 when I was in London to confer with Lord Knollys and Brigadier General A. C. Critchley, the chairman, and chief executive of BOAC respectively, to see what could be done in helping to frame the future, I noted in my diary:

> Formation of Empire Post War operation now being planned, and groping for a suitable British aeroplane. Saw Bruce who greatly in favour of all in together operation and not old Sectional operation. Knollys and Critchley also in favour.

This was United Kingdom policy at the time of the Chicago Conference and on into 1945. There was a great deal of sounding out between the U.K., Canada, Australia, New Zealand, and also with India and South Africa. The Commonwealth countries conferred at Montreal and again in London and in these conferences Dan McVey, the Australian Director-General, played an important part.

Then on 26th February 1945 the Australian Labour Cabinet approved a policy which foreshadowed the post-war set-up of Australian participation in international air transport. It was very close to a complete reversal of the policy with which the Australian delegation had gone to Chicago:

   (i) That Australia should have a representative on the Commonwealth Air Transport Council (CATC).

  (ii) That for the United Kingdom-Australia air service via India, the Australian Government will stand firm in the decision taken that the service shall not be operated by a joint operating Corporation representing the United Kingdom, India, Australia and New Zealand, but should be on the basis of parallel operation by selected U.K. and Australian operators, each operating through services between U.K. and Australia.

     On this basis the route would be operated by fully reciprocated services, with mutual assistance through the joint use of ground facilities for handling aircraft and passengers and with the pooling of revenue and resources, thus avoiding unnecessary duplication.

 (iii) That the Australian Government will join with the New Zealand and United Kingdom Governments in the formation of a joint operating organisation to operate services across the Pacific, such services being in parallel partnership with services operated by a Canadian organisation with provision for pooling of resources, sharing of revenue etc. as in the case of the Australia-United Kingdom Service.

  (iv) That the standard clauses on the lines of those agreed at the Commonwealth discussions should be adopted for in any bilateral agreements negotiated by Australia.

Efforts were continued for a closer interest in combined Commonwealth operations, Dan McVey and others suggesting that an ideal solution might be for an Empire unit to operate an express mail and passenger service, leaving the Commonwealth units to run their slower and more comfortable passenger services. Discussions were continued at the Commonwealth Air Transport Council meeting held in London in July, 1945 which was chaired by Lord Swinton. The Australian delegation was led by McVey, and I attended as an adviser. There was not much real progress, however, for Canada threw a bombshell into the proceedings by declining to join the other Commonwealth partners in the operation of pooled air services.

    This means that when the time comes, after the Japanese war, for Australia, New Zealand and Britain to operate, on a share and share alike basis, a trans-Pacific air service between Australia and Canada, via New Zealand and Fiji, Canada will reserve the right to operate her own national air service to Australia and New Zealand.

    Canada's decision to take an independent line was not disclosed in an

9

official statement summing up the conclusions of the conference, supplied to the press by the Ministry of Civil Aviation.

*Sydney Morning Herald*, 18th July 1945.

The Canadian attitude finally sealed the fate of the formation of a Commonwealth operator on the world's aerial highways. It was at this conference that Dan McVey also shocked some of his listeners when he spoke of Australian and QEA aspirations, asserting that the day would come when Australia operated her own service all the way to London. In December 1947 our new Constellation aircraft operated right through, but happily in pool with BOAC.

The meeting of the Commonwealth Air Transport Council was followed by one of a committee of operators, but this proved of little value because there were at the time no definite policy decisions. The period was rather one when policies were being thrashed out. After the London discussions I attended the first executive committee meeting of IATA, in Paris, which opened on 30th July 1945 with John C. Cooper in the chair. The most important decision was the appointment of a director general. A number of names having been mentioned, the acceptable possibilities were narrowed down to Sir Frederick Tymms, Director of Civil Aviation in India, and W. P. Hildred, Director of Civil Aviation at the Air Ministry. A sub-committee, consisting of John C. Cooper, J. R. McCrindle, John Slater and myself, was appointed to interview the two men and make a final recommendation, with the result that W. P. Hildred accepted the position.

Earlier it had been decided that the headquarters of IATA should be at Montreal where ICAO had its centre. The result was an association of great importance of the two heads, Edward Warner and W. P. Hildred. The executive committee transacted at this Paris meeting a good deal of important business including the formation of key committees to cover financial, legal, technical and traffic problems, and the setting up of a skeleton organization. At that time there were forty-two airline members of IATA and eighteen associates.

The Bermuda Agreement six months later, followed quickly by a series of sixty similar agreements, authorized the official inclusion of rate matters in terms of reference of the IATA Conferences.

> This provision for government review did even more; it created definite responsibilities to governments and, by the same token, removed the Conferences from the absolute control of the General Meeting which had been a feature of the old IATA. *IATA, the First Three Decades.*

Thirteen days after the close of our Paris Executive Committee meeting, on 15th August 1945, Japan capitulated; but already a splendid start had been made in preparation for peacetime international air transport.

## ⟫ 2 ⟪

## *Post War Problems—a Scratchy Start*

s 1944 drew to a close I was busy in London having daily interviews
with people such as Arthur Drakeford, Sir Frederick Tymms,
D.C.A. for India, Air Marshal Richard Williams (later Sir Rich-
ard), Brigadier Falla, chairman of Tasman Empire Airways, Essington
Lewis the B.H.P. head, Sir Keith Smith, Lord Swinton and William
Hildred and especially with Lord Knollys and Brigadier Critchley, the
BOAC heads.

I spent Christmas at the Critchleys' Sunningdale home where I met
Lord Ashgrove, head of the London Transport Authority and Lord
Brabazon of Brabazon Committee fame. I played golf with "Critch" and
his wife, the former Diana Fishwick, one-time lady champion of England.
The bitter white frost that blanketed the whole course caused me to
remark that a red ball would be easier to find than a white one!

The New Year was ushered in with Jerry Shaw, the pioneer cross-
Channel commercial pilot. We dined at the Cafe Royal, and then at
midnight sallied forth to Piccadilly Circus to see the fun. As was their
wont, the Scotsmen went into action. When Big Ben struck, its booming
notes coming over the frosty air to proclaim midnight and the New
Year, we were standing on the Piccadilly Circus pavement. Scots revellers
roared by in cars festooned with shouting hangers-on, and there we saw
an incident I have never forgotten.

An elegant top-hatted gentlemen, escorting a lady in dazzling white
furs, was standing alongside us when one of the elderly flower girls, a
feature of the Circus in those days, ran across from her bleak stand and,
as the last notes of midnight rang out, confronted the toff and, shoving
her hand out, shouted, "Shake 'ands, Guv'nor. It's New Year. Shake
'ands." The elegant gentleman, disdaining the poor creature, took not a
blink of notice. Then, as the flower girl repeated her invitation, he slowly
turned his back on her. Then shouted the flower girl, "Yer won't, won't
yer? Well—take that, you old bastard!" And she up and booted him hard
in the bottom.

The year 1945 was a busy one for me. I was three times in England
and twice in North America, somewhat of a record for civilian air travel
in those war days when air travel priorities were hard to come by, and an

11

aeroplane flew less than half as fast and was only a fraction as comfortable as one is today.

On 7th January I had my fiftieth birthday, playing billiards with Keith Smith at the R.A.F. Club. Next day I left Euston Station for Prestwick where I was to take off for Montreal on my return journey. On the 17th January I was at Burbank in California where I first flew in an early Lockheed Constellation then going through its initial trials. It was piloted by test pilot Wagner and a special permit was necessary from the military authorities. We all wore parachutes, though if anything had gone wrong, how we would have got out of the aeroplane in mid-air I do not know. Greatly impressed, I wrote in my diary: "Extraordinarily good aeroplane".

An amusing incident, indicative of the mishaps attached to wartime travel, occurred in the early morning of the same day that I made the momentous flight in the Constellation. I had arrived at the Beverly Hills Hotel at 5 a.m. after flying all night from Chicago with TWA. Roger Lewis, the Lockheed representative, had brought me in from the airport, but at this hour not a single bed at the hotel was vacant. Roger was not to be defeated and it was arranged that for the time being I should have the head chef's room, as he was away on leave. Hardly had I fallen into an exhausted sleep in the chef's comfortable bed when someone opened the door and there stood the chef, having unexpectedly returned from his leave. He took my intrusion in good part and on numerous visits to this famous hostelry I had many a laugh with him about the incident.

By the middle of the year I was back again in London to attend Commonwealth Air Transport meetings in what might be termed a frustrating period of attempts to secure decisions. I was supported by our accountant, C. O. Turner, and by G. U. Allan who was stationed in London as our technical expert, and later manager. Back in Sydney, George Harman carried on excellently as acting general manager. Sir Fergus McMaster was chairman of the board but in very ill health, and A. E. Rudder as vice chairman acted a great deal for him.

On 10th July 1945 I wrote to George Harman from London: .

> QEA is quite definitely becoming an international organization and must play its part in line with similar organizations. I have had it impressed on me on this visit that QEA is:—
>
>  (a) Strong in actual practical operation
>  (b) Weak technically
>  (c) Weak from a public relations, contact, Conference attending point of view.
>
> This must be mended.

12

We were struggling to form a new post-war Qantas. I went on to write:

> I hope the Bridge Street purchase is being gone on with. If this property is not bought we are faced with hiring floor space at high costs.

We were then struggling in Shell House to meet the rapid expansion of staff and improved facilities. The purchase was gone on with and the small three-storey Bridge Street building was acquired from our friends, Burns Philp, for £A25,253. A modest new office area of 12,800 square feet was put to good use. In 1957 this building was sold to Wilhelmsen Agency for £A115,000, the first of a long line of profitable deals. The last of these, in 1966, gave Qantas control of virtually a whole city block, dominated by the old Wentworth Hotel site.

I made, for those days, a wonderfully fast trip back from Hurn to Sydney by Lancastrian mail plane, a converted bomber. It was not well converted for passenger use, and I noted in my diary:

> Exasperating indeed to pass on a beautiful evening so close to Marseilles, which lay on our windowless blind side.
> This aeroplane will be a standing reproach to those concerned till it has—
> (a) Windows on the port side
> (b) A rack for clothes and light handbags and hats.
> The tragedy is that the job could be done by a local tinsmith and carpenter in a day, given a few simple materials.

This might be thought unfair comment, in view of England's magnificent, undivided war effort, but about this time C. G. Grey, the famous editor of *Aeroplane and Aviation* had written to me:

> When you have time to write, do tell me who is responsible for that absurd sideways seating in the Lancastrian. I asked Avros about it and they said that BOAC insisted on it. Then I asked BOAC and they swear they had nothing to do with it and that it must have been a freak of MAP's.
> Anyhow, the picture of nine V.I.P.s sitting solemly in a row, as if on a bench in the House of Commons, all staring out of one side of the machine and not able to see anything on the other side, is ludicrous.
> The poor wretched steward's pantry is a crime against humanity. Even if you select your stewards for their littleness, you could have difficulty in getting them small enough to squeeze between the refrigerator and the electric cooker so as to get into the crew's quarters. I know the Lancastrian is only a makeshift and a stopgap, but it need not be a laughing-stock.

Of course, the explanation was that the wartime Ministry of Aircraft Production was still in absolute control; and priorities, with the desperate shortage of materials, still ran high. The real tragedy was that, nearly two years later, in February 1947, when ANA commenced its South Pacific Service between Sydney and Vancouver with DC4 aircraft, all that

British aircraft interests had been able to offer had been the Lancastrian. It was, of course, not for want of trying that the British aircraft industry was in no condition to compete with the U.S.A. as the war ended. The British were finding it difficult to make up the lee-way lost, but as the obsolescence period of air transport aircraft was still extraordinarily short, to be one or two years behind a rival was fatal.

In 1942 the Brabazon Committee had been set up in London under the chairmanship of Lord Brabazon and functioned for some years, taking evidence from manufacturers and operators, deciding on new types to be built, and then making recommendations to the Air Ministry for final decision. The new types gone on with under this scheme met with varying success, the huge Brabazon, the Saro Princess and the Tudor being flops, while the Vickers Viscount, designed by Sir George Edwards and commenced in 1945, went on to a clear world leadership in the medium range, medium payload class, as the world's first successful turbo-prop aircraft. The Viscount was the Class IIB Specification of the Brabazon Committee. It was powered with four Rolls Royce Dart turbo-prop engines, and later models carried some sixty-five passengers at 360 m.p.h., a very good aeroplane of its day.

England had at this time Frank Whittle (later Sir Frank), the brilliant young Royal Aircraft Factory engineer who before the war had been working on his straight jet engine, and who in 1942 produced the B26 and then the Goblin, which later went into service. This was all far ahead of work being done in the United States on the jet engine, and Whittle's work proved to be of great benefit to engine manufacturers in that country because, as the result of the wartime agreement between the U.K. and the U.S.A., not only Whittle's designs but his engines went across the Atlantic.

The De Havilland Comet was Type IV of the Brabazon Committee, and work was commenced on this revolutionary plane in 1944, a tremendous amount of study and design work by the De Havilland team going into this great imaginative project before the prototype was first successfully flown on 27th January 1949, the world's first civil jet transport, and powered by De Havilland's own engine, the Ghost. History records how nearly this type swept the world. But it was the first, the pioneer, and met with much tragedy till the later Comets made their appearance. By this time the U.S.A. had caught up and were on the point of turning out their Boeing 707s and DC8s, being greatly assisted by the experience gained in the Comet.

The Comet 1 was deficient in range for intercontinental operation, but succeeding models repaired this deficiency and carried some sixty passengers at 500 m.p.h. cruising at 40,000 feet.

It was not long before I left Sydney again, this time on 26th September 1945, accompanied by my wife and Bill Nielson, one of our senior traffic men. We left Mascot aerodrome for San Diego, California, by R.A.F. Transport Command Liberator under the command of Flight Lieutenant Donaldson. I had a struggle to obtain a travel priority for my wife but it was high time that the long years of my wifeless overseas trips were broken. She was the only woman passenger and got a thrill out of it, visiting the captain in his cockpit at midnight away up over the wide and lonely Pacific. She admitted to a shock when he said that it was his first trip across in command!

At Montreal, we attended the first annual general meeting of IATA under the presidency of H. J. Symington. There interesting and important plans for future conduct of the world's international airways were proposed. The new articles of IATA were accepted, the new leading statute in the aims and objectives stating:

> To promote safe, regular and economical air-transport for the benefit of the people of the world, to foster air commerce, and to study the problems connected therewith.
> To provide means for collaboration among the air-transport enterprises engaged directly or indirectly in international air-transport service.
> To co-operate with the International Civil Aviation Organisation and other international organisations.

Not empty words. Through the years ahead IATA was to prove itself an international body which, for once, really worked. A few years later, in *IATA and Friendship*, I was to write:

> The greatest and most important function of IATA is the opportunity which the Association gives for friendship, understanding, and resolving of differences between 66 airlines representing 35 different nations. . . .
> It is up to us to see that we make it work and set an example to other societies of nations, because the members of IATA who carry on the work of the pioneer inventors and developers of the aeroplane bear a big responsibility for this shrunken world of today.

Through IATA the opportunities for understanding and friendship amongst the world's airways' fraternity were outstanding and significant. They resulted from the policy set by the Director-General, Sir William Hildred and Lady Hildred, and the early great presidents of the organization. The executive committee met twice a year and the annual general meeting took place once a year in widespread places of the world. The tradition was that wives should attend, the host airline providing entertainment. The presence of the women was what I was to refer to as "one of the great intangibles of IATA". Lady Hildred was a leader in the friendly association, and my own wife during the twenty years of meetings, from Montreal to Sydney and finally in Vienna in 1965, made her valuable contribution to international friendship.

At meeting after meeting I was to see airline representatives arrive "with a chip on their shoulders" about some real or imaginary injustice, only to leave at the end of the meeting with understanding and friendship, if not always with that full satisfaction which is rarely secured by any one of us. A vote on a contentious subject was rarely taken at the annual general meeting of IATA. It would be left to the traffic conferences. It was a complicated and perhaps subtle machinery, but it worked, and was undoubtedly well oiled by the presence of the ladies of IATA at the annual gathering.

Another highlight of my third overseas journey in 1945 was when I delivered before the Royal Aeronautical Society the inaugural British Commonwealth and Empire Lecture which I entitled "Australia in Empire Air Transport". Then there was the agreement with BOAC and the Air Ministry for the operation of a provisional BOAC/QEA partnership and for post-war services on the Kangaroo Route with Lancastrian and Hythe flying boats until more up-to-date aircraft were available. The QEA job was then to get our Civil Aviation and government authorities to agree. They were somewhat reluctant because of unavoidable economic deficiencies in the temporary plan.

On my way home to Australia, at the Galle Face Hotel in Colombo, while waiting for a Lancastrian connection, I wrote my "Report to the Chairman of Directors of Qantas Empire Airways on activities in London between 5/11/45 and 12/12/45". This was followed up in Sydney by my "Recommendation to the Board of Qantas Empire Airways, reference the order of aircraft for the Empire Route in which we are interested". My recommendations were accepted in a QEA board meeting in Brisbane on 27th December 1945, when it was decided to approach the Australian Government recommending the order of Constellation aircraft. This was one of the most momentous decisions in the history of QEA.

We had discarded the much hoped-for Tudor II, then in the final prototype construction stage, as uncompetitive, already obsolete, and uncertain in performance. This decision came as a shock to the Australian authorities for the Department of Aircraft Production at Fishermen's Bend was at this time building the Tudor II. The financial loss must have been high.

When hostilities ceased with Japan, or soon after, a through Mascot-

16

Hurn Lancastrian service was operating to a twice-weekly frequency by BOAC and QEA, we being responsible for the Mascot-Karachi section which flew via Learmonth to Western Australia and across the Indian Ocean. The through schedule was a fast one of 67 hours against the old flying boat time of 8½ days. We also operated Liberator aircraft twice weekly between Perth and Colombo, a Brisbane-Manila service with DC3 aircraft under charter to No. 322 Troop charter wing. This opened in November. There was a three times weekly Mascot-Lae service with DC3 aircraft as we had taken over the old Carpenter's contract. Flying boat charters were conducted as required to such places as Singapore, Noumea and Fiji.

In Australia we continued to operate our old route from Brisbane to Darwin and Cloncurry to Normanton with DC3 aircraft, and Flying Doctor Service flights from Cloncurry and Charleville with D.H. Dragon aircraft.

Negotiations had been proceeding for some time between the Australian and U.K. Governments, and between BOAC and QEA to restore the old England-Australia partnership route to a proper post-war basis. This entailed a swing back from the Indian Ocean route to via Singapore.

Following an inter-governmental agreement, QEA signed an agreement with the Australian government, which provided for pooled aircraft between BOAC and QEA. We were to operate the Lancastrian aircraft from Mascot to Karachi, and Hythe flying boats between Rose Bay and Singapore. The agreement was to remain in force for twelve months from 12th May 1946 and was described as Phase I. Phase II was described as a later stage when aircraft of a more modern type would be introduced. The inter-governmental agreement provided for sharing the cost of the two new services, the Australian share being estimated at £A712,812 per annum.

This financial arrangement, as far as we were concerned, was one of cost plus, profit being assessed by a rather complicated formula which ensured a modest return for the work undertaken. It was not a very satisfactory arrangement for either side but necessary for what was a short transition stage from war to peace conditions.

When the Japanese air blockade had been broken, our unique wartime trans-Indian Ocean service had been conducted with conspicuous freedom from accident, but on one of the last flights before the swingover to our pre-war route through Singapore we had the misfortune to lose a Lancastrian aircraft.

Captain Frank Thomas, one of our most able commanders, when flying from Ratmalana in Ceylon to a scheduled stop at Cocos, reported

17

his position when 690 miles north-west of Cocos Island. He was having a normal night crossing but, with showery weather, reported at Cocos Island. Then there was silence. Not a sign of the aircraft was ever seen. There is not a conclusive theory as to what caused its loss except that it was the result of lightning coupled with a fuel leak. These converted wartime aircraft often smelt strongly of petrol fumes in their after-section. In all, a total of 13 aircraft flew 437 hours covering 72,105 miles in an elaborate search, but without result.

The loss of Frank Thomas was greatly mourned, as was that of his crew, First Officer N. M. McClelland, Navigation Officer A. A. Nuske, Radio Officer W. D. McBean and Flight Steward C. A. Porteous.

By one of those quirks of fate, one of the five passengers was J. Dobson, son of Sir Roy Dobson, head of the Avro Company who built the aeroplane. We felt quite upset about it all.

In the switch-back to our old route via Singapore, until the Hythe flying boats took up on 16th May 1946, we operated between Singapore and Mascot twice weekly with Liberator aircraft. The first service left Mascot on 7th April 1946 under the command of Captain J. A. R. Furze, Captain J. G. Moxham taking over from him at Darwin. On the first eastbound trip, our Liberator was commanded by Captain J. N. Murray out of Singapore, and from Darwin to Mascot by Captain R. J. Ritchie.

The three-times weekly service operated by Lancastrian aircraft between Sydney and London commenced from Mascot on 9th April, Captains J. W. Solly, G. P. Hoskins and E. R. Nicholl flying their sections to Karachi, where the aircraft was handed over to a BOAC crew.

When the Hythes came on, Sydney and London were connected by an express Lancastrian service in 67 hours, and a slower but more luxurious flying boat service taking 5½ days. The Hythe flying boat, manufactured by Short Bros. of Rochester, was, in fact, a much improved Empire flying boat such as we used pre-war. The new boat was more powerful, had a greater range, and carried a greater payload consisting of 22 passengers and 4,000 lb. of mail and freight over economical 1,000 mile stages, cruising at 175 m.p.h. The old spacious promenade deck, a feature of the Empire boat, had been retained, and there was sleeping berth accommodation for sixteen passengers as the aircraft flew day and night over the long run from Sydney to London.

This, then, was the make-up of our provisional post-war services: a good "scratch" emergency operation, costly, but re-establishing a reasonable mail, passenger and freight service for the public. However, the employment of new, up-to-date aircraft now available in the U.S.A. and unavailable from other sources had become an urgent issue.

18

## BCPA and TAA Enter the Picture

THE FIRST shot in the Australian airlines struggle for survival and power came in 1945 with the passing of the Australian National Airlines Bill. This was directed at securing a Commonwealth Government monopoly of all Australian domestic services. It was primarily directed against Australian National Airways Pty Ltd. Since 1936 the policy of the company under the direction of Ivan Holyman (later Sir Ivan) had been, with financial assistance from various shipping companies, to absorb other airlines in order to obtain new routes. We were also involved because the legislation involved loss of our traditional Queensland inland services, by now of secondary importance to us, but with a sentimental significance.

ANA reacted to what virtually meant its elimination by challenging the Act in the High Court which, in December 1945, declared parts invalid. The Chief Justice, Sir John Latham, gave as the Court's unanimous judgment that the Act was valid "except insofar as it would prevent the issue of airline licences to anyone except the Australian National Airlines Commission for an interstate service between the same stopping places as a service of the Commission, or would bring to an end existing airline licences of that kind." To that extent the Court decided that provisions of the Act were invalid.

The Federal Government continued to hamper the operations of ANA and its several associates. Among these were intra-State operators still under the jurisdiction of their State governments, though it was the Commonwealth which issued the licences, provided the aerodromes and facilities and exercised general control.

In February 1946, A. W. Coles, M.H.R. (later Sir Arthur), one of the Independents who had put the Liberal Government out of office in 1941, was appointed chairman of the new Australian National Airlines Commission, and W. C. Taylor, a personal friend of the Prime Minister, Ben Chifley, was appointed vice chairman. It was a hectic day in the House of Representatives when the appointments were announced, but Coles and his fellow commissioners proceeded with vigour to prepare for operations which commenced on 9th September 1946. During this interesting period Dan McVey, as Director-General of Civil Aviation, implemented the Chifley Government's policy.

One morning at our old Shell House offices my telephone rang with Arthur Coles at the other end asking if I could recommend Lester Brain for the position of general manager of Trans-Australia Airlines (TAA), the trading name of the Australian National Airlines Commission. While expressing great regret that we should lose such an important executive officer, I could only say that I knew of no more highly qualified man. For over twenty years Lester Brain had served Qantas and QEA from the pioneer days. He was keen, expert on all operational and kindred matters, and, above all, he was loyal to the organization and everyone in it. He was good with staff and understanding.

So, with our good wishes, we lost a man who had played a large part in earning for QEA a high reputation in the things that matter and which achieve lasting success. As general manager he began work on 3rd June 1946, the Australian National Airlines Commission's first employee. With him went John Borthwick as his personal assistant, and Doug Laurie on the traffic side. Three months later TAA's first flight was made on a DC3 between Melbourne and Sydney. Lester Brain's new salary of £3,000 per annum was in those days a handsome sum and was well above our Qantas levels.

The next big event in these formative years was of vital interest to QEA. In Montreal in 1944, the operation of a joint British Commonwealth Air Service across the Pacific was discussed. The proposal was brought to a head at a conference which opened at Wellington, New Zealand, on 28th February 1946. Among the imposing array of civil aviation dignitaries, Australia was represented by Arthur Drakeford and Dan McVey; the United Kingdom by Lord Winster, Minister for Civil Aviation, and George Cribbett (later Sir George), the Director-General; and New Zealand by Frederick Jones, Minister for Air, and T. A. Barrow, head of his department. Lord Knollys was also present as an adviser, and on the sidelines were Sir Leonard Isitt of Tasman Empire Airways (TEAL) with A. E. Rudder and I representing QEA. Canada was not represented, and reserved the right to operate a parallel service.

The central figures at this conference were Dan McVey and George Cribbett, both fine tacticians and drafters of motions. The result of the conference was the formation of British Commonwealth Pacific Airlines (BCPA) to operate from headquarters in Sydney an airline across the South Pacific to San Francisco and Vancouver. The new company was registered in New South Wales on 24th June 1946. Capital was £A4,000,000 of which 50% was held by Australia, 30% by New Zealand

The new board meets at Shell House early in 1947. *Standing, left to right*—Daniel McVey, director, Sir Keith Smith, director, R. E. Fulford, secretary. *Sitting, left to right*—W. C. Taylor, vice chairman, Hudson Fysh, chairman and managing director, C. P. N. Watt, director, H. H. Harman, general manager (*Photo*: QEA)

QEA Lancastrian at Iwakuni in the Japanese winter (*Photo*: QEA)

Lancastrian training accident at Dubbo, N.S.W. Total destruction by fire (*Photo*: QEA)

and 20% by the United Kingdom. Arthur Coles was appointed chairman, Sir Leonard Isitt a director, and Sir Keith Smith represented Lord Knollys in the U.K. interests. At the same time the shareholdings in TEAL were rearranged to conform with that of BCPA.

The new Commission was responsible to the South Pacific Air Transport Council (SPATC) and later to the BCPA Policy Committee representing the three countries concerned. By reason of the policy effect of the 50% United Kingdom holding in QEA and our resultant lack of modern aircraft, we temporarily lost out in our ambitions to operate or share in the coming operation across the South Pacific Ocean. QEA, which should have operated under charter to BCPA, was weak; for all we had to offer were Lancastrians. The new BCPA had no aircraft but it had been decided that no time should be lost in making a start and Holyman's ANA, which now had DC4 aircraft, were commissioned to operate under charter, a start being made on 15th September 1946. ANA continued until BCPA got its own aircraft delivered and commenced to operate with DC6 aircraft on 25th April 1948 when Holyman was unkindly left high and dry.

At the time of the formation of BCPA I had already been a director of TEAL for six years and had some experience of this kind of operation which I considered as being most inefficient. I noted in my diary on 3rd July 1945 that I had attended a meeting with Lord Swinton, Lord Knollys and Sir William Hildred when the question of joint Empire unit operation was discussed, and recorded:

> I stressed that a show with several split-ups cannot compete with a unified single show. Difficulty of Empire Agreement.

When BCPA was formed my expressed opinion was that it was an ideal which would not work. In view of the inevitable competition for traffic between BCPA eastbound and QEA westbound, Australia would soon be competing against herself.

Closely following the Wellington conference, on 8th March 1946, an important conference took place at Canberra with Dan McVey in the chair. He and George Cribbett were again the principals, with BOAC represented by Lord Knollys and QEA by myself. The conference was called to discuss the urgent problem of effectively continuing the BOAC/QEA England-Australia air service partnership, which was beset with problems because of lack of suitable and economic aircraft. The British Aircraft Ministry insisted on British aircraft, and the Australian authorities objected to the high cost to them of continuing with Lancas-

C

trian and Hythe aircraft when nothing else was coming up in the future acceptable to the U.K. except the untried and unpromising Tudor II.

The minutes of the meeting quote me as saying:

> In his view, the Tudor II which had hitherto been considered to be suitable for this second stage, would be outmoded almost as soon as it came into service. He regarded it as inferior in performance and earning capacity to the Constellation and urged strongly that, in his view as an operator, it would be essential to equip with the latter aircraft if QEA were to be in a position to compete successfully with other operators between Europe and Australia, including KLM operated Constellations, and with the competing Trans Pacific-U.S.A. and Trans Atlantic Services.

A deadlock in the discussions seemed likely when McVey and Cribbett took up all the loose ends out of the room and returned with a draft agreement, well achieved by these two experts, and acceptable to all as a compromise. The U.K. Ministry still stuck to the Tudor II desperately but unrealistically; we wanted Constellations. The compromise was:

> A decision on the type of aircraft to be operated in the second stage (the first stage being the already operating Lancastrians and Hythes) should be postponed until a date not later than September 1946.

The timing was very important to us in our fight to secure Constellations in the months ahead; and a tactical advantage had been won by the Australian members of the committee in forcing a time limit for the production of an acceptable British aircraft.

In those far off days I did not receive many compliments and so I was gratified when, in answer to an appreciative note I wrote Dan McVey on the outcome of the Canberra conference, he sent me a letter which read, in part:

> I should like to say that you stated the case for QEA with clarity and force and your Board of Directors should feel satisfied that their views were ably presented.

While these and other discussions were going on the Australian Government was preparing to purchase from the U.K. Government the BOAC holding in QEA. The old form of partnership, which had been of the greatest assistance to Australia in establishing overseas air transport connection, had now served its purpose and QEA was rightly headed for a much needed clean up.

Half the directors on the QEA Board were BOAC nominated. Our chairman, Sir Fergus McMaster, was in very low health and he, and F. E. Loxton, the other Qantas nominee, were not greatly interested in the big expansions of the future which were the only alternatives to our going out of business. The suggestion was made that the old Qantas company, which was still in existence, should re-open as an operator and go into business in Queensland as an intra-State operator. I had a hard time holding the fort, and senior staff in the company wondered where it would all end, and if they would find themselves out of jobs or in rival organizations.

Sir Fergus, our doughty fighting chairman, came temporarily back into the arena in a time of crisis. On 22nd March 1946 I wrote to him after a most unsatisfactory board meeting at which I do not think he was present:

> What is your word to me and to the other Executive Heads in this hour of crisis and of alarms, when faith, confidence and courage are required? Are you going to lead us to the victory I and other Executive Heads are determined to ourselves lead in?

Eight days later I was attending an important talk in Melbourne at which Arthur Drakeford, Dan McVey and Arthur Coles were present and co-operation between BCPA and QEA and similar matters were discussed. At this meeting I put up the QEA plan to operate immediately to Japan and China. Coles raised no objections except to state his view that BCPA should later take the route over from us, and also take in all the island services to the north-east of Australia. So here, in BCPA, we had a new and serious rival. A few years later, when TAA in their early stages were not doing too well, BCPA made a number of passes at QEA which had become wholly Australian Government owned. We were indeed saved only by Chifley who, I noted, replied simply to the suggestions, "I have given my promise to Fysh." And Ben Chifley kept his word.

In my note on this interesting meeting I recorded Coles as remarking that I had turned down the post of Director-General of Civil Aviation. I do not recall this as being strictly correct, though no doubt it was on the cards should the Government have decided on the demise of QEA and gone for the two operators, BCPA and TAA, both chaired by Arthur Coles who had his delusions of grandeur. Hectic times now long past and forgotten.

On 12th April 1946 we officially put in our application to operate a regular commercial service to Japan and China. This was our first move towards the opening of our service to Tokyo which was to pay off handsomely over the years to come, QEA being the only operator.

During the building up of the TAA and BCPA organizations it was inevitable that we should lose some of our skilled staff. After losing Lester Brain, John Borthwick and Doug Laurie to the government's TAA, we lost our secretary, Ivan Lawson, who went to BCPA as accountant. Alec

Barlow from ANA was elected manager of BCPA and J. N. Kemnitz secretary. George Harman carried on ably as QEA's general manager, but he was nearing the retiring age. This was not altogether a happy period for our top executive staff. George Harman and the chief engineer, to say nothing of myself, had to wrestle with a personal executive difficulty. Those who stayed saw it through, and no doubt the organization, at least in some directions, was all the better for the time of conflict, though worse off in other respects.

The departure of Lester Brain left C. O. Turner, manager of the accounts section, well in line after Harman. Turner had proved himself useful to the board and management through his expert knowledge of accountancy and finance, and in the presentation of estimates. He assumed importance in his specialized field and rounded off the effectiveness of the organization. Vastly ambitious, he was to become one of the key men in our expansion where he made an important contribution. He had a brilliant brain and there lay his great effectiveness.

In the re-organization under George Harman as general manager, Ian Esplin became secretary, Turner became assistant general manager, Captain Bill Crowther operations manager, Fred Derham chief accountant, Verdun Sommerlad staff superintendent, and E. Bennett-Bremner publicity manager, with Bill Nielson continuing as head of the traffic and commercial section.

A change also took place in the Civil Aviation Department on 10th June 1946 when Dan McVey concluded his foundation-laying two years' term as Director-General and his place was taken by my old World War I chief, Air Marshal R. Williams, who had been retired as head of the RAAF.

In England, Brigadier Critchley had resigned as chief executive of BOAC, and Air Commodore Whitney Straight had taken his place. That great British DCA, Sir William Hildred, had resigned to devote himself to the task of building up the post-war IATA. In New Zealand a notable TEAL appointment took place when G. N. Roberts, a former Air Commodore in the RNZAF, was made general manager.

At this time a controversy took place concerning new equipment for the outmoded Short flying boats which had carried on across the Tasman for six years without accident. We pressed hard for the DC4 type which would have given a wonderful passenger service and proved profitable for this run; but as land planes could not serve the capital city of Wellington, where the aerodrome was too small for the DC4, it was decided to continue the Auckland-Sydney and Wellington-Sydney services using the new Short Tasman Class double-decker flying boats. These carried thirty passengers and gave a better service than the old boats but were costly to operate.

It was a time of intense re-organizing and re-equipping. A pertinent comment on the resignation of Dan McVey was that made by the Sydney *Sun*:

> Resignation of the Director-General of Posts and Telegraphs, Mr Daniel McVey [he held the two posts of Director-General of Postal Services and Director-General of Civil Aviation from 1943] from the Commonwealth Public Service and, incidentally from one of the biggest undertakings in Australia, is a matter for every tax-payer to regret.

The leader went on to express the opinion that big men could not be expected to remain in the Public Service while salaries remained niggardly. Further resignations later resulted in a long overdue rise in status and remuneration for heads of Departments.

I do not think the Chifley Government was at all happy about McVey's resignation. He became managing director of Standard Telephones and Cables Pty Ltd, the first of many top positions he was to hold in industry. The Government had an opportunity to correct, in some degree, their loss, and on 2nd September McVey was appointed a director of the then wholly government owned QEA.

## ❧ 4 ❧

# The Fight for Constellations

I NOW come to deal with that period in 1946 and 1947 when QEA emerged from its war years of decimation, doubt, and sometimes near despair in securing the go-ahead from the Australian Government to order the aeroplane of its choice, the Lockheed Constellation, and then in becoming a fully fledged Government-owned instrumentality. At the same time there was a complete reorganization from the board of directors down in a way which saw us fit and ready to tackle the great things which were to lead the organization from strength to strength as world and Australian air transport developed apace.

Ever since my first flight in a prototype Constellation in January 1945, and my initial contacts with those remarkable Lockheed leaders, Bob and Courtlandt Gross, two former Boston bankers, I had been Lockheed-minded. Our technical expert, Scotty Allan, also reported favourably on the Constellation with its unprecedented range of 5,000 miles, its carriage of passengers in pressurized comfort, and its low operating cost of pence per passenger miles. Dan McVey had flown in the aircraft in its early days, and so had his successor, Air Marshal Williams. We had good support from those two but many difficulties had to be overcome before we received the final consent of the Government.

In the first place, we had to meet the terms of the Canberra Agreement which provided for a decision on new aircraft for the England-Australia route by "a date not later than September 1946". Our friends in England were fighting a delaying rearguard action in the hope that the Tudor II would prove acceptable to Australia. The Tudor II was at that time the forlorn hope for the British in international transport. When it was recognized as unsuitable for the North Atlantic run because of an expected defective range, BOAC received the go-ahead and ordered the early type Constellations. It was still hoped though that the Kangaroo route to Australia and the South Africa route, with their shorter stages, could be saved for the Tudor II.

The U.K. also was desperately short of U.S. dollars and this was crippling their post-war recovery. Countries such as Holland and France were able to go ahead and order modern American aircraft on a large scale. One could understand the British position, but should Australia have to suffer with the Mother country?

26

Australia, of course, was also desperately short of U.S. dollar exchange. The question was: Where did the priority lie for the order of expensive international-type aircraft as against oil, motor cars and lorries, newsprint and a host of other essential commodities? The Bank of New South Wales, which I approached, promised an initial overdraft of £A300,000, and this backing allowed us to proceed with assurance in our first submissions.

Then there was the question of whether the QEA executives could convince our own board, equally divided as it was between BOAC and Qantas members. And, indeed, there was doubt in regard to our own Qantas directors. I was now vice chairman, acting often for the ailing Sir Fergus McMaster.

Lastly, even with the backing of McVey and Williams, there was the task of convincing Ben Chifley, Prime Minister but also Treasurer, and Arthur Drakeford, Minister for Civil Aviation, who were under pressure from the U.K. Government to prevent an Australian order of Constellations.

In our early negotiations with Lockheed, and in evaluating the Constellation, we had C. J. (Tal) Davis, head of Australian War Procurement in Los Angeles assisting us. It was in December 1945 that Lockheed made their first offer. This was also discussed in London with Scotty Allan. The offer was for the Constellation 49, the type being the converted civil version of the military C69. Then came the first developed civil aircraft in the model 649.

TWA, the great backers in the Constellation venture, had started their North Atlantic operations with the 49 in January 1946. They were followed by BOAC with their 49s on 1st July 1946. KLM had ordered, so had Air France.

Then right in a critical stage of our negotiations a series of faults developed in the Constellation, and during a training flight in the U.S.A. an aircraft caught fire and was destroyed. More fires were reported, most of them being traced to installation and electrical problems. All Constellations were grounded between 1st July and 30th August. This was a blow to us as it cast doubt upon the suitability of the aircraft. Undeterred by what we regarded as surmountable teething troubles, we went ahead. The essential decision to order Constellations was made in Australia during the time the aircraft were grounded. We felt this was unique and showed the supreme confidence of our own technical heads and of those of the Australian Government.

As time went by, we decided to wait for a more impressive model 749, which had the bugs out of it when we took delivery in 1947 and commenced to operate.

The Lockheed offer with which we finally went to our Government was most attractive. It foreshadowed the system of "pay as you earn" that became, with modifications, general in regard to the large aircraft purchases of the future. The basic cost of each aircraft was £A284,532. Our total investment to put four aircraft into the air, plus fittings, spare engines and airframe parts and equipment to keep them in the air was estimated at £A2,151,572 which was considered a huge sum for the QEA of those days.

Lockheed's terms for the aircraft purchase were 15% on order, 10% on delivery and the balance in thirty-six promissory notes, repayment to be spread over a four years' term at an interest rate of 2%. This was called the long-term dollar plan and was a most favourable offer which was open for 30 days from 28th June 1946. We went to work with a will.

Performance figures differed in the circumstances of altitude, range and throttle openings; but for our purposes the 100,000 lb. all-up weight Constellation 749 with its four Wright engines could carry a load of 13,200 lb., including 44 passengers, at 275 m.p.h. over a range of 2,700 miles, the extreme range of the aircraft being 5,000 miles. The accommodation for passengers included 22 bunks. No other aircraft of the day could approach this specification.

The final drama of the Constellation commenced in July when on the 27th Fergus McMaster cabled Lord Knollys stating the clear intention of QEA to do its utmost to proceed with the Constellation order, and giving our reasons. Lord Knollys replied on 18th August, stating that he had interviewed—

> . . . the Minister for Civil Aviation, Lord Winster, and that if QEA wished to procure Constellations for operation on the Australia-United Kingdom route, they could not object and appreciated the considerations.

Lord Knollys went on:

> But H.M.G. must now consider carefully implications of any proposal to introduce Constellations on Empire Route, particularly its effect on principle of parallel operations and on United Kingdom South Africa Service.

He asked if it would be possible for QEA to obtain dollar exchange for two or three Constellations to help them out of their real dollar difficulty. We did our best but without avail for Australia was still very short of U.S. dollar exchange.

Great opposition to the order for Constellations was gathering in London, and on 14th August I wrote to Lord Knollys who, at this time, was unhappily being ground between two forces, for he was still under Air Ministry orders:

I am afraid that any further inclination to stall may have dire effects later if we get into difficulties through continued lack of decision, and I do urge that further delays be avoided.

On 20th August came a cable to Fergus McMaster from Lord Knollys:

For your information H.M.G. now received cable from Australian Government officially proposing Constellations stop Minister here views proposals with grave concern and Government is replying stating implications of this plan are being urgently reviewed stop it is hoped no final decision will be taken until further communications have been sent.

At this crucial period I had a continuing correspondence and many interviews with Air Marshal Williams, the new DCA, who was helping in the fight. A particular issue was the misleading figures which the Air Ministry had sent out comparing the Tudor II, yet unflown, and outmoded anyway, with the Constellation. This caused resentment among our authorities and helped us considerably.

On 4th September I cabled poor Lord Knollys:

Would urge you to secure urgent Air Ministry action cable true Tudor Constellation figures to Australian Government and face position which must surely otherwise rapidly deteriorate and end in serious misunderstanding.

I also had correspondence with our Prime Minister and Arthur Drakeford on the difficult and contentious subject. The last paragraph in a letter I wrote Ben Chifley on 1st August 1946 read:

We are now at the eleventh hour of decision and while we are confident that this matter will turn out all right, a decision allowing us to plan and get ahead with the spares programme would be of almost incalculable help to the QEA organization and its future.

I had a long correspondence with Drakeford and Chifley. It began to look as if we would win; but in the face of such strong opposition from the Labour Government in London there was no final decision.

And then I managed through Arthur Drakeford to secure an interview with the Prime Minister. This took place early in September at Victoria Barracks, Melbourne, not a usual place for the P.M. to be, and I still do not know how he came to be there.

I first saw Arthur Drakeford, after which he went in alone to the P.M. Then a long fidgety wait before at last I was ushered into the presence. A visit to any P.M. is always something of great import to a person such as myself. Such a man has the weight of the country's affairs and problems on his mind.

Smoking his pipe as usual, his puffs floating upwards in the still, rarefied air of the Barracks, Chifley invited me to sit down. In front of him on his pad lay the leaves of an urgent telegram. He did not waste words. He and Drakeford had made up their minds and did not want to hear any more.

Said Chifley, fingering the telegram, "You see this? It is an urgent telegram from Clem Attlee, Prime Minister of England, begging us not to go on with those Constellations you want."

A pause, a smile, and then he said, "Well, anyhow, I have decided. We'll give it a go."

I strap-hung the St Kilda cable car back into the city and, treading the heady air of success, walked up the steps of the G.P.O. and wrote out a telegram to Sir Fergus McMaster in Brisbane.

Two cables of congratulation came to me from two friends and helpers in London. They repose in my scrap book. One from Keith Smith reads:

> Now you have really started something. Congratulations your personal triumph.

The other from Scotty Allan reads:

> Enthusiastic congratulations on consequence your perseverance.

When I cabled Lord Knollys on 12th September, announcing the decision in favour of the Constellations, I concluded:

> It is our great desire to maintain the closest possible bond with British Overseas Airways Corporation and in preserving old friendship such as will be able to stand on an economic basis against competition.

This was an aspiration we in QEA really felt and strove to live up to in the years ahead.

Purchase of our Constellation fleet, with its vital significance for the competitive well-being of the organization, was the last big deal while we remained a private concern before the acquisition of the U.K. shareholding in QEA by the Australian Government, and then, the Qantas shareholding. Playing a principal part in the Constellation deal as I did, and in view of the coming re-organization of QEA, I had been practically on trial for my own future. It was a matter which did not bother me greatly at the time because of the heat of being in action.

Time was running out for the old set-up for several reasons, but principally because of the impossibility of combining the wishes and policies of the two governments and, at the same time, produce a first class competitive service operated on a sound basis. It was in a way just evolution, but what hurried on the changes was the insistence of the Air Ministry in London on preference for British aircraft, even when these were not able to compete with those procurable elsewhere. Another factor was the steeply rising capital investment which necessitated government backing in contracts, subsidies, or, as it turned out, mail rates, which was to be our new basis of payment made possible by the Constellations. Many overseas international airlines had been nationalized, including BOAC under a Conservative Government, and clearly a change had to take place here in Australia.

A difficulty had arisen when Lockheed asked for a government guarantee for the P.N.'s connected with the Constellation purchase. Our government would not guarantee a private firm, though the U.K. and Dutch governments had, I believe, guaranteed BOAC and KLM in their Constellation purchases. Lockheed gave way, but later a problem occurred when the P.N.'s could not be discounted in the U.S.A. and the matter came back to us for possible arrangement in Australia.

The dollar position was very acute in 1947 and we were held up over the urgently needed fifth Constellation and more spare engines, and were constantly in touch with our government authorities and Norman Watt, secretary to the Treasurer. Those were the days when QEA organization was halfway through the nationalization fence, and the change in authority made finalization of the financial provisions for our Constellations order with Lockheed difficult.

Lockheed still pressed the matter of the P.N.'s and the whole negotiation had to be reviewed by the Treasury. This resulted in Ben Chifley making a decision that the P.N.'s should be paid off by the Government. I remember I was horrified at the idea of paying off a loan at 2% interest before the due dates, for where could cheaper money be obtained? But it was argued that it was an indebtedness anyway, and so the deed was done. No doubt Lockheed had better use for the money and were delighted, the credit of Australia and QEA rising steeply.

In September 1946 Bill Crowther, our operations manager, had established a link trainer at Mascot, a significant happening in view of the great mechanization of pilot training which was to develop over the years ahead.

Then, before the end of the year, I left for Cairo to attend the second annual general meeting of IATA, and Scotty Allan, Bill Crowther and I had preliminary discussions with BOAC executive heads on an operations level, tackling the problem of future co-operation between BOAC and QEA on the England-Australia route. There was little result because government policy was not finally defined at that stage.

## ❦ 5 ❦

# Crisis and Change—Government Owned

IN LOOKING BACK on the turn of events which saw the rise of new and powerful formations, which profoundly affected contemporary history, and even in considering our Australian air transport undertaking which was now to go through a complete transformation, it is remarkable to reflect how dependent these things are on the whim of fate.

It had been the lot of the Federal Labor Government, during its long term of office from 1941 to 1949, to completely re-organize Australian air transport on a basis which was to prove permanent in its essential features. It is interesting to speculate on what might have taken place if the Liberal-Country Party coalition had not lost office in the 1941 rumpus.

In the first place, TAA would, undoubtedly, not have come into being, though such a government organization might have come some years later, and with it the present two-airline policy. Ivan Holyman's ANA would have proceeded on a triumphal way. The continued unfavourable attitude of the Labor Government drove them into a decision to cease operations. They did so but were without a buyer for the airline when it was up for sale. When the Liberal Party came into office, it was in an embarrassing position as there was almost a universal public demand for two main domestic operators, to provide beneficial competition. At this stage Reg Ansett, who was operating smaller domestic services, rescued the Government by buying ANA and forming Ansett-ANA. This organization has continued to operate under the Government's two-airline policy.

In respect to QEA—would we have achieved our Constellation order? I think so. Would a Liberal Government have bought out the BOAC holding in QEA? I feel so; but undoubtedly a coalition government would not have acquired the Qantas holding in QEA as the Chifley Government did, and the QEA undertaking could well have become a joint Qantas private enterprise and Australian government-owned undertaking with perhaps an increasing predominance of governmental capital and control as the years passed.

Actually, when Labor went out of office and shortly after the Liberals came back into power in 1949, my board was requested by the new Minister for Civil Aviation, Thomas White, to investigate the desira-

32

bility of reintroducing private capital into the QEA structure. We firmly recommended against the proposal and the matter was dropped. The great majority of the international airlines, the large chosen instruments of governments, were government-owned. History has confirmed that for a country like Australia, with its limited private capital resources, the present set-up has proved most effective.

My record of the events which resulted in the nationalization of QEA begins with a letter I wrote to Lord Knollys back in September 1945. I informed him that during an interview with Mr Chifley I had been told by the Prime Minister that a memorandum was going to Cabinet recommending acquisition of the BOAC shares in QEA. Fifteen months later, on 6th December 1946, a Bill called the Qantas Empire Airways Agreement passed both Houses in Canberra and authorized the purchase of the BOAC holding. No price was mentioned in the Act, but I believe it turned out to be 30s 9d for every £A1 share. This was 9d above the valuation by BOAC of their 261,500 shares in QEA.

In introducing the second reading of the Bill in the House of Representatives, Arthur Drakeford, after giving an historical survey of Qantas Empire Airways, said:

> It is proposed that in 1947 the Australian service shall extend to London, and operate in parallel with British Overseas Airways Corporation service along the same route.
>
> In these circumstances, it is logical that the Government owning 50% of the shares in Qantas Empire Airways shall be the Commonwealth Government, rather than the United Kingdom Government.

In a tribute to BOAC I made what I felt was an appropriate announcement:

> The Bill for the acquisition of the BOAC shareholding in Qantas Empire Airways Limited has now been passed by the Australian Parliament. In recording this important change, the Company wishes to acknowledge, with gratitude, the invaluable and, in fact, unique aid given by BOAC to the organization which pioneered Australian overseas and international air transport, a work in which Mr A. E. Rudder, BOAC representative in Australia, and Vice Chairman of QEA, has been closely identified. A very happy and progressive partnership has existed since 1934, when the original route out of Brisbane to Singapore was commenced.

Apart from the policy angle, the purchase of these shares looked like a profitable investment for the Australian Government. We had paid regular dividends since the formation of the company in 1934 and our profit for the year ended 31st March 1946 had been £54,061, with a 7% dividend. For twenty-two years, the original company, and then QEA, had enjoyed one of the highest business ratings in Australia for an unbroken run of profits. They were modest profits, and modest dividends, but we enjoyed a high measure of stability with constant progress despite the often hazardous and uncertain nature of our business.

When it came to the matter of the Australian Government electing directors to take the place of the three BOAC directors, Arthur Drakeford extended to me the courtesy of asking me to discuss the question with W. C. Taylor, a Sydney solicitor of the firm of Crichton-Smith, Taylor and Scott. Bill Taylor, at the age of thirty-eight, was appointed vice chairman of QEA, and later played an important part in Australian air transport direction as he was also vice chairman of TAA and on the board of Tasman Empire Airways.

The other appointees were G. P. N. Watt, then deputy secretary of the Australian Treasury, and a director of TAA. He also played an important part in the future. The third man was our old friend, Sir Keith Smith, of Vickers Vimy fame, and I was heard to remark that the appointment to the board of a "capitalist" like Keith Smith was a good omen for the future. Sir Fergus McMaster carried on as chairman, myself as managing director, and F. E. Loxton as the other Qantas nominated director.

So there was little disturbance and away we went, as we thought, with a new and permanent set-up, preparing to call for new capital to take care of our share in the Constellation order. It was planned to increase authorized capital from £500,000 to £1,500,000, and to call for new subscribed capital, offering to existing shareholders two shares at par for each share held. This would bring in about half a million pounds, leaving a similar amount to be subscribed by the Federal Government. We estimated it would take approximately £1,000,000 to finance the new Constellation operations.

As our shares were then being traded on the Stock Exchange at 33s. and our future was assured, the proposal looked to be a good thing for the existing shareholders, something tangible for their long pioneering efforts. J. B. Were were to underwrite the issue.

Things were not to go that way, for the Commonwealth Government bought out the Qantas shareholding before the issue took place, and one of the first acts of the Government after the take-over was a grant of £1,000,000 overdraft from the Commonwealth Bank.

In looking back on these events, I feel that one of the reasons why the Chifley Government bought out the Qantas shareholding was because of this pending capital issue. This would have been of great financial benefit to our old shareholders for, with the Federal Government holding virtually guaranteeing security, the privately held shares would have a great financial future. This would have led to difficulties. Apart from that, the position was too much for Chifley and his colleagues to accept when they had sweeping plans for the nationalization of the private banks and other undertakings.

Chifley's great ambition was to gear Australian enterprise to the good of the people as a whole, and his honest, self-sacrificing attitude was directed by that vision. But even the great have chinks in their armour and, with Chifley and his colleagues, this lay in their denial of reward in money or in honour to those who performed outstanding service to the community, whether it was in arts, crafts or business. This weakness was revealed in the refusal to support the recommendations put forward from England, and by myself, for recognition of the magnificent work of our wartime pilots, especially those who operated the Catalina service to Ceylon. This denial of recognition was, and still is, a fault in Labor policy when even the Soviet Union has accepted the need to reward human endeavour.

Yet in my political contacts over the years, two people who impressed me as truly great and not self-seeking, were Ben Chifley and his wife.

It seems appropriate to mention here the friendship between Chifley and Bill Taylor which led to Taylor receiving his airways appointments and becoming a power in the behind-the-scenes Labor forces, acting as an astute listening post for the Prime Minister as did Major Morton and others for Churchill.

Taylor was the son of a shearer father from Rylstone, a staunch A.W.U. man. The family moved to the Sydney suburb of Ryde where Bill was born, the youngest of five children. He passed out of Fort Street High School well and became a solicitor, specializing in the Industrial field and beginning his career in a strong Labor atmosphere.

At a time when the Labor Party was at a low ebb in public favour and performance because there were too many office holders and internal dissensions, a prime mover in the backstage rehabilitation campaign was Chifley. His work on this clean-up programme took him to two barristers who were immediate recruits and in their chambers in Phillip Street Chifley discussed the ticket which was being prepared for the forthcoming A.L.P. elections. When he had been informed of the names of candidates, he turned to one of the barristers and said, "Well, why shouldn't your younger brother be on the list?" The suggestion was accepted and W. C. Taylor went on the ticket. His barrister brother was Stanley Taylor, later Mr Justice Taylor, the other barrister being W. J. McKell, later Premier of New South Wales and then Governor-General of Australia.

So began the close association and friendship between Chifley and Taylor, and only their intimates knew how often Chifley, from his home town of Bathurst or from Canberra, used to telephone Taylor at his home in Mosman sometimes several times a night. Chifley's inner sanctum at Canberra was always wide open to his friend, and often the two would lounge, yarning under a tree in the Sydney Domain, both with their pipes going.

Chifley had a high aptitude for attracting loyal associates, and they reciprocated. One of the closest friendships, which resulted in effective Civil Aviation administration, was between Chifley and Arthur Drakeford, not a brilliant man but of a kindly and loyal disposition who, working in close harmony with Chifley, was an effective Minister.

On visits to Canberra, which I haunted in those days, and while I was in Arthur Drakeford's office when the House had risen at lunchtime, Chifley would walk in and after a few brief words, settle down on Drakeford's couch for a nap before tackling the business of the afternoon in the House. The two formed a most effective combination. The mutual confidence which grew out of these informal contacts was to react in favour of a new and workable constitution for QEA.

Both Chifley and Drakeford had been railway men, engine-drivers steeped in the tradition of their service, and in the movement to secure better working conditions for their union, the Australian Federated Union of Locomotive Enginemen (AFULE). Drakeford had been Federal Secretary in the early 1920s and Chifley an active member. Chifley had a meagre basic education, but with determination to fit himself for greater things, he attended night school at Bathurst, read avidly, studied economics and kindred subjects.

During the early months of 1947, when the new board of QEA commenced to function and the financial arrangements for our new Constellation order were still being discussed, the possibility of the Federal Government acquiring the Qantas shares in QEA came to light. Fergus McMaster was too ill to tackle the problem. Loxton expressed his views. I held dual roles as managing director of QEA and vice chairman of Qantas. McMaster and Loxton were all for a great effort to carry on as we were. This was also my wish. All sorts of dire consequences to our pioneering effort—now, as we thought, well on its feet—were predicted should the organization become fully government owned. In the past, government-owned enterprises, particularly in Queensland and in the field of transport, did not have an encouraging record. It was predicted that failure of our enterprise would come about. All would be at the whim of our political bosses, and personal directions from Canberra

Lockheed 10 in a crash at Condamine, Queensland. They all walked out. (The aircraft was carrying nine passengers and was commanded by Captain D. A. Tennent. One engine failed and height could not be maintained on the other. The occupants escaped injury because the aircraft slewed round after impact with trees, the final impact being taken backwards—a good argument for the advocates of backward-facing seats.) (*Photo*: QEA)

First Constellation arrives at Mascot, Sydney. *Left to right*—Captain E. C. Sims, Hon. A. S. Drakeford, Captain C. McIntyre (Lockheeds), Hudson Fysh, Sir Keith Smith (*Photo*: Laurence Le Guay)

Constellation *Ross Smith* at Canberra. W. C. Taylor, Prime Minister J. B. Chifley, Captain
E. C. Sims

would override the discretion of the board. TAA was reported to be in difficulties. Perhaps the Government had its eye on QEA, a profitably operating, established organization, to minimize expected losses on TAA.

It was in this atmosphere that I prepared a review which I took to Canberra on 22nd April 1947 and which was passed on to the Prime Minister after discussion with Drakeford and Taylor, now vice chairman of QEA. The review was in three parts, the more lengthy one advocating a continuation of the present QEA set-up and setting out arguments. The second one explained broadly the conditions in which Qantas would be willing to negotiate, should the Government decide to acquire the shareholding in the company, and expressing continued interest in making a success of the undertaking under any such new ownership. The third briefly mentioned some suggested overall conditions for carrying on the company in the event of government purchase. QEA would carry on under the same name, doing the same work, with proper protection for staff in the continuation of the pension scheme and salaries and conditions.

Mr Chifley granted me an interview on 23rd April, when I found his mind was quite made up on the acquisition of the Qantas shareholding. Back in Sydney, I wrote a long letter to F. E. Loxton in Brisbane, extracts from which read:

> I regret I found the Prime Minister's mind firmly made up on the question, and such as making it quite useless to pursue further argument to the contrary.
>
> What has caused the Government to change its mind now is mainly on the question of finance, concerning provision of new capital, which is growing into a very big thing for QEA, and its application from the Government point of view to the new QEA set-up.
>
> Also with TAA, BCPA, TEAL, TCA, BOAC, SAA, and NZNA, all totally government owned, the QEA set-up, as it is now, is out of step with every other main Empire operating set-up.
>
> After some 27 years of Qantas pioneering in Air Transport, during which we have seen the original small struggling enterprise grow into the concern QEA is today, the present position is regrettable indeed, specially for myself, but I am afraid it is the penalty, if it can be put that way, of growing too big, and with further inevitable great advances ahead in an industry that is closely bound up with Government interest, and with National and International relations which are primarily the affairs of Government, and which are both controlled and operated by them in every Empire unit except in Australia.

There was no arguing against this, and on 6th May I wrote to Mr Chifley and, concerning the attitude of the shareholders, said:

> Though I do not like intruding myself into these considerations more than can be avoided, the fact cannot be escaped that I am heavily personally

involved in this whole question, and a good deal depends on my attitude. I have already handed you personal notes in Canberra which set out my views, but which, of course, did not take any fully developed form.

You mentioned in Canberra that, should QEA become a wholly Government concern, it would be the wish for me to carry on, but, as you will realize, consideration of this would be dependent in the first place on the deal accorded to the Qantas shareholders, to the present Qantas staff, and the status and measure of management control accorded to the organization in the future.

I urged early notification of the Government's intentions, to which the P.M. replied that an early decision by Cabinet could be expected. On 15th May I received the following letter from H. C. Barnard, Acting Minister for Civil Aviation:

> I have to inform you that the Government, after full consideration of the developmental programme and greatly increased capital requirements for extension of the Empire Air Service conducted by Qantas Empire Airways Limited, has decided that it is desirable that the operating company should be entirely Government-owned.

The Acting Minister asked for immediate attention, which we gave, and on 23rd May the Qantas board officially agreed to negotiate, in fact ratifying the conferences which were taking place between F. E. Loxton and myself for Qantas, and G. P. N. Watt and Air Marshal Williams for the Commonwealth Government. We received from Watt and Williams a definite offer of £1 13s. 4d. per £1 share, an offer they were prepared to recommend to the Prime Minister, who was also Treasurer. A meeting of the Qantas Board on 26th May accepted this offer, subject to agreement by the Prime Minister and ratification by the Qantas shareholders.

After his long and gallant fight against ill health, our chairman, Sir Fergus McMaster, at last felt that he could not carry on any longer in that position. In fact, his position was untenable, with one big change after another being decided in his absence. He had written to the board at the meeting on 23rd May 1947 and I was elected to the position of chairman and managing director. Press releases were agreed upon, and on 27th May I made the following announcement:

> The decision of the Commonwealth Government to purchase the Qantas private shareholding in QEA has come as the result of greatly increased expansion and capital requirements for the latter organization, and is in line with Government policy and with previous action by all other main Empire units, where we see British Overseas Airways Corporation, British South American Airways, British European Airways Corporation, Trans Canada Airlines, South African Airways, New Zealand National Airways Corporation, Tasman Empire Airways Ltd., British Commonwealth Pacific

Airlines, all owned by their respective Governments or groups of Governments.

The taking over of principal airlines in the various British communities is not confined to Labour Governments only, but follows a common trend of political thought, and represents the will of the people, which must prevail in democratic countries. . . .

Qantas, originally founded by Queensland enterprise and shareholders, is the oldest name in air transport in the Empire, and probably the second oldest in the world, and the organization has been one which from its humble beginning has tried to carry on in this realm, with honour, the world leadership won in the air by the Australian aerial pathfinders, and the Australian Flying Corps and RAAF in their own spheres, and now we must accept the changes, which time prescribes in all things.

The Qantas Empire Airways organization and what it is and stands for, is something which was not built in a day, and its continuance on a basis which will enable it to continue to function with efficiency and success, is something which the present Government has in mind.

The Board Meeting held on the 26th May made the momentous decision accepting the purchase price of the Qantas shareholding in QEA. The valuable, historic name passed to the Government though we had been denied any goodwill value in the sale.

On 29th May I flew to London to join in talks with BOAC on the finalization of an entirely new partnership agreement which was to provide for the "application of the principles of parallel partnership" on the Empire route between Sydney and London. This was not easy as we were in the initial stage to operate Constellations, and BOAC Lancastrians and Hythe flying boats, entirely different types, with different economics and passenger appeal.

C. O. Turner had been in London before my arrival, assisting Captain Johnston, Deputy Director of Civil Aviation, while, for the United Kingdom, George Cribbett was in the chair as Director of Civil Aviation, assisted by Atherton of BOAC. I found that preliminary agreement had been reached and that Turner had been of considerable assistance to Captain Johnston and BOAC in what were difficult discussions.

The arrangements agreed upon at these meetings were later agreed to by the Governments, the chief provisions being that BOAC and QEA should operate their own services between London and Sydney, revenue should be pooled and shared each year on the basis of actual capacity ton miles flown, thus eliminating competition. Each partner should stand its own costs. Rates and conditions and other difficult details were thrashed out. The agreement was to be subject to six months' notice on either side.

Thus a new and effective partnership arrangement came into being, leading in an essential development of the old partnership provisions first inaugurated in 1934. The agreement envisaged carriage of a surcharged mail and payment to the operators on the basis of gold francs per ton kilometres. The death knell of that great and ambitious venture of 1938, the Empire All Up Mail Scheme, was thus finally sounded.

On 17th June I left Heathrow Airport by BOAC Lancastrian for Sydney.

## ❊ 6 ❊

## Exit Qantas

I FOUND on my return to Australia a good deal of press and political criticism of the Commonwealth Government's purchase of the old Qantas private shareholdings. This was to be expected because of strong opposition to Labor's far-reaching plans for nationalization. It was the issue of nationalization of banking that ultimately led to the rejection by the electors of the Chifley Government.

Criticism of the acquisition of the Qantas private shares was, no doubt, sharpened by supporters of Holyman's ANA which had desperately offered to operate services to London without government assistance, and to lower the fare from £400 to £170. We had heard of such offers before and they were to come from world-wide sources well into the future, but they never came to anything. No guarantees to maintain the offers were ever given. It was what I called "the art of airline penetration".

R. G. Menzies had this to say in the House:

> Commonwealth control of Qantas Empire Airways would not mean a better running of the services. Nobody could suggest that Qantas was not one of the best run airlines in the world, and that its shareholders were not responsible for a marvellous pioneer work. They come in later and reap the benefits of the pioneers.

The *Sydney Morning Herald*, in a balanced leader, did not oppose the change, but thought that QEA might well have carried on as a fifty-fifty show, and expressed fears for efficiency in the future. The Sydney *Daily Telegraph* was likewise fearful of the future and felt QEA profits might be used to offset TAA losses. The Sydney *Bulletin*, in a vigorous article under the heading "Exit Qantas", stated:

> At midday, October 2nd, at the Wool Exchange, Brisbane, there died Qantas. . . . Cause of death, asphyxiation, caused by socialism, a virulent disease transmitted by raucous demagogues.

And so it went on, a flood of praise for the old Qantas, but not a word in support of Chifley and his government for doing what Fergus McMaster and I knew was the correct thing, having regard to the limited Australian capital resources. It was a step that was to be amply justified in the future.

On 27th June 1947 a meeting of Qantas directors agreed to the take-over terms, subject to agreement by the shareholders, who endorsed the proposals at an Extraordinary General Meeting held in Brisbane on 5th July. Meanwhile, the Commonwealth Government had taken over on 1st July, a convenient date, from which the new organization was in business.

It was ironical that on 12th July, twelve days after the takeover, a strike of workers took place at our Rose Bay flying boat base. Except for a stoppage in Darwin, this was the first strike in the twenty-seven years' history of our organization. I do not know if the takeover had anything to do with the strike, though at that time unionists were inclined to think the Labor Government was a fairy godmother. It was a belief that ceased when the Government took strong action in the coal strike of 1949. In any case, labour conditions at Rose Bay were very unsatisfactory, some men working under State awards, others under Federal awards. There were members of different unions, with different awards, often working together on the same benches. There was also an internal struggle for power among the union leaders. Some two hundred men went out, and flying boat services to England, and by TEAL to New Zealand, had to be cancelled for a few days before a settlement was reached.

One of the most interesting letters I received at this time was from C. G. Grey, the famous editor of the *Aeroplane*, in which he wrote:

> Just a line to sympathise with you on the demise, translation, absorption, sequestration or what not of your beloved offspring, Qantas. Anyhow, I hope that you have cleared a nice packet out of it.

I see by the records of the Liquidator that I then held 1,235 one pound shares, and my wife 400 shares, for which we received 34s. 4d. a share, along with the other shareholders. Further than this I received no financial compensation, for the pioneer company had no founders' shares or anything like that.

I had started off with 600 shares. Then on 30th June 1923, in our dark days, I acquired another 45 shares as the result of an amusing incident in the Longreach Club. One of our shareholders, holding ten shares, was speaking gloomily about the future of the company, and I ended the discussion by saying I would take his shares and toss to see whether I gave him ten shillings or £1 a share. I won and acquired the ten shares cheaply. Two other shareholders then spoke up and said I could have theirs also at the price and I accepted the offer. The names of the three shareholders were S. S. Clark, A. P. Ridley and J. W. Sinclair. I remember that the barman, Joe Woodman, also held ten shares which he was always very proud to own.

I built up my holding gradually through new issues and purchases to 1,675, later, apparently, selling 440 shares in a time of financial stringency.

At the time of the takeover, the Qantas capital holding in QEA was 261,500 one pound shares. It is interesting to note that in 1966 the paid up capital of QEA had, in nineteen years, grown to £19,658,822. As from 1947 with government ownership QEA was in an extremely sound position and paid regular dividends. Should QEA have remained a fifty-fifty Qantas-Federal Government affair, the issue after issue of new shares would have been of great financial benefit to the private shareholders. This, I feel, would have been too much for the Government to accept. There would have been inevitable argument and conflict on matters such as dividend rates.

As it turned out, the pioneer shareholders, in which my family and I were included, and the founders of the company, missed receiving any adequate financial reward. Nobody made anything out of the pioneer concern, Qantas, perhaps least of all Fergus McMaster who led the company along lines of extraordinarily high and patriotic principles and was extremely hard on himself.

The board of the Queensland and Northern Territory Aerial Services Limited (Qantas), having decided to recommend to the shareholders liquidation of the company, on 2nd October 1947, the shareholders met at the Wool Exchange Building, Brisbane, for the 27th annual meeting. This was followed by an Extraordinary General Meeting which voted unanimously for a dissolution. I took record of all present, of everything said, and the financial details. This record is in a bound folder entitled *The Last Day of Q.A.N.T.A.S. Ltd, 1920-47.*

In all, sixty-one shareholders were present, among whom was a fair sprinkling of QEA staff. I had always encouraged the staff to take shares in their employing company. In the absence of Sir Fergus McMaster, who was too ill to leave his home, I was elected to the chair, and either as chairman or personally held an absolute majority of the proxies, representing 263 shareholders against 54 held by other members.

It was an historical and harrowing occasion and I remember facing the meeting with a great deal of tension. The business of the annual general meeting proceeded smoothly, the main business being to review the activities of the company during the past financial year, trace the doings of QEA, confirm the dividend of 6% already paid, fix directors' fees which, incidentally, to my chagrin, were distributed equally amongst directors.

A special retiring allowance of £2,500 was voted to Fergus McMaster.

I had drafted a special resolution to cover this, which was carried; a number of shareholders, including Sir William Glasgow, F. E. Loxton, Alan Campbell and Norman Bourke, spoke in high praise of the tireless work done by Sir Fergus for Qantas.

I was also determined to obtain some financial recognition for H. H. Harman, the man who had carried on as secretary for many years for an annual remuneration of £25, then £75, and who had worked tirelessly in the winding up process. A retiring allowance of £250 was voted him, but not without dissension. Eric Donaldson, one of our veteran pilots, supplied a list of nineteen names of pioneers in the company who, he felt, should receive a cash recognition. Laudable as the idea was, we could not entertain it; but Donaldson stood his ground, as he always did, and the vote to Harman was passed with his dissent.

Then followed the Extraordinary General Meeting where the motion was put that we go into voluntary liquidation. When the resolution was carried unanimously, a number of rather emotional speeches were made. After tracing some of the early history of Qantas, I said:

> It has been a most interesting and, in fact, a wonderful association, particularly with Sir Fergus McMaster. You hear all sorts of stories about how the Company started, and who started it. You hear all kinds of versions, but I think, if you really wanted to single out one man who supplied the first spark of this Company, and who first had the idea, it is undoubtedly Mr P. J. McGinness (applause). He is the one who supplied the first spark, and then the others came along.
>
> Sir Fergus gave wonderful help. I remember going to the Longreach Club in 1921 and talking to another director who said, "Well, we will have to close down, what hard luck," but Sir Fergus then spoke up and said, "I am damned if we will close down," and so it was that your Company went on to what it has achieved through the years.

I thanked Mr A. N. Templeton and Mr F. E. Loxton for what they had done and the shareholders for their confidence, and then traced the world-wide trend in the nationalization of international air transport organizations:

> Your directors also had to look at the difficult years ahead, and, in trying to make a contract for the operation of a service to England with Constellation aircraft, they found that QEA, only partly private enterprise owned, had to make a contract to work in with completely government owned airways such as BOAC. It was a position so difficult that it became untenable.
>
> Although it is very sad to see the Old Show go out after all these years, you have had a good deal from the Government—otherwise we would not have recommended acceptance to you. The Government has always had a high regard for the company, Sir Fergus McMaster and your directors, and we got an amicable deal from them.

Ladies and Gentlemen, on behalf of the board and myself, I would just like to say goodbye to you.

A SHAREHOLDER. Usually, when a company winds up, the name is forgotten. Qantas Empire Airways will still be carried on under a new management, and we hope this will always continue.

MR A. E. SHARP. Goodbye, Hudson, so far as the company is concerned; but you are our friend for life. . . .

MR FYSH. Thank you for the sentiment. I cannot say all of it is quite true as regards myself.

MISS MACANSH. I'm looking forward to your book.

MR C. E. THOW. Qantas will not vanish—the name liveth for ever more.

MR FYSH. We will do our best to keep it so.

MR E. S. N. BOURKE. Ladies and Gentlemen, I propose that we move a vote of thanks to all directors.

This was carried, by acclamation.

MR FYSH. Thank you, on behalf of the directors. I now declare the meeting closed.

Our stalwart Board members, Fergus McMaster, F. E. Loxton and A. N. Templeton, not to mention the shareholders, many of whom were of twenty-six years' standing, deeply felt the passing of the old Qantas. There must have been quite a bit of feeling that, with only myself as a founder and director to go with the new set-up, I had landed a good job for myself. It was natural that I should feel more than a little unhappy about this.

At the end of the meeting, in a tense atmosphere, Loxton, Templeton and I sat down to decide, as was usual, in what way the £500 voted for directors' fees should be split. Sir Fergus McMaster was to get his usual £200, but I felt that as vice chairman, and the one who had led in the difficult negotiations connected with the wind-up, I should receive more than last year's equal split of £75 for Loxton, Templeton and myself. This was opposed; I stuck to my guns, claiming that as acting chairman I had a casting vote. The other directors would not agree. They walked out and this meeting was never recorded. Anyhow, how could we hold the usual post-annual general meeting directors' meeting, when, meanwhile, the company had been wound up?

The liquidator was later in difficulty, and I settled the matter by meeting him and agreeing to the same split in directors' fees as that made the previous year. It might be thought that I came out of the incident with discredit, but Loxton, Templeton and I were good friends later. They had hated the passing of Qantas, and I did not blame them.

The Commonwealth Government now confirmed me in my previous position as chairman and managing director of Qantas Empire Airways.

W. C. Taylor was vice chairman, G. P. N. Watt, a director, and a new director, A. R. McComb from the Civil Aviation Department was appointed from 16th August 1947, but resigned as from 30th December on his appointment as deputy secretary general of ICAO. On 2nd December 1947 our old friend, Dan McVey, was appointed a director, and for many years gave distinguished service. The new board settled in and, in association with our new authority, a cleaning-up process commenced which decided the basis for our organization for the years ahead.

In June 1948 Arthur Drakeford introduced a Bill into the House of Representatives to authorize the Government to invest another £2,000,000 in Qantas Empire Airways Ltd. In doing so he traced the present position of QEA and the greatly extended work which faced the organization. As might be expected the Bill was criticized by the Opposition as being "another burden on the unfortunate taxpayer". It was "the obituary notice of a splendid public service" and so on. The fuss was purely party political and in opposition to the wider plans for nationalization which were envisaged by the Labor Government.

At the end of 1948 we turned in our first profits under government ownership, a good one of £79,900. Under the heading, "If You Must Socialise" the Sydney *Telegraph* commented:

> Happy Qantas family. No airlines commission, no direction from political bosses who claim knowledge of the airline business. . . . Perhaps Qantas is the blue-print for success in nationalised concerns.

Qantas Empire Airways was, and is, a unique, wholly owned government instrumentality, the Commonwealth Government having acquired all the shares, but permitting the concern to continue under its old name as a limited liability company with its head office in Brisbane. General meetings, however, were only a formality, control being exercised through a financial directive.

Board members had a hand in helping to draft the directive which was issued by the Minister for Civil Aviation on 1st May 1949. The Minister was to appoint the directors, the financial directive going on to say:

> The Board of Directors appointed by the Government is charged with the responsibility of directing the operations of Qantas Empire Airways Limited, in accordance with the Government's Civil Aviation policy, as communicated by the Minister from time to time, and also with the responsibility of ensuring the proper use of public monies invested in the Company.
> Within the framework of this Directive the Board is authorised to direct the affairs of the Company as it thinks fit, with due regard to the practices in existence prior to Government ownership.

Then followed provisions in regard to capital and other financial matters. Problems which had to be considered included the relationship of QEA as a government-owned instrumentality with TAA and the Commonwealth Public Service, questions of salaries, staff pension schemes, and the possible payment of staff bonuses. The question of higher salaries and the handling of industrial problems were two of the main difficulties in our relations with the Commonwealth Government.

Nevertheless the directive was a good document and I was gratified by the first paragraph in the preamble:

> In assuming full ownership of Qantas Empire Airways Limited, the Government is fully conscious of the value of taking over a going concern, an efficient established organisation with many years' experience of international air transport, and it is the desire of the Government that there shall be as little change as possible in the existing organisation and the managerial and operating practices in existence prior to Government ownership.

The weakness of our position was that the company was entirely in the hands of the Commonwealth Government and at their mercy in respect to the appointment of members of the board. However, over the years, all went well; the prophets of doom were confounded. We suffered no unreasonable interference but had the strong support we deserved through our loyalty to our masters, the government of the day. Still, there lies the main danger. On the other hand our partners, BOAC, suffered from a rapid succession of new chairmen and chief executives.

David Corbett, in his brilliant work, *Politics and the Airlines*, makes an excellent comment on the question of private versus public ownership of business undertakings:

> The classical political argument over public enterprise has been whether the Government should own businesses at all. Yet what matters more than titular ownership is how the enterprise is run, who makes the decisions, under what rules and subject to what pressures. . . . Ownership does not necessarily give control; it may, in fact, affect the character of the industry very little.

But what of the United States system and the interesting and complicated control of CAB which the State Department overlaps, and where the anti-trust laws of the country also are involved and under which companies like Pan American Airways operate?

David Corbett says:

> The fact that there has been no political agitation for public ownership of airlines in the United States ought not to be misunderstood. It does not mean that laissez-faire prevails. The characteristic form of state intervention in the economy is regulation rather than public ownership, but the motive

behind regulation is often very similar to the motive behind public owner-ship in Commonwealth countries.

However, under the American system there is no doubt that the more successful air transport operators, both international and domestic, have done very well for the shareholders; by our Australian standards, fan-tastically well. Assuming that shares were purchased in 1963 and held through the glamour years of the airline industry until 1966, the approxi-mate increases are as follows:

| | |
|---|---|
| Pan American Airways | 800% |
| American Airlines | 400% |
| United Airlines | 467% |
| Delta Airlines | 600% |
| Trans World Airlines | 1000% |

The U.S.A. nomenclature and practices in share accounting, stock splits and the like, are somewhat different from our own; but it is worth noting that, in 1967, a shareholder in Pan American World Airways would have received a dividend of 40 cents on each of his 25 per cent par value shares held, and the market value of each 25 cent share at this time was $23·75*.

Pan American's first issue of par value shares was in 1932, the unit being one of $10. Since then there have been four share splits and one rearrangement of capital, finally reducing the unit to one of 25 cents. The market value of each $10 share, acquired in the original 1932 issue, would be now attracting a dividend of $6·40 per share, with a market value of $380. The number of 25 cent shares issued now stands at 16,129,643, having a book value of $23·51 per share, total shareholders' funds being $379,219,000.

The interests of Pan American, of course, include kindred under-takings such as Inter-Continental Hotels Corporation and the Guided Missiles Range Division. But it is clear that the American system of airline organization and control has been most profitable to the private ownership. In the case of Pan American, those of the 60,635 shareholders who bought their scrip a few years back have been on velvet. Fortunes must have been made inside the company itself in share options and the like.

It can be said, therefore, that under the U.S.A. system, the companies

---

* Since this was written there has been a considerable fall in the payability, potential and market value of U.S.A. city transport shares. Pan American Airways shares were quoted at $10-⅞ in April 1970. The world's large international operators seem headed for another situation of over-provision of capacity.

themselves and those participating in them have been allowed the opportunity to reap great monetary benefits, though the companies are closely identified with national policy and control. But beyond national success there has been international success. Pan American today leads the world in low air fare structure and operating costs per capacity ton mile. It is a story of fantastic success, only possible in the U.S.A. with its great pool of private capital, technical resources, efficient direction and management. Standing behind these has been the United States Government itself.

An interesting example of a successful government-private enterprise undertaking was seen in Amalgamated Wireless (A/sia) Ltd (AWA) when it ran Australia's overseas wireless communications and was also engaged in radio manufacturing and kindred activities. In 1945, when British Commonwealth countries nationalized their radio communications, following talks between Lionel Hooke (later Sir Lionel) of AWA and Mr Chifley, the Australian Government took over the wireless communications side of the business, forming the Overseas Telecommunications Commission (OTC) and in 1946 sold their shares in AWA to the public, AWA has a splendid pioneering history and a high record of service, but, as may be imagined, the old partnership arrangement led to political difficulties at times.

In this section I have traced the laying of important post-war foundations in Australian air transport and in the conduct of international air transport. The period closes with the now wholly-government owned Qantas Empire Airways poised to operate with the new Constellation aircraft through from Sydney to London, but under the old management. Some twenty years on, an enthusiastic builder of words coined the phrase "Architect of Qantas' post-war advancement", but attributed it without reading history. There is no doubt that the true architects of this post-war period were, in the first place, Ben Chifley and Dan McVey, influenced by the times in which they planned; and assisted—or perhaps at times confused—by the advice of the leaders of their operators. We, ourselves, put forward a well-nigh continuous stream of suggestions which assisted in the final outcome.

The QEA organization, as the years passed, seemed to exhibit little change in its objectives, its outlook and direction, though governments changed and direction changed. Together we went forward, as would a firm of architects in which there was a number of architects working together for the same end.

## ⁂ II ⁂

*Girt in our new constitution, and armed with the epoch-making Lockheed Constellation, the ocean bridger, we gathered in Japan and South Africa.*

*Diverse and enterprising in many new developments, in keeping with our spreading industry, we made things grow. We also saw the coming of the world's first civil jet—the Comet—pointing to a new and fascinating future in air transport.*

Early air hostesses—Sally Kellow, Marjorie de Tracy, Joan Firman (*Photo*: Qantas)

H. H. Harman, general manager, presents Dobell portrait (*Photo*: J. R. T. Richardson—Richard McKinney Studio)

Hon. H. L. Anthony dispatches first trans-Pacific service by QEA from Mascot, 15th May 1954
(*Photo*: Qantas)

The Queen and the Duke of Edinburgh arrive at Mascot by QEA (*Photo*: QEA)

# We Operate to Japan

IN THE LATER half of 1947 and on into 1948 many long-planned advancements in our service took place. These proved so demanding that I was unable to attend the IATA annual general meeting held outside Rio de Janeiro. It was the only AGM that I missed in all the years. Bill Nielson, our traffic manager, took my place, with my son, John Fysh, as his offsider.

The dying days of the war had found John near completion of his pilot's training in the RAAF. He then applied to join the QEA flight staff, but failed to pass his eyesight tests which were more exacting for Civil Aviation than for the RAAF. On 16th July 1945 at the age of nineteen he joined QEA as a commercial trainee and had a year's experience with BOAC in London, followed by a year with TWA in the U.S.A. When he arrived back in Sydney his first job was that of chief cargo officer. Later on he was posted to Japan where he became manager for Japan in 1954, the first of a series of overseas postings before he returned to Sydney.

Changes in Civil Aviation leadership which affected us took place about this time, principally the coming of Air Marshal Richard Williams as Director-General of Civil Aviation. Sir William Hildred had gone from the U.K. Civil Aviation Authority to head of IATA and his place was taken by Sir Henry Self as Permanent Head of the Ministry of Civil Aviation, who was followed in 1947 by Sir Arnold Overton, Lord Nathan being his Minister.

Changes were also taking place in BOAC. On 1st July 1947 Sir Harold Hartley took over from a disillusioned Lord Knollys. Sir Harold Hartley was a sixty-nine-year-old scientist and, in addition to other important positions, had been Controller of Chemical Warfare in the first world war. A charming personality, a terrifically dedicated worker, he was no less than seventh in line of succession as BOAC chairman. Whitney Straight, who had enjoyed a brilliant record in the RAF in the second world war, a prominent car racing driver and sportsman, came in as chief executive in place of General Critchley.

QEA itself was exhibiting a new look under government ownership. The new board consisted of Norman Watt, Dan McVey and Sir Keith

E

Smith, with W. C. Taylor as vice chairman and myself as chairman and managing director. With these personalities, knowledge and contacts, it looked a formidable combination. R. E. Fulford was board secretary at this time, H. H. Harman general manager, with C. O. Turner as his assistant. Then came W. A. Baird as works manager, W. H. Crowther as operations manager, C. W. Nielson as traffic manager, G. U. Allan, controller of technical development, and F. C. Derham as chief accountant, holding Turner's old job. N. A. Black was manager for Queensland, where we were still carrying on and developing our inland domestic services until the new TAA felt able to take over.

Overseas, ANA were still operating the Pacific service for BCPA, and with their eyes still turned towards an operation to England via India, commenced the negotiations which were to bring them into Air Ceylon and later into Cathay Pacific Airways in Hong Kong.

An important development across the South Pacific was the Pan American Airways service to Sydney. The first official flight took place when the DC4 Clipper *Kit Carson* left San Francisco on 17th March 1947 and arrived in Sydney on 21st March. Before this flight, Pan American had operated weekly charter flights from 21st January, and the first mail-carrying flight had arrived in Sydney on 26th February. This new service was a challenge, and so was the BCPA service which competed with our Kangaroo route via India for European traffic.

At this time BOAC and QEA had a monopoly of Australian westbound overseas services. KNILM, the Dutch Indonesian post-war operator to Australia, was unable to restart because of disruption in the Indies. Indeed, we had no competition on the Sydney-Singapore end of the Kangaroo route until Air France opened their service in December 1950, to be followed by KLM in December 1951.

There was great activity in our Australian regional overseas services in the immediate post-war period, when military operations were giving way to civilian replacements. As a result of their war experiences the outlying communities were demanding air connections. We were active in our service to New Guinea, our service from Sydney to Lae being extended to Rabaul, and internal services in the Pacific Islands were increased.

Perhaps the most isolated of Australian territories, the former penal settlement of Norfolk Island, 1,041 miles north-east of Sydney, fell on difficult times at the close of the war because of inadequate shipping facilities. Something had to be done to alleviate the lot of its eight hundred or so inhabitants. The rock-girt, five miles long little island had no harbour, but it had an unsealed airstrip, so the Australian authorities arranged with us to commence a regular fortnightly service with Lancastrian aircraft, the first service being inaugurated on 14th October 1947. Captain L. R. Ambrose was in command, having as his crew Captains P. J. Miller and G. P. Wright, Engineer Officer G. Grant and Radio Officer W. R. Clarke.

Even with the limited passenger accommodation of the Lancastrian, the new service proved a boon, mainly in the carriage of passengers and urgently needed supplies, and with the return carriage of fresh vegetables and passionfruit for which this garden island is renowned. It was in 1856 that Queen Victoria offered facilities on the island to the Pitcairn Islanders, descendants of the mutiny on Bligh's *Bounty*. They were transhipped there, lock, stock and barrel, and their descendants with their romantic story, the grim buildings of the convict era now set in peaceful countryside surroundings, together with the stately Norfolk pines, make the island an attractive tourist resort.

We also commenced operations on a charter basis from Sydney to Lord Howe Island, about 482 miles from Sydney. With an area of six square miles the island is half the size of Norfolk Island. It had no harbour for vessels of any size, no suitable area for a landing strip, but enjoyed a large coral lagoon which, except at low tide, was suitable for flying boats.

Trans Oceanic Airways, of which P. G. (later Sir Gordon) Taylor was chairman and Brian Monkton managing director, were already operating an irregular service. Our request for permission to operate to Lord Howe meant competition and was bitterly opposed, the giant QEA against the pygmy Trans Oceanic. The Civil Aviation Department issued a licence to QEA but as the island was part of the State of N.S.W. it was necessary also to obtain a State permit. This was granted on a charter basis and each trip had to receive local sanction. We sought the opinion of Sir Garfield Barwick, then in private practice, which, though of course not conclusive, was that Trans Oceanic could not legally restrain QEA from operating.

Meanwhile we had purchased the first of a number of Catalina flying boats from the RAAF and the work of reconditioning was being carried out at our Rose Bay workshop. The civil Catalinas proved most acceptable to passengers. They had fourteen comfortable chairs and specially cut observation port-holes. A small washroom was provided, though galley arrangements were primitive. We were to employ five of these aircraft on our island services and in New Guinea where they did good work until small amphibian aircraft became available.

Our first survey flight to Lord Howe Island was carried out by Catalina VH-EAW on 20th November 1947 under the command of Captain J. L. Grey. The opening flight on 3rd December had to return to Sydney without alighting because of bad weather. On the 9th December the first successful flight was completed, Captain Grey being in command, having as his crew Captain E. R. Nicholl, First Officer I. C. Peirce, Navigation Officer T. E. W. Howe, Radio Officer H. W. Taylor, and Engineering Officers J. C. Brady and J. P. Conway. Mail was carried to the island at ordinary rates.

The service was not to run happily and showed the difficulties of divided control of air services between the Commonwealth and the States. Trans Oceanic Airways either did not come under the control or was able to flout the control of the Civil Aviation Department. While they allowed 50 lb. of free luggage for each passenger, QEA was forced by the Department to adhere to the usual limit of 35 lb.

While we were planning and developing these regional services, our eyes had been firmly fixed on a regular operation which would link Australia with Manila, Hong Kong, Japan and China. The bringing of our plans to fruition depended on political developments following the chaos of war, and the availability of suitable aircraft and dollars to buy them. Years before we had proposed a service to China on the great circle route to the U.K. The shortening of the journey to London by some 1,200 miles had always attracted us; but until the present day we have been defeated by political considerations in China and Russia. After the war, in June 1946, we submitted a definite plan to operate DC4 aircraft on a route Sydney, Darwin, Manila, Hong Kong, Tokyo.

Australian forces then formed part of the British Commonwealth occupied area in the southern part of the main island of Japan, Bofu being the principal base. Since November 1945 the RAAF had operated a courier service linking Australia and Japan, using Dakota aircraft. No. 86 Transport Wing had done a splendid job carrying passengers and troop mail; but demobilization had been pushed along and the opportunity came to us to take over the service from the RAAF.

Air Marshal Richard Williams was, of course, a great help in securing the service for QEA; and Lieutenant-General H. C. H. Robertson, Commander-in-Chief ("Red Robbie"), in thanking No. 86 Wing for their work, welcomed QEA. No DC4 aircraft were available, so again we started a post-war service with that old stop-gap, the Lancastrian.

Neil Geike was in charge for us at Bofu, and on 16th December 1947 our Lancastrian VH-EAU departed from Mascot on the opening weekly flight, under the command of Captain J. G. Morton, having as his crew Captain A. R. H. Morris, Captain F. T. Bryce, Navigation Officer G. H.

Parsons, Radio Officers H. Hocking and W. R. Clarke. After calling at Darwin and Manila, the aircraft landed at Bofu on 18th December, carrying some 1,200 lb. of Christmas mail for the troops, and six passengers.

This first civilian service between Australia and Japan was greeted in force at Bofu by Japanese newsmen and photographers. Sheets of copy and exposed film were rolled into tiny metal capsules and, attached to carrier pigeons, were soon in Tokyo where headlines appeared in the newspapers.

Winter conditions were bleak at Bofu. There was no hangar accommodation, and often accumulated snow had to be shovelled off the icicle-encrusted wings of the Lancastrians.

Some relief was given when the frequency of the service was stepped up to twice weekly. On 4th April 1948 the nearby renovated Japanese aerodrome of Iwakuni came into use by us. Then on 15th October 1948 the service was extended to Tokyo. Following Neil Geike, Dudley Dunn was our No. 1 man in Japan, to be followed by Nowell Jones, and then John Fysh was posted as manager in August 1954.

Until recent times QEA had the sole service, which continuously improved in aircraft and importance, in passenger, mail and freight volume, and which did much to accelerate the cultural, trade and tourist relations between the two countries. The first really significant development did not take place until service to the Australian Occupation Forces ceased to be the main consideration and, in 1949, five Skymaster aircraft were purchased, some of which were employed on the run. The greatly added capacity for mails, passengers and freight, and the provision of up-to-date meal services enabled us to cater for traffic to Manila. The Philippines were now recovering from the devastating economic consequences of a long war and the Japanese military occupation.

It was vital that we should include a stop at Hong Kong, also recovering from the war with Japan. This was to be the world renowned British free trade crossroads of the Orient, and it was also important that we should make a link there with the BOAC service operating from London through Singapore. On 17th March 1949 a QEA Skymaster landed at Kai Tak airport under the command of Captain E. C. Sims on an initial survey flight, carrying an imposing array of company officials led by Captain W. H. Crowther, operations manager.

Satisfactory traffic rights, the basis of successful aerial operations, were always a jealously guarded national asset, and the United Kingdom, with their local authority in Hong Kong, were being particularly difficult. The stage had been far from reached where QEA could get workable traffic

57

rights from Hong Kong to Tokyo and Manila. Our Civil Aviation Department was experiencing difficulty in obtaining permission from the McArthur regime in Tokyo for us to replace the Lancastrians with Skymasters. Overcrowding of the Tokyo Haneda airport was one reason cited for delay. The intervention of the Prime Minister, Mr Chifley, finally cleared the way, and on 22nd November 1949 our Skymasters went in and our real commercial services commenced.

To return to the Hong Kong service, our first regular service commenced from Sydney on 26th June 1949 and flew over the route Sydney, Darwin, Labuan, Hong Kong. Captain J. M. Hampshire was in command of Skymaster VH-EBM, and he had as his crew Captains A. R. H. Morris and R. D. Mears, First Officers Lindsay and Sommerville, Navigation Officers E. C. Richards and J. Hodges, Radio Officers H. W. Taylor and J. E. Hills, and Flight Stewards R. Hogan and A. McAlister.

It was from this basis that our service to the Orient developed till it was welded into an efficient, organized, through-service, omitting the call at Labuan. Constellation 749 aircraft were put on the run in 1954.

A few years previously I should have been obliged to be on the spot myself to organize the service to the Orient. Now my duties chained me to my office desk in Sydney, and it was a group of active young planners who arranged for the opening of the routes to Japan and Hong Kong. Not until April 1951 was I able to visit Tokyo with my wife. We had not been to Japan before and we saw it in the stage of its rehabilitation under McArthur and fast approaching full autonomy. We were taken to the Marunocchi Hotel, still under the control of Australian forces. The U.S.A. forces were in possession of the famous Imperial Hotel.

I remember an amusing incident when our early morning tea was brought in by two delightful, trim little Japanese girls dressed in smart uniforms. Later, when chatting to the manager I asked him, because I was always interested in hotel service and efficiency, why *two* girls brought the tea in. He very quickly answered, "Oh, we have strict rules here, you know. Safety first! Safety first!"

On a later visit to Tokyo, my wife and I stayed at the Imperial Hotel in the charge of the world famous hotelier, Inumaru. There, the morning tea was brought into our luxurious suite by an elegantly dressed Japanese girl progressing forward on her knees.

What a lovely country Japan was then, with the last of the spring cherry blossoms on the trees, and up at Hakone, where we stayed at the Fujiya Hotel with its views of the famous mountain, the hilly countryside was clothed in green after the winter. The Fujiya was run by another famous hotelier. Each room was identified by a flower instead of a number; ours was the fuchsia. We swam in the "Pool of Eternal Youth", sampled the unsurpassed cuisine, and enjoyed an atmosphere of cultured patronage which earned, from me, the classification of No. 1 in the world. Now and again, in my travels, I have classified world hotels, others ranking from time to time as first, and each for peculiar types of dignified personal service. These have been the Beverly Hills in Burbank, the Berkeley in London, the Imperial in Vienna, and the almost incomparable Royal Orleans in New Orleans. The Mandarin in Hong Kong was, of course, well up on the list. Here in Australia, we have always been behind in top hotel accommodation and though we are now moving towards higher standards, we know nothing of the charming hospitality to be found in the older countries.

On a later visit to Tokyo I was accorded the Freedom of the City, in recognition of our early post-war service to Japan, but I was never able to find out what freedoms, if any, the honour entitled me to. The presentation was made on 13th May 1955 by the Governor of Tokyo, Mr Seiichiro Yasui, when I was presented with a beautiful gold key in which the arms of the city were incorporated. This was only the 35th key to be presented to that date and was the only one ever presented to an airline head.

We left Japan greatly impressed by the country and the people, and convinced of its remarkable tourist attractions and of the part which Japan was destined to play in the future. Coining a phrase, I dubbed the country "the England of the East".

Continued friendship and co-operation between Australia and Japan will be important for the future, and it was a privilege for QEA to have brought the two countries closer together by air. The Australian international airline increased the volume of those two vital ingredients of contact, trade and tourism. The present need is for more Japanese tourists to visit Australia to establish a correct balance.

## ✦ 8 ✦

## *Enter the Lockheed Constellation*

THE YEAR 1947 was a hectic one for all our senior officers. In addition to the regional and Orient services, we were preparing to operate the sophisticated Constellation 749s on our most important route, the Kangaroo route to England.

We had seen the cap and goggle days, the coming of cabins, washrooms, and with the Handley Pages, restaurant services, the multi-engined DH86, the commodious Empire flying boats, the DC4 Skymaster, and now the Constellation. This aircraft incorporated so many advances that it ushered in an entirely new era in long distance travel. The broad oceans were flown at great speed, in pressurized comfort, and comfort in seating, ventilation and heating; with the ushering in of quick-freeze food service, and an enhanced carrying capacity at a reduction of operating cost per ton mile. The Constellation itself was a thing of beauty, whether on the ground or in the air, with its sleek long fuselage gracefully humped, dolphin-like, at the fore end, and its trim, triple-tail fins and rudders. A truly great aeroplane of its day, backed up by its compatriot, the DC6. There was nothing in the world to beat the Constellation.

We had quite a contingent of the Lockheed people from the factory at Burbank, some fifty in all, and Scotty Allan was "Officer in Charge Constellation Project". Ten of our pilots and six first officers went through a five weeks' technical course at the Lockheed training school, and undertook flying training there. In addition, Captains E. C. Sims, D. F. MacMaster, K. G. Jackson and R. J. Ritchie did a special course in the new technique of instrument landing at the Pan American World Airways Flying School at La Guardia, New York.

In Sydney, on the ground, the Link Trainers were at work, and in the air two Wackett trainer aircraft. Captain W. H. Crowther, as operations manager, had all this work under his control. On the engineering side, Arthur Baird was engineering manager with D. H. Wright as chief engineer. The latter handled many of the complicated problems that had to be overcome in dealing successfully with the sophisticated and touchy monster. Handling of the power plant, the Curtiss Wright 2,500 H.P. C18-BD1, raised the important issue of spares procurement, both in the overhaul shop and in the air where flight engineers became members of the crews for the first time.

A contingent of engineers was sent off to the U.S.A., led by D. B. Hudson, and backed up by N. W. Roberts, A. J. Littlejohns, J. A. Upex and G. J. Aldous, with M. Meyers on the radio side. R. A. Scott looked after spares and other procurements until D. Armstrong came along, to be followed by E. J. Cloherty. Training and familiarization took place at Burbank and at the Curtiss Wright factory in Woodbridge, New Jersey, outside New York, and at their propeller plant. Sam Irwin was our Curtiss Wright contact for many years in the U.S.A. and, in Australia, Ernest Heymanson, the Lockheed agent, was to prove a great strength in future years.

N. V. St Leon was one of fourteen QEA men sent to the U.S.A. travelling on a "Bride" ship of eight hundred women; our chaps were the only men passengers on board. St Leon ultimately became a QEA captain of aircraft, the only ex-engineer, apart from the late Arthur Baird, to get his pilot's wings with the company. He topped things off by marrying one of our first air hostesses, Patricia Burke.

On the important instruments and electronics side, the leading QEA man was George A. Roberts who spent some time in the U.S.A. studying the complicated systems incorporated in the Constellations.

The building of the aircraft was, of course, watched closely by our people. Then there was the decoration of the machines, the choice and fitting of passengers' chairs and sleeping bunks, the decision on the galleys and ovens for handling frozen food. Spare engines were ordered and dispatched, together with aircraft and engine parts, with a continuing supply of the latter for our Mascot overhaul shop. Under the efficient supervision of Scotty Allan, and with hard work by all concerned, the general procurement and delivery side had gone to plan. Harman, Crowther and Turner visited Burbank.

Later, I made a personal visit to Lockheed's which I always found an uplifting experience, and the interesting problems of the present, and the fantastic future, were discussed with Bob and Courtlandt Gross and their executives. What wonderful people we found Lockheed's through the years, inspiring the greatest respect and confidence.

In the years I write about, Australia had not yet taken her full place in world affairs. This was partly why a visit to Burbank was always such an interesting affair. I remember with amusement an incident which happened on one of my all too brief visits. At our Burbank office, the conversation turned to how everyone owned at least one car in the Hollywood-Los Angeles area, otherwise they could not get to work. The women local staff at our office all arrived in their cars. They were mostly in debt and in strained circumstances until next payday came along. One lady, whose wage was two hundred dollars a month, was mentioned as having difficulty in meeting payments on her modest second-hand car. On my next visit, I asked how things were going with the lady. Had she been able to keep up her payments? I was met with the reply, "Yes, she's paid it off." I said, "Oh, she must be relieved now she is out of financial worry." The reply came quickly, "Good heavens, no. She's in deeper than ever. She's just put a deposit on a new Buick."

This seemed to be how those who had wage-earning power were living in America. It was promoting big business. Nothing seemed to be built to last, as I found out when I heard about a refrigerator going wrong in one of our staff-rented flats in San Francisco. "Throw it out," said the owner. "We will put a new one in." A saying that has always stuck in my mind is: "America's economy is built on waste."

Another never-to-be-forgotten incident occurred when I was invited out to dinner at the home of a Lockheed technical man. We called at a shop on the way to his home, and just as one would buy a loaf of bread or a pound of butter, we bought the whole dinner, pre-cooked and deep frozen, to be thawed out for our meal.

I was given a ride on the Los Angeles helicopter circuit, sitting on the mail bags, as mail only was carried. We landed on the Central Post Office roof, taking on the mails which came up in a lift and which were automatically weighed. On the circle of heliports, the timetable between stops provided for times such as seven minutes, thirteen minutes, nine minutes in the air. It was a memorable experience twenty years ago, though common enough today.

Our aircraft began to roll out at Burbank, with their gleaming, newly-painted names: the *Lawrence Hargrave, Harry Hawker, Ross Smith* and *Charles Kingsford Smith*. The new names reserved for the next two Constellations were *Bert Hinkler* and *Horace Brinsmead*. Soon the delivery flights would begin while in Sydney the preparations to receive, service and operate the aircraft were near completion.

In Shell House, Sydney, there were scenes of extraordinary activity, for this was the nerve centre for the operations of our commercial and finance sections. At Mascot, our engineering workshops had been renovated, the wartime extension of the overhaul shop, which had been put up by the RAN, having been purchased for £4,000. Here Jack Avery was in charge, preparing to cope with what proved to be a difficult and temperamental engine. Initial production of overhauled engines was to be three a week. Our instrument and electrical shop was brought up to date, instruments being in the charge of George A. Roberts. The Constellation had numerous advanced instruments, new to us, including the radio compass. Each aircraft had no less than 125 electric motors, though I am told the true number was never ascertained, for they were always finding another one! Power assisted controls were one of the new features.

We started off with 50% spare engines. These quickly increased to 100% because of unexpected failures which, in the dark days, rose to 52% of engines removed before reaching their time-expired running time of some 800 hours. Spares were sent out along the Kangaroo route, relief engines being flown on the Australian end in Liberators, BOAC looking after the UK end with KLM doing the overhauls at their renowned overhaul shop at Schipol, perhaps the most advanced overhaul shop of its day. KLM were both efficient and reliable and helped us out of many a difficulty. An innovation that came later was when one of our Lancastrians was fitted out as an engine carrier with a special Qantas designed engine pod slung under the fuselage.

Rose Bay flying boat base proved the site of yet another initial venture, when our first frozen food factory was built there with Ron Edwards in charge. Supplies were processed to be put aboard our Constellations and for shipping along the route as far as Singapore. Cahills, a Sydney pioneer in this field, helped us in our initial stages. Then we were visited by "Bushy" Hedges, that lovable character in charge of BOAC catering. Lyons of London were the leaders in the early days of frozen food catering. In their factory outside London they erected their famous "glider", an aeroplane cabin mock-up where pre-quick-frozen meals were served to potential customers who incredulously handled solid bricks of soup which quickly turned into piping hot liquid steaming up from the plate. Ron Edwards put on a dinner party at Rose Bay where all these mysteries were revealed to wondering diners.

Our frozen food production went on through the years from strength to strength. In 1950 our St Mary's Quick Frozen Food Centre was opened up with H. M. Ross as manager. There a staff of thirty produced up to two tons of food daily. In 1956 the plant was moved to Mascot where it was conveniently centred in a passenger services building. In 1966, the jet age, some 287,700 meals were produced.

The decision was made to employ air hostesses on the Constellations in addition to flight stewards, a combination of personal and skilled friendly service which has gone on through the years to earn for Qantas international aircraft a passenger approval unsurpassed in the world. J. Martin and others laid the foundations of acceptable friendly service right through from the old flying boat days.

When the decision to employ air hostesses was made, advertisements were placed in the newspapers, with the result that our employment section was swamped by 2,000 applications. These had to be fined down to the initial nine required. The qualifications required were:

| | |
|---|---|
| Age | 22-27 years |
| Nationality | British subject |
| Education | Intermediate Certificate or higher |
| Height | 5' 3" to 5' 6" |
| Weight | In proportion to height—maximum 9 stone 7 lb. |
| Medical | Nursing certificate (fully trained) or current holder of St John's First Aid Certificate |

Bruce Hinchcliffe of the staff department had the heavy task of eliminating the unsuitable candidates, then Bill Nielson, traffic manager, came into the picture and George Harman, general manager, and there was a final line-up of girls before this tribunal in which was included Lady Hudson Fysh.

The nine girls chosen were Misses Margaret Lamb, Patricia Burke, Rosetta Allison, Irma Wharton, Marjorie de Tracy, Joy Daniell, Margaret Calf, Joyce Bruce and Adrienne Gudlinger. All had previous experience as air hostesses with either TAA or ANA. Miss Marjorie de Tracy was appointed senior flight hostess, and she has headed this important section of our passenger service right through the years and seen the number of air hostesses grow from the initial nine to 129 in 1966. Some amusement was, of course, caused by the two names Calf and Lamb.

Not long after the original selection a further six were chosen, their names being Misses Margot Umphelby, Patricia Moffat, Pamela Waddell, Margaret McLachlan, Joan Algie and Lilian Heal. Pamela Waddell and Margaret McLachlan came from the ranks of QEA staff and the others from domestic airlines.

A rigorous training was commenced on 5th January 1948 with a school at Rose Bay and familiarization flights abroad. On 8th May the first air hostess to serve on Constellations left Mascot for London.

The plan of combining air stewards and hostesses was a success from the start, and it was a great help that we had a well trained and dedicated group of stewards with an honourable tradition dating back to the time of the old Empire flying boats. At the end of 1947, J. Martin was head steward of a staff of fifty-four. A few of the excellent team were A. Graham, F. Shell, K. O'Flaherty, S. Moll, S. Preece, H. Smith, S. Andrews and A. de Courcy. By June 1966 the air stewards numbered five hundred.

Passengers all over the world, and a grateful directive and management of QEA, attested to the extraordinarily good work of our stewards and hostesses. As the passenger today steps inside the entrance of a big

Boeing jet he or she is met with a genuine smile of welcome; the pleasure to be of service, which is so rare today. No tips; the dignity of labour. And so it goes on throughout the trip, whether it be the serving of a sumptuous dinner, helping to look after a baby or an old lady, or inquiring of a restless passenger in the small hours of the morning, "Would you like an extra pillow or an Aspro?"

The establishment of a service such as the Constellation makes heavy demands upon the office staff. At Shell House, timetables had to be worked out and printed after the decision on stopping places and night stops, accommodation for passengers and crews arranged, and a new passenger fare fixed. The printing presses ran hot on new menu cards, timetables and tariff folders, passenger and advertising material of all kinds. Management and the accounts section met the new decisions by re-planning, budgeting and revised accounting.

For all of us there are a few great days which always ignite our memories. A golden day for me was 10th December 1919 when I saw Ross Smith's Vimy appear as a fast growing speck out over the Timor Sea, coming in to land on Fanny Bay aerodrome at Darwin. Another great day for our small welcoming group was 14th October 1947 when at Mascot aerodrome, at about 1.15 p.m., we saw our first delivery Constellation—the *Ross Smith*—appear in the distant sky and then circle the aerodrome in all its gleaming outlined beauty, and come in to land, taxiing to rest in front of the welcoming party headed by Arthur Drakeford, Minister for Civil Aviation, who, later, his face wreathed in smiles, spoke of his Government's determination to keep Australia in the forefront of international air transport through the agency of QEA.

As the *Ross Smith* had come in to final position on the tarmac, Captain E. C. Sims, the commander, put his airscrews into reverse pitch, which moved the Constellation backwards. This made the onlookers gasp, and the press reported that it had never been done before in Australia. The *Ross Smith* had flown from Burbank to Sydney in 33 hours flying time and 43 hours elapsed time. These were commercial records then.

There followed a visit to Canberra where W. C. Taylor and I showed the Constellation to the Prime Minister and other notables. An amusing press photograph of the visit showed Ben Chifley sitting next to me in the cabin, his inseparable pipe in his left hand and a flaring match in the other. The caption appearing with the photograph read:

> Smoking is prohibited in an aircraft when it is on the ground, and Mr Hudson Fysh, Managing Director of Qantas, had to remind the Prime Minister that even the famous pipe must be extinguished.

We then took the Constellation to Melbourne, flying from Sydney in 97 minutes against a 25 m.p.h. head wind, but breaking the previous commercial record by six minutes.

With its many new features, all designed for extra speed and comfort, the Constellation immediately appealed to the imagination of the public. Here are some of the basic figures for the model 749 as we received it, though, of course, they were constantly improved during the lifetime of the type, as increased power was obtained and all-up weight was lifted. All figures are approximate:

| | |
|---|---|
| All-up weight | 102,000 lb. |
| Wing span | 123 feet |
| Length | 95 feet 1½ inches |
| Height | 23 feet |
| Wing area | 1,610 feet |
| Power plant | 4 Curtis-Wright C18-BD1 engines of 2,500 h.p. |
| Maximum cruising speed | 318 m.p.h. |
| Service ceiling | 26,000 feet |
| Passenger capacity | 38, with bunks for 20 |
| Payload, long range | 14,000 lb. |
| Normal range | 3,000 miles |
| Maximum range | 4,800 miles |

Actually, our aircraft, when placed in service on the Kangaroo route, carried a payload of 12,120 lb. over stages up to 2,500 miles, with seating accommodation for 38 passengers. There were also four seats in the promenade lounge.

An interesting feature of the Constellation 749 was the speedpak, a boat-like cargo container which, when loaded with up to 4,000 lb. of freight, was lifted electrically and clamped under the body of the aircraft. This resulted in the carriage of a greatly enhanced payload when operating over shorter stages and without any significant sacrifice of performance.

The final preparation for commencing the service was a proving flight from Sydney to London and back, Captain R. J. Ritchie commanding the *Ross Smith*. Then came the great day of 1st December 1947 and the ceremonial at Mascot airport when the opening Constellation service was dispatched to London. At 10.6 p.m. Arthur Drakeford, Minister for Civil Aviation, made a speech, as did Air Marshal Richard Williams, Director-General. Then Mr Bradley, the Deputy Director of Posts and Telegraphs, handed me a special mail bag which I handed to the captain of the aircraft. The 29 passengers went aboard and, as the *Daily Mirror* put it next day:

> Finally, the Constellation, like a great firefly, winged its way into the night—but let us stick to the Drakeford formula, for therein lies the prospect of Puck's promise, as in "Midsummer Night's Dream", being realised: "I'll put a girdle round the earth in forty minutes."

The crew leaving Mascot on this opening flight of the *Charles Kingsford Smith* consisted of:

| | |
|---|---|
| Commander | Captain K. G. Jackson |
| | Captain A. A. E. Yates |
| | Captain J. C. Pollock |
| Navigation Officer | A. J. Hughes |
| Radio Officer | B. P. Beresford |
| Engineering Officer | D. E. Brown |
| Flight Engineer | E. J. N. Jackson |
| Flight Steward | A. Cain |
| Flight Steward | A. Gragan |
| Flight Steward | C. Bussell |

At Karachi, Captain D. F. MacMaster took over as commander and landed at London on schedule at 12.35 p.m. on 5th December.

The first London-Sydney service left on 7th December and was satisfactorily concluded on the 11th, under the command of Captain D. F. MacMaster on the first stage and Captain A. A. E. Yates on the second.

At the time of opening this new service the one class fare between Sydney and London was £A325, or £A585 return. The freight was £2-12-0 per kilo. The airmail fee was 1s. 6d. per half ounce, a special commemorative cachet being struck by the company.

The timetable between Sydney and London was an interesting compromise. The bunks were not used, so as to accommodate the large number of passengers. Two nights were spent in the air and two on the ground at Singapore and Cairo. This slowed down the journey to just under four days but made the trip more comfortable. Once weekly in each direction was the original frequency.

An interesting consignment on the opening service to London was 2,000 lb. of food parcels, many of which were sent by QEA staff to their opposite numbers in BOAC. In 1948 the Lord Mayor of Sydney's food parcels fund was sending 15,000 parcels weekly, some £800,000 being spent in this way in two and a half years.

With the introduction of the Constellation service, a new phase in air travel between Australia and the U.K. and Europe had begun, and a really significant traffic flow. The service was soon stepped up to three times a fortnight. Then, during a memorable trip to Ireland which I had with Sir Harold Hartley, BOAC bought five Constellations from Aerlinte Eireann Teoranta, whose new government, elected on a platform of strict economy, cancelled the Trans Atlantic programme of the defeated government. We bid for but were unable to secure some of these aircraft for ourselves, so leased one from BOAC who, with the other four, commenced a parallel Constellation service to Australia in place of the old Hythe flying boats and Lancastrians. This was the beginning of a very satisfactory partnership for some years. Much was to be heard of the Comets and Britannias before the coming of the Boeing 707.

To turn to another page of the story at this time, while searching through old records for material for this chapter, I came upon two references to Mornington Island and the Flying Doctor Service which showed that the old-time days of romance in our operations were not yet over:

> Qantas pilots on Flying Doctor Service in Queensland have to be good all-rounders. Recently, the Flying Doctor based at Cloncurry performed an urgent operation at Mornington Island. The patient was a native woman with a burst appendix. The operation took place at night on a table in the Mission House. A weather official acted as anaesthetist, and the pilot as "assistant surgeon". The operation was successful. Paying tribute to both men, the Flying Doctor stated, "With a short talk and a few written instructions given them before the operation, they formed as good a surgical team as could be found in a city hospital."

Then, in December 1947, for the ninth year running, we dropped a special parachute Christmas mail and special Christmas gifts from the Australian Inland Mission in Sydney, on the lonely outpost of Mornington Island, away in the Gulf of Carpentaria.

The Royal cabin (*Photo*: QEA)

Flight stewards Harold Smith and Kevin O'Flaherty polish up aboard the *Horace Brinsmead*
(*Photo*: QEA)

Catalina VH-EAX blown ashore at Lord Howe Island

Remains of Catalina VH-EAU after Rose Bay explosion on 27th August 1949

## ❖ 9 ❖

## *Qantas Security*

In the barnstorming days of the early 1920s, Security for Qantas meant the night watchman sleeping in our Longreach hangar, or, at some outback town such as Windorah in the Channel country, a hastily engaged "bushie" sleeping under the wing of our pegged-down plane. The Old Timer would have his little campfire twinkling, and the mosquitoes buzzing in their millions from the nearby swamp. The old man's duties were to keep stray cows and horses from chewing the wings of the old BE2E and to prevent local enthusiasts from writing their names on the fuselage, or putting their feet through the fabric wings in an endeavour to climb up and explore the mysteries of the pilot's cockpit.

We had in those years our share of disturbing incidents as when a prominent Brisbane business man hired a Puss Moth, flown by Arthur Baird, for a tour of country districts. When over Toowoomba the passenger made desperate efforts to open the door and jump out, but Baird restrained him. This was possibly the first case in Australia of attempted suicide from the air, though several important people overseas, including the "Match King", had committed suicide from an aeroplane. Our client, back in Brisbane, solved his domestic troubles by jumping to his death from a tall building.

With the introduction of our Constellation service it was necessary to establish a properly constituted security staff. BOAC had started one in 1946, KLM, TWA and others had done the same. Qantas, now operating long international services, and daily, if not hourly, breaking through the national barriers each country had erected in its customs, migration, health and monetary controls, needed a security branch for its orderly progress.

Cargo thefts were taking place on the Sydney-London run; there was petty pilfering of tools and stores at our bases. More spectacular was the disappearance at the Rose Bay flying boat base of the fur coat of a director's wife which she had left in the luggage rack. As on a previous visit this director's suitcase had been dropped overboard from the luggage launch, sparks flew over the loss of the fur coat.

The security branch was formed while George Harman was general manager. Gordon Fraser, later to be known as "First Flight", started as

69

F

security superintendent with twenty night-watchmen. During the next few months C. V. Owers, a retired police inspector, joined the new branch as supervisor of guards and watchmen, and H. H. Miller, a Shanghai fire brigade officer, became our fire officer.

Gordon Fraser proved a good choice, for he is still head of the now greatly expanded security service. He was a product of the New South Wales police cadet training system, which he joined in 1936 straight from school at the age of sixteen. In 1947 the Criminal Investigation Branch appointed him to concentrate on airline work, and in this way he came into touch with QEA.

A security service performs an essential function, but can easily get out of hand and become a menace if allowed too much power. This has never happened with QEA Security, though, unavoidably, friendships were strained in the course of duty. The understanding and human approach of Gordon Fraser, the man in QEA with the most sensational secrets in his keeping, was the guiding force behind the smooth and successful working of our security branch. If ever he gets around to writing the story, it will be a bestseller.

The duties of the service in an international airline are varied and important. One, of course, is the safeguarding of aircraft against sabotage, particularly in times and places of political unrest, but also against cranks. There were the special precautions to be taken with royal flights, a number of which we carried out in an atmosphere of the most careful watchfulness. Other duties of the service involved the prevention of theft of mails, cargo and passengers' effects, the investigation of thefts and losses, the checking on new appointees. There was the necessary fire and security patrol of hangars, workshops and offices, guards being supplied with walkie-talkie equipment and radio-equipped vehicles. Smuggling had to be guarded against; assistance given to the company's legal section. The duties were complementary to those of the local police and most of our recruits came from the New South Wales police force.

Matters involving criminal or suspected criminal action of a serious nature were handed over to the local police. The company was concerned with operating an airline, not a police, fire brigade or customs force.

One of the most sensational happenings in our long history was the blowing up of the Catalina flying boat VH-EAW which sank at her Rose Bay moorings. The loss occurred just two months after our Catalina VH-EAX had been damaged beyond repair in the lagoon at Lord Howe Island. We had been operating to the island for eighteen months and had seen traffic build into something worthwhile.

On 23rd June 1949 our Catalina and one of Trans Oceanic Airways were riding at their moorings on the lagoon when in a "blow" our flying boat broke her moorings and went ashore. On a previous night the TOA flying boat had broken adrift but was returned safely by the crew who had remained aboard. In the case of our Catalina, reliance had been placed on the three inch manilla rope mooring pennant, and the storm pennant of galvanized stainless steel cable, with a breaking strain of 38,960 lb. Mooring buoys and pennants are the responsibility of the Department of Civil Aviation, and following the loss of VH-EAX there was a great deal of correspondence to determine responsibility for the accident. Should we have had a crew aboard? What caused the supposedly stout cable to break after the rope pennant went?

The cable had been passed as fit on the 7th April by a Civil Aviation officer and again on 1st June. Yet on 23rd June the steel cable had parted. The result of investigations by the Defence Research Laboratories was the finding that:

> At positions adjacent to the fracture the inner surfaces of each strand were badly rusted; the galvanising had been completely removed from all wires and a red corrosion product had accumulated between the strands.

The failure had come at the point where the cable would be alternatively in and out of the water, and where corrosion could be expected; but I am not aware, myself, of the interesting point of difference between corrosion and rust.

This loss placed us at a great disadvantage but we were able to continue with the service until when, at 2.22 a.m. on Saturday morning, 27th August 1949, the Catalina VH-EAW blew up at its Rose Bay moorings with a roar that woke me in my home at Wallaroy Road.

At first, it was thought that the problem facing Gordon Fraser and his assistants was an internal matter, an accidental explosion. But when the shattered wreckage was fished up from the bottom of the bay, an apparatus, foreign to the aircraft, was found under the seat of the flight engineer. Sabotage was so clearly indicated that further investigation was handed over to the police, Detective Sergeant Alridge of the Arson Squad taking over.

The apparatus consisted of a piece of fruit case board, measuring approximately 18″ by 9″ by ½″, through which several holes had been drilled. Attached to the board by means of string and fishing cord was an alarm clock, a six volt lantern battery, and a vibrator coil similar to that used on an old T model Ford car. There was no sign of a lead to an explosive charge and it was assumed that the unit was designed primarily

71

to throw a spark. From a reconstruction, it was assumed that this was done by leaving a bare wire at the back of the alarm clock, against which the winder of the alarm struck as it rotated when the alarm went off, causing sparks to be thrown from two wires at the top of the coil. No traces of explosive were found on the aircraft but it was discovered that a locking device had been broken on the port side fuel gauge. The starboard side fuel flow meter was broken, allowing petrol to drain into the engineer's compartment. It was assumed that the apparatus threw a spark; this had ignited the escaping petrol fumes and an explosion and fire had resulted. It was a very neat job, but the perpetrators had not expected the apparatus to be recovered virtually intact.

In the City Coroner's Court evidence was given which led to the arrest of an executive officer of TOA and his trial before Judge Curlewis on a charge of causing malicious damage to a flying boat. A strong alibi was submitted and the defendant was acquitted.

The years have passed on, and no one is now likely to be apprehended for the serious crime which undoubtedly occurred; but those concerned, whoever they were, are no doubt still living with the incident, either chuckling to themselves, or being haunted by remorse, according to their natures.

The whole affair was an unfortunate episode for both TOA and Qantas. Trans Oceanic Airways had come into being as a result of P. G. Taylor meeting a group of young and enthusiastic ex-wartime pilots at Rose Bay, as he put it, "struggling gallantly with an obviously hopeless attempt to start an airline." Their determination appealed to him and he decided to help them. This resulted in TOA operating on a better basis with more capital coming in and the Clan Line taking an interest. Unfortunately the larger established airlines were fighting to establish their position, and ANA were in the process of gaining control of whatever airlines they could. We were determined to secure our own position in all services in and out of Australia, and in this we had to oppose TOA in services to Lord Howe Island and New Guinea. In the circumstances of the times the new operator had no chance of survival.

The security services of the airlines could operate within the regions of their jurisdiction, but it was soon necessary for International Air Transport Association to move in and attempt to keep infringements of the traffic regulations under control. With some reluctance on the part of Sir William Hildred, the executive committee of IATA brought into being an enforcement section, R. Feick being appointed chief enforcement officer. This new branch was at first gingerly referred to at the annual general meeting of IATA as an "inspectorate", but the executive meant business and in the years to come a ceaseless war was made on chiselers, fare undercutters, evaders and the extremely cunning tricks made to circumvent the laws of IATA and to steal a march on competitors.

What made action imperative was that some suffering members were complaining to their governments and this could only lead to unpleasant international consequences. IATA had wisely recognized its responsibility to enforce rates and conditions of traffic which it had itself laid down.

A Breaches Commission was set up to hear cases of infringement and to report to the executive committee, recommending when necessary an appropriate fine. The committee then made a final decision. Later amendments to the rules left the matter of fines, within limits, to the Breaches Commission which was kept extraordinarily busy, collecting through the years fines totalling $US5,347,150 which offset the cost of the enforcement section. QEA remained unfined until 1966 when the genuine error of a traffic officer in weighing a freight consignment brought a fine of $US1,000.

During a discussion in the executive committee of IATA, when things were particularly bad, I remember that I made the casual remark that QEA had never been fined. A member, with a smile, observed that my board could not have felt very proud of me!

Breaches mainly consisted of undercutting agreed fares and rates. At one time, in South America, as much as 40% could be procured off an air fare. Dealings between some members and accredited IATA booking agents also proved extremely sinful.

Airline security officers were bound to become involved in these IATA matters in bad areas, but Australian business practices were usually remarkably clean and unsophisticated, and our security branch was never seriously called upon. Our security people, however, had to deal with a constant flow of interesting or sad cases. I remember the loss of a valuable instrument which had been consigned from Switzerland to Sydney. When the case was opened, all it contained was a large stone of exactly the same weight as the instrument. Months went by trying to find out, amongst other things, which particular country that type of stone came from.

Then there was the interesting legal argument arising from the consignment from Sydney to Hong Kong of a valuable Dachshund bitch in pup. At Singapore the bitch was there all right and obviously "expecting" but at Hong Kong she had undoubtedly whelped. Where were the pups?

73

They had vanished and it was surmised she had eaten them. Who was responsible for the loss—the consignor, the carrier, or the consignee?

Gold, which has had such a fascination for man over the ages, is now rarely seen in coin or pure bulk form. The world's gold reserves are hidden away under every security device known to man. So it is understandable that the transfer of gold from country to country is conducted in the strictest secrecy, and that air transport has proved the most effective medium, the cutting down of transit time enabling great savings in interest.

Through its history QEA frequently carried gold, and at one time we flew the bulk of gold won out of New Guinea. BOAC were engaged in the carriage of gold in a big way, and one of the first attempts at a large robbery was made at London airport about the time we were launching our security service. It became known to a gang of thieves that BOAC were lifting large consignments of gold and a bribe of £1,000 was offered to a former BOAC security guard, then working in the cargo warehouse at London airport, to place sleeping tablets in the evening meal of staff handling the strongroom when next a large consignment came through. The ex-guard informed BOAC security, with the result that they and officers of Scotland Yard laid a trap. The warehouse staff was replaced by police officers who pretended to be lying asleep when eight or nine gangsters entered and attempted to seize £300,000 worth of gold. A fight followed, they were captured, and all received long jail sentences. To prevent reprisals from gangland on the man who reported the matter, BOAC and QEA security got together and, with my concurrence, the man was given a job at one of our most remote bases under an assumed name.

Not always were BOAC and QEA to be so successful in foiling gold thieves and smugglers.

Aircraft now have become so commodious, with large cargo compartments, that stowaways have come to rival the onetime romantic stowaways at sea. A book could be written about the exploits of air stowaways, successful and unsuccessful, and often of a novel and amusing nature. There comes to mind the case of Bas Wie, the twelve-year-old Timor boy who on 7th August 1946 arrived at the Darwin airport huddled up in the retractable-wheels recess of a Dutch Dakota aircraft. Perhaps the first case of an attempted stowaway out of Australia occurred on 20th November 1949 when a Qantas watchman, Jack Butcher, apprehended a lad of seventeen who was attempting to stowaway on a KLM aircraft. As no act of Parliament seemed to cover stowing away on an aircraft, he was simply charged by the police as being "an uncontrollable young person" and released on a bond by the Children's Court.

The first person in Australia to be actually convicted of stowing away on an overseas aircraft was a twenty-four-year-old Englishman who had worked for us at Berrimah Camp, Darwin, for a few weeks. He secreted himself on top of the cargo stacked in the hold of a Comet. When the aircraft arrived in Sydney and the hold was opened up, the stowaway who was dressed in our regulation white uniform with a red cap, pretended he was one of the local hands. He was challenged by Kevin Andrews, a Qantas employee at Mascot, and promptly made off. Our security people discovered that the stowaway had consigned his possessions from Darwin to Sydney by TAA and he was picked up very simply when he came to claim his baggage. In his statement to the police he said that he considered the Comet a suitable aircraft for stowing away because of the pressurized hold. He had walked aboard the Comet at a suitable time, through the clothes closet and then through the sliding door into the hold. It was a case of careful planning that had gone wrong. He had money in the bank to pay the £50 fine imposed by the magistrate.

On two occasions, university students, on pranks, have managed to sit in seats in the cabin and avoid the count. Then there was a most disturbing case when a mental patient at Honolulu, thinking he was on his way to his native U.S.A., made a stowaway on a Qantas aircraft bound for Sydney.

At Tokyo, when Nowell Jones was Qantas manager there, as our Skymaster came to rest after a flight from Australia, a man leapt from the cargo hold and sprinted for the airport building where he disappeared through the customs area. An investigation of the interior of the hold showed that someone had travelled in the aircraft for a considerable distance.

Later, came the sensational cases of stowaways travelling in boxes as freight. A notable case was the consignment from Rome to Cairo by the United Arab Diplomatic Corps of a man tied up in a box. Air India had a stowaway in a box from London to Perth. Qantas, not to be outdone, had a stowaway from Sydney to San Francisco who got away with it, leaving a note in his empty box signed "Dick the Fox". He later approached our manager in San Francisco seeking payment for the favourable mention he made of Qantas in the story of his adventure which appeared in *Life* magazine.

Smuggling by air will, of course, be always with us, but the aim of airways security is to keep it within reasonable proportions. The temptations put in the way of air crews and cabin crews have often been great. A case comes to mind when, some ten or more years ago, one of our cabin stewards was apprehended at Mascot on his way to the shower-room after completion of a trip. It was found that he had two hundred watches fastened to his legs with medical bandages.

A notable theft was that of a "repatriation" parcel of $100,000 in U.S. currency consigned from the Hong Kong-Shanghai Bank of Hong Kong to the Anglo-Crocker Bank. The money, which was stolen from our traffic office safe in San Francisco, was later recovered.

Undoubtedly security is an important part of our airline's responsibility, and the work done by the section has been very effective. Whenever a passenger walks across the tarmac to board an outward bound Qantas airliner and sees the alert, uniformed security officer on duty, he or she cannot fail to experience a sense of confidence in the company.

## ❖ 10 ❖

## *Qantas and the Hotel Business*

A S I LEAF through the bundle of records before me, the story of how we came to take over the old Wentworth Hotel in Lang Street, and develop from it the great, modern building which bears that name, appears one of the most fascinating in the history of Qantas.

The story begins soon after our Constellation services got into full flight and the traffic flow was leaping. At Sydney, our focal point, we were completely unable to cope with the increasing stream of passengers demanding modern hotel rooms. It was a serious blot on our service and a hindrance to our progress. Nothing new in hotel accommodation was offering, yet what a fight we had to establish it ourselves. This was the time of my most intense activity as chairman and managing director of QEA. I was constantly travelling oversea; I saw the need in Sydney, and I made it my personal business, with the assistance of the board, to remedy the position.

The need was clear; but, as a government instrumentality, with a new Liberal Party Government in office, our position was difficult. We had been created by their opponents. Would we be allowed to do the things that were obviously essential to our success? Would we be trammelled and retarded under an uncompetitive and unenterprising political control, the slave to the whims of reactionaries? No doubt, in the circumstances of election promises, the situation needed careful examination. Time, some ingenuity, plus some good supporters in Canberra, ultimately won us the victory.

In 1950 we were each day seeking accommodation for eighty passengers, tiny figures now, but in those days significant, for Sydney's first-class hotels had only some 800 rooms to cater for all accommodation needs in the growing city. Of these rooms only a small proportion had private bathroom facilities. We had a block of rooms at the Australia Hotel, but this proved quite inadequate, and often embarrassingly so, for when overflows occurred as they frequently did, protesting passengers had to be sent out to second-class hotels.

We set to work to acquire our own accommodation, but in the face of extraordinary opposition. Actually we were far from new to the business. Airlines operating internationally, through countries with different standards of hygiene, had to face the problem of providing acceptable

77

food and accommodation for passengers. This occurred not only at nightstops but at the terminal traffic centres. There was also the provision of food and beverages aboard the aircraft. The second problem was met by quick frozen food catering aboard the aircraft and in this Qantas had been most successful. The first could only be met by the airlines themselves providing first-class hotel accommodation where it did not exist.

The crucial issue was in fact that the volume of air traffic which could be carried was limited by the accommodation available on the ground. This was a fundamental principle of travel way back to the old caravanserai days. KLM were active in overcoming difficulties, so were Pan American Airways who formed their wholly owned subsidiary Intercontinental Hotels Corporation, which went on to operate a great chain of worldwide hotels fundamental to their business.

We had been catering for passengers since the 1920s when cups of tea and sandwiches were tendered to our helmeted and goggled clients at stops along the Queensland route. Harry Corones' daylight tea and sandwiches at Charleville, and McMaster's morning tea at Winton were famous. In 1934, with our first overseas service, came meals at selected stops, or cardboard box lunches aboard. At this time our clifftop nightstop cottage at Darwin was in full swing. In 1938, with the Empire flying boats, came full meals aboard, served by stewards in restaurant style from heating containers holding pre-cooked meals. Then, with the Constellations, came the ideal solution in the provision of quick frozen food, delightfully fresh, though perhaps first cooked in our St Mary's kitchens months before.

In 1950 we had leased the Queen Wilhelmina Hotel in Djakarta to look after transit and emergency night-stop passengers. At Singapore we made emergency arrangements with the Raffles Hotel but refrained from acquiring an hotel interest, though we were close to joining with the Hong Kong and Shanghai Bank in a project to erect a modern hotel.

At some outlying stations, staff and air crew accommodation was a problem, particularly so at Darwin and Lae. Soon after World War II we felt we had to do something at Darwin, which was civically one of the lowest grade towns in Australia. On 9th August 1946 we purchased the former army hospital at Berrimah, outside Darwin, for £4,813 and let a contract to John Stubbs & Sons for a renovation job to cost some £34,000. A great deal more money was put into the establishment which became quite a show place, a home from home which my wife and I always found a delight to visit. It was under the control of E. H. Godlinion and his assistants. This airways village, for a start, housed some 130 single staff and 32 married families. There was a comfortable mess hall, a recreation hall and a swimming pool. There was comfortable accommodation for lay-off air crews, and up to forty passengers could be put in single rooms all with their own shower facilities. No one who stayed at Berrimah Camp, as it was sometimes called, will forget the hospitable and tranquil atmosphere so apparent there. Having served its purpose, after the big jets were flying through Darwin, Berrimah was discarded in favour of a staff housing scheme in the town.

At Lae, our headquarters in New Guinea, we created our own village of 26 houses with central mess and staff, passengers' lounge and other amenities. The Qantas architects, Rudder, Littlemore and Rudder, were prominent in all these works, and so was our fast-growing property section under Hudson Shaw, general services superintendent.

These activities took us very close to the hotel business. We had considerable experience in providing a friendly service as temporary hosts to the travelling public. At that time, in the retarded development of the idea of "service" in Australia, good hotel service in this country was almost non-existent. It was something that I was anxious to get my hands on, for I realized how essential it was if Australia was ever going to attract tourists. At this time I felt the Dutch were the most effective hotel operators in the world. They had the right ideas of welcome and attention, though in the air QEA could equal the best.

We looked over Petty's Hotel and found it unsuitable. Then one day, I don't know how it happened but I suppose we had expressed interest, Charles Maclurcan, managing director of the Wentworth Hotel walked into my Shell House office and offered to sell us the hotel. Several others were interested, including Ansett and the Federal Hotel group, but he said he would like us to have the Wentworth as QEA would give his traditional staff a better deal than a hotel group. It was a friendly approach, confidence was established at once.

When negotiations commenced, Sir Norman Nock was chairman of the Wentworth Hotel board but was away on an extended overseas tour. Charles Maclurcan was managing director, the other directors being Mrs F. C. Postle (sister of Charles Maclurcan) and Colonel D. H. Dwyer.

The hotel was situated on historic Church Hill, on a piece of land once owned by W. C. Wentworth, father of the New South Wales Constitution. In 1854 Wentworth rented from a Mrs Onge No. 3 Church Hill which she conducted as a boardinghouse. It was formerly part of Underwood's Buildings where in 1849 the Colonial Treasury was situated. In 1851, in the roaring goldrush days, the first Gold Escort arrived to the tune of wild cheering from the assembled crowd. A Mrs Mary Hayes, who

79

was the next occupant, obtained a liquor licence. The hotel was burnt in 1888 but Mrs Hayes built the lower part as we know it and changed the name from Wentworth House to Wentworth Hotel.

In 1901 the Maclurcan family came from the Queen's Hotel, Townsville, and Donald Maclurcan, retired master mariner, took a twenty years' lease from Mrs Hayes with the option to purchase. He died in 1903 and the lease passed to Mrs Hannah Maclurcan who, with her associates, formed Wentworth Hotel Limited in 1912 to take over the freehold. Her son, Charles Maclurcan, had in 1911 carried out his early radio experiments from the roof of the hotel and his was the first station in Australia equipped to maintain communication with ships at sea. The hotel buildings were added to and greatly improved by the company and in 1920 was built the palatial ballroom which was a feature of Sydney's social life for many years.

Mrs Maclurcan died in 1936, having left her mark as a grand and adventurous lady of the hotel business. Her parties and receptions, where she held court, were famous, and as a good Queenslander I well remember meeting her when she gave a reception for Bert Hinkler after his record-breaking solo flight from England.

Charles Maclurcan became managing director but in a bad time, and the hotel had to face under him the depression of the 1930s which nearly forced a closure. The Bank of New South Wales decided to take an interest and Sir Norman Nock, chairman of the board, determined to pull the hotel out of its troubles. He succeeded but the spirit and adventure of the old days seemed to have gone, and the hotel did not regain its glamour despite Sir Norman's ambitious plans, one of which was to construct a connection with George Street. Much needed to be done to the old building, and the principal shareholders, the Maclurcan family, were anxious to quit the business.

Following a valuation of the property and a financial survey by C. O. Turner on 24th November 1949, I submitted a memorandum to the board of QEA recommending outright purchase of the Wentworth Hotel property. The Board approved, and then came the blessing of Ben Chifley and Arthur Drakeford who, however, pointed out that as the Federal elections were due in a few weeks, no financial decision could be made until the new government was in office. I wrote on 22nd December confirming the position.

At the elections the Chifley Government was defeated, largely over the nationalization issue, and we were confronted by the Menzies Government elected on a private enterprise platform. T. W. (later Sir Thomas) White, the old World War I airman who wrote *Guests of the Unspeak-*

*able*, a man with extreme views on the necessity to limit government participation in industry, became our new Minister, and we were to have a torrid time with him over some of our projects during his term of office.

On 10th January 1950 we submitted to our Minister the proposal to acquire the Wentworth Hotel, and on the 14th I received a telegram stating that the proposal had been before Cabinet and was turned down. Cabinet seemed solidly against us. It was too soon after the election and we seemed to be at a dead end.

So, in an effort to overcome the "private enterprise" difficulty, we then went ahead with a scheme to form a separate company in which we would participate with private shareholding. In this we received expert legal assistance from our old friend and adviser, Cliff Minter, of Minter Simpson & Co. A plan was evolved in which a company would be formed, giving QEA the control that was essential, but offering an attractive preference in dividends to the private shareholders. This would be an inducement to taking-up of shares and also satisfy the Stock Exchange as to listing.

In June 1950 we had our plans ready and, knowing we now had a number of Ministers on our side, on 6th June when White was overseas, we made a submission to R. G. Casey (later Baron Casey) who was Acting Minister for Civil Aviation. The matter was deferred until White's return and on 26th June we were informed by him that Cabinet had rejected our proposal, the Minister expressing surprise that we had acquired an expensive option on the hotel. The option was £4,000 for one month, which was to come off the purchase price in the event of a deal. Courtaulds had made an offer to purchase, Federal Hotels and Ansett were interested, and there was an intriguing offer by undisclosed U.S.A. interests at an advance price to our offer. We were determined not to give way for upon our success in this issue hung other ventures and our whole future. I find it fascinating to look over the mass of old letters, to be read in the context of the times. From a letter of 5th September to my Minister, Tom White, I quote:

> Whatever happens now outside of QEA acquisition means the accommodation will be totally, or greatly, lost to the BCPA, TEAL, BOAC, QEA requirements, and the control of the accommodation will be lost to Australian interests should the U.S.A. authorities get it.
> I trust you will not mind my thinking on paper on this matter, and as I know you like a story, perhaps some may appreciate your quoting the saying, "If someone gives you a dog, you should not starve it."
> P.S. On the other hand, if it is thought we are ticky, by all means pull them out.

The day before I had written to A. W. Fadden (later Sir Arthur), Federal Treasurer and a grand supporter of QEA enterprise:

> It seems to me that we have proved our case over and over, and that the real objection is one of principle in respect of our constitution. If this is so, should it not be our constitution that is under consideration, but not that the work of your national overseas operator be endangered.

I might add that an interested Prime Minister, R. G. Menzies (later Sir Robert) was kept fully informed also.

By our intense representations we were sure of increased support in Cabinet, and our plan was again resubmitted. Once again the result was a telegram from White rejecting the proposition. Menzies was overseas at the time, and I received a telegram the next day stating that the matter would be submitted to the Prime Minister on his return.

The result was that on 15th September 1950 a telegram was received from White giving approval for the plan to acquire the Wentworth Hotel, but turning down our application for our proposed £242,223 building at Mascot. A rumour at the time was that the Wentworth Hotel scheme had been approved only on the casting vote of the Prime Minister. Among those who certainly helped us were Arthur Fadden and Harold Holt. At the time of the deal the Board of QEA comprised W. C. Taylor, G. P. N. Watt, Sir Daniel McVey, Sir Keith Smith and myself.

The basis for the purchase and re-organization of the hotel is interesting. Capitalization was low at 50,000 one pound shares, total assets amounting to £116,428. The value of the freehold property was in at cost of £107,972 and was worth much more as a marketable asset. The Wentworth had experienced a good year in 1950, returning a net profit of £16,067 and was a profitable undertaking at a considerably higher capitalization, so a sale price of £5. 10s. a share was agreed upon, with a total of £275,000.

When QEA had bought the shares, the Wentworth Hotel continued to operate under the same name, but was wholly owned by the new holding company, Qantas Wentworth Holdings. Nominal capital was £500,000, out of which were issued for public subscription 125,000 £1 "A" class preference shares and 160,000 "B" class shares taken up by QEA. Under the articles QEA nominated three directors and the public shareholders two, thus giving full control to QEA.

As an offset to this control, the "A" class shares were to have a dividend preference which was so worded by Cliff Minter in the articles as to provide at the end of each financial year for the private shareholders to receive out of the profits a dividend at the rate of $4\frac{1}{2}\%$ in priority to the "B" class shares.

The "B" class shares were then to be entitled, out of the balance of such profits, also to receive $4\frac{1}{2}\%$ dividend; and thereafter any surplus profits for distribution were to be divided equally between the "A" and "B" class shareholders. As the lowest dividend paid was $5\frac{1}{2}\%$ in the first year, we never had to bring this preference provision into operation.

Qantas Wentworth Holdings Ltd was registered on 17th November 1950, and commenced business with the following directors: W. Hudson Fysh, chairman, Sir Keith Smith and H. H. Harman nominated by QEA, and Sir Norman Nock and C. D. Maclurcan elected by the private shareholders. Charles Maclurcan, who had agreed to stay and help the new direction and management, was in actuality managing director. Oliver Rule continued as manager. The QEA members of the board worked under a directive from their main board which, although businesslike, was liberal in its terms.

The new hotel company continued to work well for twelve years until Kenmaster Holdings Ltd, wholly owned by QEA, came in and purchased the "A" class shares in Qantas Wentworth Holdings Ltd in preparation for the vacation and demolition of the old hotel and the erection of the new hotel at Chifley Square which operates under the old name.

So there I was in 1951 an active chairman of the Wentworth Hotel, running a pub, and I reflected what my mother would have thought had she been alive. In the old religious tradition, she would not even take shares in a brewery or hotel. To many minds of her generation the old-fashioned pubs were sinks of iniquity, with drunks hanging around and the six o'clock swill. What I had in mind with the Wentworth was that there was now an opportunity to show what a good hotel could do in service to the public. There proved to be little need, as in the evolution of the business and with wiser legislation, a great change for the better was taking place. Well run hotels and motels were within a few years to cater efficiently not only for domestic travellers but for Australia's share of world tourism which became of increasing importance.

When the new board took over, the old Wentworth had 113 rooms with beds for 161 people, the average permanent staff being round about 150. The hotel needed modernizing for our requirements, as far as this might be done in an old building. The QEA directors were insistent on this, and my own principle had always been that a satisfied client was Qantas' first objective. We had then to "spend money to make money" and Sir Norman Nock helped us in this with his valuable advice, his intimate knowledge of the Wentworth, his close scrutiny of costs, costing and budgeting, and the financial progress of each feature of the hotel, whether it was the house, dining room, bar, or banqueting service.

83

We were fortunate in securing as permanent manager Stanley Mc-Neill, a man from the north of England, an ex-RAF air crew, who had emigrated to Australia and come to the hotel from Beetle Elliot Plastics Ltd in Melbourne. He was recommended to us by L. W. Farrer, secretary of the Residential Hotels Association.

The work of developing the old Wentworth Hotel was a most satisfying experience. The hotel constantly increased its service to QEA, profits rose each year. It was a success story which served as a useful preliminary to the larger venture to come. By 1953 we opened the Corroboree Room for functions in what had been the old Tudor Room. In the same year the block of land adjoining the hotel was bought with an eye to extension, and operated as a profitable double-decker car park. The ballroom annexe was altered and in 1955 was turned into a passenger pick up and set down station leased to QEA. International passengers passed straight from this depot to their rooms in the hotel.

By 1955 the bathroom project was completed, the Wentworth being the first hotel in Australia to have full conveniences for every room. In the 1956-58 period, air-conditioning and T.V. sets were installed in all suites and many rooms. All bedrooms had been reconditioned and redecorated under the guidance of Mrs Hilda Abbott. The diningroom had been improved and a modern kitchen installed adjacent to it, doing away with the old method of bringing up food in lifts from the depths below.

Other innovations were the popular Tavern snack bar and major alterations to the main bar adjoining the lounge. A modern lift was installed. Stanley McNeill could feel well satisfied with all his hard work and that of his assistants, J. Baljeu, an experienced Dutch hotel and catering man, and O. K. J. Bacon who was in charge of the house. Room occupancy maintained a steady 98% year in and year out. Functions were a popular service of major importance.

On the death of Sir Keith Smith, R. R. Law-Smith came on the board for QEA in 1956 and Stanley McNeill became managing director in 1957 on the death of C. D. Maclurcan. J. W. Lyons became secretary in place of K. D. Gowans.

But the board was frustrated in its desire to erect a new, modern hotel on the Lang Street site. Sydney was still hopelessly short of accommodation, but the time was far from ripe for the great expansion we believed necessary. It was too soon after the political rumpus of 1950. Little could be done beyond drawing up preliminary plans and preparing estimates.

A dramatic step forward was taken when Qantas acquired the Union Club land in Elizabeth Street. The club was rebuilding and, to secure

The infernal machine

Landing passengers from Catalina *Island Chieftain* in five-knot current at Kikori on the Sirebi River, Western Papua.

Loading housing timber at Bulolo (*Photo*: Qantas)

Our Lae village (*Photo*: Qantas)

A Mt Hagen chieftain we met

finance, land not required was for sale. It was next door to Qantas House, and for future expansion and a city passenger pick up and set down terminal, the chance was not to be missed. We acquired the site for £515,000. Athol Townley was then our Minister and approval to purchase was received from him on 13th April 1955. W. C. Taylor and C. O. Turner were the prime movers in this profitable deal.

The Wentworth Hotel board was still employed with plans for the erection of a modern building alongside the old one, and a proposal had gone to the Minister. This was turned down by Cabinet on 29th June 1955, and our attention was then directed to a plan for erecting an hotel on the Union Club site. The battle was on in earnest, and it was not until six years later, on 11th August 1961 that, after difficult and intense representations, we received permission to go ahead from the Minister, Senator S. D. (later Sir Shane) Paltridge, to whom we owed a great deal for the favourable result, as we did to Athol Townley whom we first approached with the plan in May 1956.

Senator Paltridge and his Director-General of Civil Aviation, D. G. (later Sir Donald) Anderson, faced an onslaught from the QEA board. A number of Cabinet Ministers were solidly against the project and there was very strong opposition by hotel interests, led by L. J. Hooker, Federal Hotels, with the support of the so-called first-class hotel interests in Sydney, including Korman who was building the new Chevron Hotel.

The need for an airlines hotel was overwhelmingly clear to us; we felt that we had an unanswerable case. Pan American Airways, KLM, SAS, JAL, and other airlines were actively erecting hotels for their clients. In 1960, Australia had 70,000 visitors a year from overseas and there were only 1,839 first-class rooms in Sydney to accommodate them, and few of these were first class by overseas standards. The established hotel businesses screamed that they would be put out of business, but did little to improve the position. In Canberra, it was the old story of whether a government-owned or government-controlled organization, even with private capital participating, should be maintained in a hitherto private enterprise field.

Shane Paltridge decided to call the protesting hotel interests and QEA together in what was termed an "Hotel Investigating Committee" under the chairmanship of Sir Daniel McVey. The discussions were at times difficult. I well remember Stanley Korman, chairman of Stanhill Holdings, interviewing me and I had Bob Law-Smith come along in support. Korman was getting into financial difficulties and wanted to sell us the Chevron Hotel at Kings Cross. We said we were not interested, it would not suit us. Pressed hard for a reason, I said, "We feel it

G

is the wrong place for our needs. We want the hotel in the main city area." Korman came back quickly with, "What, in the wrong place! I am a man of the world. I know. It is in the right place."

When things looked desperate in September 1958, I wrote to Don Anderson:

> All I know is that if we can't get ahead—and it has been a long row to hoe already—then some of us are just going to sit down and cry our eyes out.

In May 1959 Cabinet approved our scheme in principle, subject to a further investigation by the Minister. But we were not out of our troubles yet. In June 1960 Cabinet turned down our latest proposals at a time when I had not succeeded in bringing in BOAC, and the P & O Orient lines, whose support would have helped us considerably. Later in 1960 we were again turned down in Canberra.

Not until 11th August 1961, to our great jubilation, did we receive the go-ahead from Senator Paltridge, and the long fight, in which we had put up alternative scheme after alternative scheme, was over. I wrote the Minister a letter expressing the thanks of our board for his assistance and confidence. At the same time I wrote to the Prime Minister, R. G. Menzies:

> Apart from the obvious need, and the assistance to tourism, for some time I have realized that the real issue lay in regard to whether Qantas was to go ahead in enterprise and competition with its competitors, or whether it had reached a high water mark from which it would inevitably recede.

Here is the success story of our operation of the old Wentworth Hotel on the principles of "spend money to make money", the giving of increasingly better service to clients, the keeping of charges fully competitive, and making adequate provision for reserves:

| Year | Profit £ | Dividend % |
|------|----------|------------|
| 1951 | 12,786 | 5½ |
| 1952 | 20,485 | 5½ |
| 1953 | 25,733 | 5½ |
| 1954 | 32,074 | 7 |
| 1955 | 32,734 | 8 |
| 1956 | 33,140 | 8 |
| 1957 | 43,092 | 9 |
| 1958 | 43,330 | 9 |
| 1959 | 45,950 | 12½ |
| 1960 | 48,442 | 12½ |
| 1961 | 46,489 | 12½ |
| 1962 | 47,342 | 12½ |

Then came four years of operation under the control of the transition company, Kenmaster Holdings, when the profits were fully maintained.

Without going into too much detail one may say that the new hotel was organized and financed by the formation of a transition holding company called Kenmaster, which acquired the "A" class shareholding in Qantas Wentworth Holdings, paying those private shareholders £2 for every £1 share held, and, where they wished, re-investing the money in the 7% preference debentures in the new hotel. The "B" class shares were also acquired from QEA at 35s. a share. The final reconstruction came when the new hotel carried on again under the old name of Qantas Wentworth Holdings Limited, with a board of directors consisting of Sir Roland Wilson, chairman, R. R. Law-Smith and Sir Norman Nock, Stanley McNeill going across as general manager supported by John Baljeu.

The QEA board delegated their chief executive, C. O. Turner, to organize for the erection of the new 448-room hotel. Intensive work was done by a hotel committee, under the chairmanship of W. H. Crowther, on which also sat S. McNeill, J. Rourke, J. R. Coates, E. C. Brown (project secretary) and C. W. Porter, H. H. Harman having been the chairman in the early days of the committee. Skidmore, Owings and Merrill of San Francisco were chosen as architects, working with Laurie and Heath of Sydney, and the contract for erection was let to T. C. Whittle Pty Ltd.

Late in 1966 the new Wentworth Hotel was completed, but not before the usual hard work and frustrations entailed in the final stages of a large hotel. Here the committee did an excellent job. The organization entailed in stopping the old hotel and starting the new was under the control of Stanley McNeill who worked day and night for a success which is a monument to his efforts.

Those familiar with the operations of boards and committees will recall with a smile how often small things occupy more time than matters of great import. It took the QEA board a solid three years to decide on the name for the new hotel! A staff competition was run but without result. The board decided, with some division, on "Royal Sydney", but there was relief when uncertainty was discovered in registering the name. I favoured "Sydney International" as expressing the hotel as it should be, and the committee agreed; but the board would not. Turner favoured "Waltzing Matilda" though this never seemed to have a chance. The names "Sydney", "Governor Phillip", "Jumbuck" and "Qantas", among many others were considered. Finally Norman Nock, in desperation, suggested a board ballot and went for "Wentworth" as carrying on the business name of the old hotel. This was chosen and agreed on the basis that it did not after all matter much what we called it; but I still liked "Sydney International".

The old Wentworth Hotel, till it was demolished in 1967, stood on an historic site in the centre of old Sydney, hard against the old "Rocks" area. The same could be said of the new Wentworth. It stands on the site of the old Robert Campbell stables, an adjunct of the famous old Wharf House. It was here that the stallion Hector, one time owned by the Duke of Wellington, stood at stud and sired colts and fillies which ran in Australia's first race meeting, held in Hyde Park, Sydney, in October 1810.

The old stables were convict built, and when they were demolished some of the bricks went to the Australasian Pioneers' Club to decorate the premises. In the stables, a cornerstone was found, bearing the inscription, "R. Campbell Jnr. 1828". This was "Robert Junior", the nephew of the original Robert Campbell. I had this stone carefully preserved and erected in the old Sydney Bar at the new Wentworth Hotel, with a suitable inscription. If a ghost walks around at the Wentworth, it will be the shade of the grand sixteen-hands Arab, Hector, who died at the age of 31 years.

Another feature at the hotel and one which has some sentimental value to my wife and myself, is the fountain standing at the entrance to the Garden Court. This fountain originally graced the gardens of an old English manor house and was chosen by Lady Fysh from a junkyard in London from where it was rescued and later erected at the Wentworth. For me it will aways be the "Lady Hudson Fysh Fountain".

I was retired from the chairmanship of QEA on 30th June 1966 and this automatically involved my position on the hotel board. So ended my association with QEA hotel ventures. The old Wentworth closed its doors on 14th December 1966. The staff went across and the new hotel opened for business the same day. An official opening was planned for early 1967 but the disastrous pilots' strike was in progress, and the opening was cancelled.

Naturally I had felt completely involved in making the new hotel venture successful and payable. In the dark days of our struggle to win the approval of Cabinet, when it was claimed that QEA would lose heavily on the venture, I wrote to Bob Menzies:

> I ask you to note that everything Qantas and QEA have gone into has been financially successful. I assure you this venture will pay also.

I had hoped to continue to serve on the board. I had ideas for expansion to key points, expansion that would have taken place long before, if only we had political sanction. But now I was not wanted. Age was

88

frowned upon; and I would, of course, have continued to be difficult. Perhaps it was best that I should go, my memorial in this field being the pivotal decision to take over the old Wentworth Hotel at Lang Park and my work in conjunction with the hotel boards and management. I appreciated being associated with Sir Norman Nock; and Stanley McNeill and I, though we were parted in business association, will always continue to be close friends.

The new Wentworth Hotel, carrying on the historic name which was given by Miss Onge 115 years ago to her boardinghouse on Church Hill, has already proved of the greatest service to QEA and in meeting international tourist needs in Australia. Today, the critics of the 1950s are all confounded and our claims made during the struggles of those years are more than justified.

## ⇛ 11 ⇚

## *Qantas in New Guinea*

IN 1946, the tide of war had rolled back from the Australian territories of Papua, New Guinea, New Britain and their great sweep of smaller islands. In the aftermath of conflict there remained the litter of war in its disintegration and chaos. The debris was scattered from Port Moresby and Lae to Rabaul, from Manus to Bougainville. The scavengers were out, cleaning up fortunes in everything from webbing belts to motor vehicles, damaged tanks and holed ships. Business was returning too in Burns Philp, Carpenters, and the Bulolo Gold Dredging Company, but it was uphill work.

The Administrator, Colonel J. K. Murray, was back in the Residency at Port Moresby, facing the problems of restoring law and order in the wide, and sometimes almost inaccessible areas beset by sea, mountain, jungle or swamp. Shipping had all but ceased, roads rarely existed, there were no air services, and the military had all but withdrawn. Colonel Murray's opinion was unequivocal:

> There is only one way to rehabilitate this country, and that is through the agency of air transport. We must act quickly.

This he proceeded to do. Part of the plan was, of course, to build strong air communications with Australia. Since April 1945 we had been operating a weekly service between Sydney and Port Moresby and Lae, and this was increased to three times weekly. Internally, Carpenters had a De Havilland Dragon aircraft in action. Other small operators started up but without much promise of large worthwhile development. For his island and waterways requirements, Colonel Murray had the temporary use of two RAAF operated Catalina flying boats. The old pioneer operator, Guinea Airways, now in conjunction with ANA, probed the possibilities of a come-back, but received scant encouragement.

Conditions in the Territories made it difficult to re-establish quickly a locally based airline of any magnitude. There were no proper aircraft, no facilities for engine overhaul and maintenance. There were no buildings worth the mention; but our service provided speedy communication with the mainland, and placed us in a position to give material assistance to the Administration.

Colonel Murray, after being in touch with the Departments of Civil

Aviation and Territories, requested us to come to New Guinea to discuss the situation. Our general manager, H. H. Harman, with O. D. Denny, assistant operations manager, an old New Guinea hand who had our Australia-New Guinea services under his wing, went to Port Moresby for a conference. This was the first step towards our internal operations which, from the ground up, were built over the years into an impressive organization.

In July 1946 I went to Port Moresby and Lae to look over the prospects myself. My wife, who wanted to see a late war area, went with me. The trip gave her her money's worth! I will always remember the sunken Burns Philp ship, *Macdhui*, lying on its side in Port Moresby harbour, and how at the Lae strip our pilot had to dodge the rearing prow of a sunken Japanese vessel. Conditions were primitive at Lae. There was a flow of stormwater rippling through the damaged Guinea Airways hangar where a crashed DC3 leaned drunkenly alongside. There was no proper accommodation, and in the evening the mosquitoes buzzed the heavy atmosphere in their millions.

Captain J. A. Bird and his wife, despite our protestations, nobly gave up to us for the night their little sisalcraft-lined, packing-case home which was mosquito netted. The refreshing shower in the morning came out of a hoisted container into which buckets of water had been emptied by native boys.

Orm Denny was with us, and we were met at Lae by Harold Hindwood, a one-time Burns Philp ship's purser and New Guinea old hand, who had joined us to take charge at Lae. In those days, Lae was one of the most undesirable places I have ever visited, and Hindwood had a difficult task ahead of him.

On 20th November our first Dragon aircraft left Brisbane, flown by Captain L. L. McNeill, who was to be stationed at Lae. He was shown the ropes by Captain R. O. Mant, one of our experienced New Guinea pilots. Captain McNeill himself had operated for us at Charleville a Dragon air ambulance of the Royal Australian Flying Doctor Service.

This small start was the outcome of discussions we had with J. D. Simpson, the capable and energetic field manager of Bulolo Gold Dredging Ltd, who gave us a contract for up to four return trips a week between Lae and Bulolo. Normally, the Dragon filled with 1,000 lb. of freight a trip, with room for one passenger on the one hour ten minutes run of 75 miles into the Highlands. The Dragon was also at the disposal of the Administration, undertaking flights from Lae to Kokoda and Buna, and from Port Moresby to Kikori. From this beginning, services spread with additional aircraft until a wide range of points was served.

The gold dredges were again working at Bulolo, and soon the wonderful pine forests were being exploited by the Commonwealth-New Guinea Timbers Ltd, who opened their plywood plant in 1954. Plywood and timber had to be taken from the Highlands to Lae for shipment, and transport by road or air had to be arranged. The wartime road between Bulolo and Lae was a rickety affair, and to reach it freights had first to be lightered across the wide Markham River at Lae. The poser of road versus air for heavy bulk loadings was finally resolved when the road into the Highlands was reconstructed, and the river bridged at Lae. Meanwhile we and other operators served well by air, and continued to do so in the Wet season when the road was blocked by landslides. Air freighting is still a vital factor in penetration where no roads exist. In my 1946 report, I wrote:

> The great final advantage in choosing air transport is that it is available to serve other fields and centres, many of which have no connecting roads and never will.

The attraction to us in obtaining contracts for flying bulk loads of timber, plywood and furniture out of Bulolo was its back-loading value, reversing the flow of freight loadings from great manufacturing centres to less developed areas. This was the economic bugbear of air freighting the world over in all developmental years. We never did discover a useful back-loading for our Australia-New Guinea service, though it was not for the want of trying. Government regulations against the importation to Australia of many items defeated us. Mud crabs, that delicacy from the mangrove swamps, were one item which I can remember, and the hubbub that ensued when I arrived in Cairns with a batch!

In 1949 I was again in New Guinea, and I noted great changes, though things were still somewhat chaotic and primitive. At Lae our new hangar was completed, and so was a passenger handling and office building. Final plans had been made for the erection of a staff and passenger housing project which, when completed, was like Berrimah, Darwin, an autonomous village, with all the amenities, including special quarters for native staff. My wife and I stood with Orm Denny on the edge of the jungle on the hill behind Lae, and there the final decision was made for the siting of the Qantas village. Behind us was the honeycombed site of the old Japanese military hospital, the entrance to which had been blown in when the Allies recaptured the town. That skeleton of secrets was never to be opened.

Housing was still the most urgent matter in the rehabilitation of the Territories. Simpson, up at Bulolo, had come to the assistance of the Administration and private business in typical style.

Having, in the old days, achieved "pre-cut" gold dredges which had been flown in by Guinea Airways when many experts were ridiculing the idea, Bulolo's engineers were not at all daunted when called upon to devise a pre-cut system in Klinkii pine. Houses of various sizes, barracks, messes and other structures were cut ready for assembly. Furniture was designed to go with the houses which were flown, trucked or shipped to many parts of the Territories.

At Lae, work had started on the erection of fourteen houses by John Stubbs to Australian design. To supplement these, we entered into a contract with the Bulolo people to erect for us twenty-four of their houses and a large amenities building, staff and passenger lounges and diningroom, all to be set up on our village site. The services building contained a laundry, motor transport shelter, powerhouse, carpenter's shop and so on. Septic systems went in, and a large water tank was erected on the hillside. Native quarters went up, and an aviary in which brilliant birds of paradise flew. The gardens soon bloomed in splendour beside the well cut lawns. The completed village housed over a hundred staff, with married and single quarters, and twenty passengers. The use of Bulolo houses was then extended by us to cover our requirements in Port Moresby and Madang.

Most of these houses, and many others, were flown down from Bulolo by our DC3 freighters. Five plane loads made a complete house. Our whole housing, amenities and airport building project cost us in excess of £300,000. It was a great amount of capital, and my board became concerned about our lack of proper security of tenure for the now expensive New Guinea internal operations. But it was all essential to establishing ourselves, the new housing making tropical New Guinea livable for our long-suffering staff.

In the three years since 1946 our one Dragon had been increased to six. We also had five DC3 freighter cum passenger aircraft and one Catalina. The DC3s had collapsible seating down each side of the fuselage for twenty-four passengers, white or natives as they came; the, at times, very smelly Highlanders being seated in the rear. Large numbers of recruits were flown down from the mountains to coastal centres, and then flown back at the end of their period of indenture. All our aircraft had a great variety of work throughout the whole of the Territories for the Administration and the public. For instance, our DC3s flew loadings from Lae to Goroka and Kerowagi where the smaller Dragons picked up passengers and every conceivable kind of freight for the outpost Highland strips, often roughly cleared up hillsides. The aircraft landed uphill and took off down because there was a mountain at the other end. It was hazardous work, and thrilling for our team of bush pilots to get off and on these strips, dodging along valleys and over ridges in a cloud-beset mountainous country. Behind the Banz strip, near Mt Hagen, Mt Wilhelm towered to its 15,400 feet.

I remember an adventurous trip my wife and I made to Nondugl. On such trips our pilots were up against most primitive conditions, with no proper accommodation or meals at the end of a mountain run when they arrived for the night at some outlandish place. The natives, decorated with bird-of-paradise feathers, put down their spears and battle axes, and humped bags of flour and boxes of provisions to the grass-thatched hut of the white Administration police officer. Often the officer was paid for his night's lodging by the pilot on his next flight bringing him up some unwaybilled welcome delicacy. There were no scales for weighing freight, the pilot made out his own waybills and load sheet, wrote the passenger tickets and took the money. In 1949 in New Guinea this was going back to our early Queensland days of the 1920s. Attempts to impose usual commercial practices were a dismal failure and became a joke. It was a primitive land where primitive conditions existed and this had to be recognized by head office in Sydney, and winked at by J. Arthur, District Superintendent for the Department of Civil Aviation based at Port Moresby, who battled manfully to produce order where possible.

We had extended our Australian DC3 service from Lae to Rabaul, landing at Finschhafen on the way on an old wartime strip, a narrow runway with dense jungle creeping in on either side. It was a scenic journey, over the long volcanic island of New Britain, the active volcano on Willaumez Peninsula. Circling Rabaul, I remember seeing under the clear waters of the harbour a large sunken Japanese flying boat. There were the remains of 122 ships in that harbour. The township of Rabaul was still in a dilapidated condition, with crashed Zero aircraft, disabled tanks and trucks poking out of the steaming vegetation that was fast covering the entrances of the tunnel systems dug into the nearby hillsides by the Japanese. At night the roads swarmed with giant snails that had been brought in by the Japanese for food but now ran wild.

Matupi, the local volcano, still smouldered after the great eruption of 1937 when Rabaul, smothered in ash, was temporarily evacuated, and a new volcano at Vulcan Island, near the far shores of the harbour, appeared. Rabaul is built on the rim of a vast volcanic crater, a precarious situation which caused the authorities to consider shifting the town. It remains the most important commercial and administrative centre of a vast complex of islands. The linking of Rabaul by air with Port Moresby and Sydney was the beginning of a system which extended over the years into a complex network from Daru to Kavieng, from Hollandia to Honiara, and from Manus Island to the Debyne Islands.

Our Catalina aircraft based at Port Moresby was flown by Captain C. G. Fox and Captain H. M. Birch to all kinds of outlandish places. My wife and I had the opportunity to accompany Captain Birch on his normal round into the vast swampy areas of Western Papua, where we flew direct to Lake Murray near the West Irian border, carrying medical supplies to the police officer stationed at the northern end of that large lake. This was the first visit of an aircraft to the lake which was surrounded by seemingly impenetrable swamp and jungle, but where a large native population existed, primitive men wearing nothing but a walnut shell, as Captain Birch put it. Natives paddled out in their canoe hollowed from a tree-trunk and manoeuvred alongside. The medical supplies went off and the mail, contained in an old sugar bag, was thrown aboard. Then we were off.

At Kikori, our next stop, Captain Birch brought the *Island Chieftain* down on the broad Sirebi River, flowing five knots, and anchored. Again a picturesque native canoe came alongside and we were paddled ashore to be entertained by the local police officer. Mail and supplies had been dropped, but when we came aboard, we found that in addition to a freight that included a consignment of mummified hands, our cabin was occupied by three hundred mud crabs. On our flight back to Port Moresby, a brief call was made at the Yule Island Catholic Mission Station.

That day Captain Birch had been some ten hours in the air. It was a good day's work and one that well illustrated the kind of work our Catalinas were doing, day in, day out, in the Territories. It was interesting to note that on the round we did, our visit to Lake Murray had meant the elimination of the usual regular call at romantic Lake Kutubu, situated in the Southern Highlands at an elevation of some 3,000 feet, a heavily populated area completely cut off except by air.

Another interesting trip was in a small Dragon aircraft to Goroka, Kerowagi, Nondugl and Mt Hagen, dodging up valleys and over ridges, with roaring torrents below, into the Eastern Highlands under the shadow of Mt Suaro and Mt Wilhelm, the highest peak in the Australian administered portion of New Guinea. It was at such places that we saw the completely primitive people in their fascinating dress and with weapons that literally never left their hands, except when they were pressed to carry a bag of provisions off the plane.

Captain Fox, who for years flew these amazing mountain runs, has some good stories about transporting goats, a beehive, or the natives who travelled accompanied by a pet pig. He recalls the native passenger who, when he looked down on his village, tried to open the door and jump out. Village committees of Meris would assemble at the landing strips to welcome their kinfolk home, feeling them all over as was the native custom, or, with some tribes, "shaking hands" by grabbing the middle regions. I was sorry that I was never able to visit Telefomin where the only male clothing or decoration was the thin end of a gourd covering their manhood. Not obscenity, nothing to be laughed at.

What amazing people these primitive highlanders were with their strange customs! But there is little new under the sun, and the old north Scotland practice of "bundling" was practised at Manus Island until suppressed by the authorities as antisocial! Manus was on our regular visiting list when we ran a courier service for the RAAF from Townsville to the island. Quite an institution of courtship and marriage existed there. The young men and girls met by arrangement in a long, low house called "the no house". It was a sort of matrimonial agency, watched over by the keeper of the house. The young couples would spend the night together rigidly and immovably bound to one another. When morning came, after what must have been a most uncomfortable night, if the experiment showed they had liked each other, well, they got married! This reminded me of a wonderful painting by Bill Dobell of a communal courting scene in the New Guinea Highlands.

During 1950 our regular services and charter flights were greatly extended. H. E. Shannon, who had come from Darwin to act as area manager, had a staff of 115 at Lae headquarters in the new Qantas village when it was opened on 2nd December by Colonel Murray. Sir Keith Smith and H. H. Harman, and Orm Denny, the manager for the airline, went from Sydney to take part in the colourful event, when the Administrator broke out the Australian flag from the village masthead. I was in England at the time, but Colonel Murray wrote to me:

> As Administrator, I am greatly helped and cheered by the vision and drive of companies which are able to bring about such a splendid improvement in Territorial facilities.

On the thirtieth birthday of Qantas, he had written:

> I should like to repeat to you how invaluable the services of your Company have been in the post-war development of the Territory and in the everyday work of the Administration. . . .
> Mrs Murray and I remember, of course, the great service to Queensland, and somehow those early days, when the foundations were being laid, seem to tie in with the great work which has been done here in the years following the desolation which war brought about.

These were heartening words for all of us in QEA who had worked so hard on the New Guinea development project, and for our staff, in the air and on the ground, who for four years had carried on in most atrocious living conditions.

Many New Guinea residents had come from Queensland, people whom we knew and admired. I well remember the great hit I made in a speech at Lae when I described the Australians in New Guinea as, "Just like Queenslanders, but more so". The New Guinea people had the fierce independence of the early pioneers, and were prone to level the most severe criticism at their Government and all in authority. We in QEA did not escape, at times, from being castigated for the nature of our services, our fares and rates, our lack of capacity, for badly delayed freights from Sydney, and so on. But I am told that after we left the Territory there was a better realization of the work we had done.

In 1952 Orm Denny went back to New Guinea, with his family, to take charge and to implement the increasing local control. What we were doing was now too big to be run from Sydney, and soon Denny was doing his own engine overhauls and aircraft repairs and maintenance at Lae. By mid-1952 we had 174 European staff in New Guinea spread over a wide area. At this time Captain E. C. Sims was assistant area manager, Captain W. Forgan-Smith chief pilot, E. P. Brown area engineer, H. R. Goodsell area traffic superintendent, G. K. Weekes area accountant, R. G. Moore general services officer, G. W. Etchells senior catering officer, while J. P. Samuels was station manager at Port Moresby with Captain C. G. Fox as senior flying boat captain. L. M. Henry was station manager at Madang, and C. G. Wade in charge at Rabaul.

Other changes in New Guinea were taking place, and in 1953 Brigadier Cleland (later Sir Donald) took over as Administrator. With him we were to continue a happy association in our development and operations. At Bulolo, Lars Bergstrand had taken over.

A great improvement took place when DC4s were put on the Sydney-Port Moresby-Lae run. To replace the over-ripe Dragons we had the three-engined De Havilland Drover which, on paper, seemed an excellent replacement, but its rate of climb performance lagged, and the type developed chronic propeller trouble. This it was found impossible to remedy without loss of performance. We suffered our worst aircraft accident in New Guinea when, just before coming in to land at Lae on 16th July 1951, Captain J. W. Speire, flying our Drover, crashed into the sea. The crash resulted from structural failure of the centre engine propeller, and Speire and his six passengers lost their lives. There was gold shipment on board, and though many tried, I do not think it was ever re-

97

covered. We had another Drover crash at Mackay in Queensland, when the centre engine propeller failed shortly after take-off. We eased out of the type.

Paradoxically, we then went right back into single-engined aircraft operation. After much consideration and obtaining the opinion of pilots on the job, we acquired four de Havilland Beaver aircraft. This aeroplane had become famous for its work in the Canadian outback and in the Army, because of the reliability of its 450 h.p. Pratt and Whitney Wasp engine, its low landing speed, and fast initial rate of climb of 1,020 feet a minute. Its stout undercarriage could handle rough runways, and, floats could be fitted. The Beaver carried, at 143 m.p.h. cruising, one pilot and six passengers.

From the Beaver we went on to the Otter, also manufactured by the De Havilland Canada Company, four of which we put into service. One Otter was very usefully operated as an amphibian, but at decreased payload and performance. Built along the same lines as the Beaver, the Otter was a larger aeroplane, accommodating a crew of two and ten passengers. Fitted with a 600 h.p. Pratt and Whitney engine, it had a greater range than the Beaver and was a better commercial proposition, but suffered from a reduced rate of climb which was a handicap in New Guinea conditions.

When we were phasing out the old Catalinas, a Beaver was fitted with floats and did good work. A Sandringham flying boat was stationed at Port Moresby. At this time, in the early 1950s, we were also operating Sandringhams from Sydney to Fiji and the New Hebrides, linking up with the New Guinea based services and providing a chain of air communications that covered all the main outlying island centres.

This marked the end of our introduction of new aircraft into New Guinea, except for the operation of Constellations on the Australia-New Guinea run shortly before we handed over to TAA in 1960. Despite all our plans, we never felt able to introduce spacious air cargo craft into the Lae-goldfields run, because without a suitable contract with Bulolo Gold Dredging Ltd we were unable, after the completion of the road, to equal the lower costs of road transport.

An interesting event occurred on 1st December 1949 when trout were introduced into New Guinea, Captain Forgan-Smith flying a batch of 20,000 fingerlings from Sydney to Nondugl in the Western Highlands for release in the Arl River. This trip was flown for the philanthropist Sir Edward Hallstrom, and the story is fully told in my book, *Round the Bend in the Stream.*

On 7th September 1953 the Civil Aviation Department having negotiated the rights, a regular DC3 service was commenced between Lae, Madang, Boram, and Hollandia in West Irian, an international service. Projected services to Nauru and Tarawa could not be started because of the lack of suitable aircraft, but our DC3, Catalina and Sandringham services flew down through the Solomon Islands, calling at points between Rabaul and Honiara, giving us another international service.

For the year 1952 we had fourteen aircraft controlled from Lae, Port Moresby and Madang, flying to 103 or more points on regular services and charters. We had our twenty-six mountain, river and wave hopping pilots flying 1,351,329 miles for the year, carrying 35,029 passengers and 1,399,548 load ton miles of freight and mails, all to an achieved load factor of $62 \cdot 992\%$.

We received £44,000 from the Government to cover our work for the Administration for the year, and expected to make a loss of £20,000. We never made much out of the New Guinea services, and directors were still anxious about the poor security of tenure from the Department of Civil Aviation, our capital stake in our Territories organization having become large, with half a million pounds invested. We maintained that, under our original "charter" from the Commonwealth Government, these services were our rights as overseas services. Papua was an Australian Territory but New Guinea was under international Mandate, and, of course, we pointed to the international aspect of our services to Hollandia and to the Solomons.

During the latter 1950s when Senator S. D. Paltridge was Minister for Civil Aviation and D. G. Anderson was his Director-General, pressure was exerted by Ansett-ANA to enter the New Guinea arena. That company had great hopes of extending overseas from Port Moresby to Hong Kong, as they had an inherited ANA shareholding in Cathay Pacific Airways, centred at Hong Kong. New Guinea had become a magnificent training ground for our young pilots before they entered on our main international route, and we fought hard against losing the New Guinea services. We repeatedly urged an extension of the Port Moresby runway and the erection there of suitable facilities, so that we could ourselves link Australia and New Guinea with Hong Kong and Japan.

It seemed, as in other instances, the Government was determined to do something for Ansett-ANA, a company full of vigour and bent on expansion. However, there was the Government's "two airline policy" to be reckoned with. Ansett-ANA could not go to New Guinea unless TAA did the same. This was evident.

It ended by our losing the battle and the Government deciding to relieve us of our services in New Guinea and in the Australian Terri-

99

tories. Our great build-up of operations passed out of our hands. We were requested to assess the value of our undertaking and then to sell to TAA, who would then operate to New Guinea in conjunction with Ansett-ANA, and operate internally, later Ansett-ANA joining in the work by purchasing Mandated airlines from Carpenter.

We had a pleasant negotiation with Sir Giles Chippindall, chairman of TAA, and John Ryland, his general manager. We agreed on a price of £A700,000 and assisted in the transfer of our New Guinea staff to TAA. On 31st August 1960, when TAA took over in New Guinea, K. H. Vial, vice chairman of TAA telegraphed to me expressing his thanks for the co-operation and assistance which made the transfer possible with the least delay. He concluded:

> Qantas' name will live on in New Guinea as a pioneer. TAA will always endeavour to maintain the standards laid down by your organisation.

Sir Giles Chippindall also wired on the taking over of our services from Australia to New Guinea on 8th May 1960:

> Thanks your gracious message. QEA last Bird of Paradise service marks end of period over Australia-New Guinea route for which you can be joyfully proud.

Amongst other matters I wrote to Sir Giles:

> We naturally feel rather sad at having to give up this operation, but from a practical side we are going to feel it most, owing to the loss of contribution to our overhead, and the loss of an invaluable training ground for our young pilots.

James Burns, head of Burns Philp, and our great friend and supporter over many years, also wrote to me expressing his appreciation. I replied:

> I think we feel this loss as much as when we went out of the Queensland services but it was wrong, perhaps, for us to have too much and what might have constituted a vast air monopoly in Australia. This would have been bad from the public point of view in the long run.

So another chapter was written and closed in the history of our organization. Perhaps the loss strengthened our main world-wide operations which were expanding rapidly. If we had been allowed to retain New Guinea, we would, for efficiency, have had to form the service into a separate organization under our control. QEA has not yet recovered from the loss of the unequalled training ground, and great sums have had to be spent in training, not so effective and of an entirely uneconomical nature.

The QEA staff in New Guinea formed a unique band, and all who

Lowering the QEA flag at Lae airport for the last time (*Photo*: Qantas)

The prototype Comet at Hatfield, England. John ("Cat's Eyes") Cunningham, de Havilland test pilot in overalls (*Photo*: de Havilland)

Off to South Africa. Captains W. L. Crowther and L. R. Ambrose on steps, with their crew. *Standing, left to right*—W. R. Clarke, radio officer, G. H. Hebron, flight engineer, A. R. Morris, deputy captain, G. Jakimov, first officer, J. L. B. Cowan, navigation officer, D. Maitland, traffic representative (*Photo*: Jo Fallon)

served there during the hectic fourteen years in which an imposing edifice was built on the debris of war can look back with pride on their contribution to the rehabilitation of the Territories.

An important daily event at Lae airport through the years had been the raising of the QEA House flag each morning and its lowering each evening. It was an effective disciplinary ceremony, bound up with *esprit de corps*. At 6.30 a.m. on the morning of 1st September 1960, Nanandai, a Papuan who had been employed by us for many years as engineering foreman, gravely lowered the QEA flag, and as the first TAA service within the Territory took off for Madang, Wewak, Manus, Kavieng and Rabaul, the TAA flag was raised.

"*Sori tumas* [great sorrow] Qantas im finish along New Guinea," said Nanandai.

H

## ⇒ 12 ⇐

## *The South African Story*

FLYING out into the unknown, the Columbus-like first aerial crossings of the world's great oceans were undertaken by undaunted pioneer airmen, most of them Australians. Then commercial enterprise followed with the establishment of regular services. Never perhaps were the pioneering and the commercial operations carried out in the one endeavour until QEA first crossed the Indian Ocean from Australia to South Africa in 1948, and in 1953 opened a regular service.

P. G. Taylor and his associates early in 1939 put to the Australian and British Governments the need to investigate a reserve Indian Ocean route for use in time of war. The governments were sympathetic, but the difficulty was to find a suitable aircraft with the necessary range. At that time the American Richard Archbold was in New Guinea with his Catalina, *Guba*, carrying out research for the American Museum of Natural History. This long range flying boat was capable of tackling the great ocean fastnesses, and Jack Percival, an associate of Taylor, went to New Guinea to see Archbold, with the result that the aircraft, complete with crew, was chartered by the Commonwealth Government to make a survey across the Indian Ocean.

After a thorough overhaul of the *Guba* at Rose Bay, under the QEA works manager, Arthur Baird, the flying boat left on 3rd June 1939. Taylor was leader and representative of the Australian government; Jack Percival was his official Number 2. Archbold, the owner, was on the flight with his pilot R. Rogers and navigator L. A. Yancy. R. Booth was in charge of radio, and there were two engineers, S. Barrinka and T. Brown.

The route flown was Sydney—Port Hedland, W.A.—Batavia—Cocos Islands—Diego Garcia—Seychelles—Mombasa, the visit to Batavia only because the *Guba* missed Cocos Islands in conditions of poor visibility and was forced to fly to Java before the emergency fuel gave out. Mombasa, the island port of Kenya, was safely reached on 21st June. Another memorable first flight across a great ocean had been accomplished, with an American crew and in an American aircraft, but under the leadership and initiative of P. G. Taylor. Taylor's report was full and contained much valuable information.

102

The long association between South Africa and Australia dates back to the days of sail when ships bound for Australia took in stores at Capetown. Captain William Bligh in the *Bounty*, on his way to Tahiti, took a variety of fruit trees from Capetown, some of which were planted by him near Cape Frederick Henry in Van Diemen's Land. These "three very fine apple trees" were the first planting in the Apple Isle. Though they probably did not survive, other fruit trees brought to Port Jackson with the First Fleet were successfully grown. On 26th June 1797 Captain Waterhouse in his *Reliance* arrived at Sydney from the Cape with sheep, cattle and horses, among them the famous merinos from the flock of Colonel Gordon at Groenkloff near Capetown.

In return, Australia sent to South Africa the wattle and the eucalyptus. John Van der Plank, a Natal farmer, when visiting Australia in 1839, gathered some wattle seeds and took them home. In its new environment the wattle flourished and by 1950 no less than 450,000 acres were established, in addition to the great areas where the wattle was used to bind poor sandy country and on treeless plains. Today the wattle bark industry is an important one for South Africa, the wattle bark extract factory at Maritzburg being the largest in the world.

The opening of the Suez Canal and the supplanting of sail by steam lessened the contact between Australia and South Africa, and until air communications were established, contact by ship was infrequent and the voyage took thirty days. It seemed wrong that two communities, at one time styled "Sisters of the South", should be so isolated, and in 1948 we entered negotiations for the establishment of a regular air service. By ship—when there was one—the journey took a month; by air service through India and Egypt the 13,869 miles journey took seven days. By our proposed service, which entailed 8,417 miles from Sydney to Johannesburg, we could do it in four days. Among the other possibilities opened up was an alternative route from Australia to Europe, taking in South Africa.

Captain W. H. Crowther, our operations manager and Indian Ocean expert, submitted to the board on 23rd June 1948 a proposal for the regular operation of a service between Perth and Durban, and suggested a preliminary survey flight in a Lancastrian. The route was Sydney—Perth—Cocos Islands—Mauritius—Durban, the longest hop being the 2,670 miles between Cocos and Mauritius. Both islands were suitable for the construction of an airstrip, but much work would be necessary at Cocos to provide for a regular service, as the RAF had abandoned their station there. The total length of the proposed route was 8,335 miles.

The possibility of a service via Heard and Prince Edward Islands was examined. This would have reduced the journey to 7,094 miles, with a longest hop of only 2,080 miles. But this would have involved expensive establishments and the difficulty of constructing strips on these small, sub-Antarctic and, at times, storm-swept islands.

We made our submission to Air Marshal Williams on 28th June and received an encouraging reply, with a warning to keep away from Heard Island, and the reminder that the 2,670 miles stage between Cocos and Mauritius was longer than the Honolulu-San Francisco hop. The Government was interested and arrangements were made for a RAF survey party from Singapore to make investigations of the air-strip and abandoned amenities on Cocos. The group was under the administration of the Straits Settlement government; a fascinating little coral atoll, it was by agreement with the British government vested in the hands of the Clunies-Ross family. J. C. Clunies-Ross held all but autocratic rights over the island with its native population of some 1,800.

The RAF Sunderland, under the command of Squadron Leader Hatfield, arrived at the islands on 16th August 1948 with a survey party led by Air Vice Marshal Storar, Director of Civil Aviation for Malaya. Our Captain L. R. Ambrose, who was later to take a prominent part in the service to South Africa, was one of the party which included officials from Singapore, and Dobree, Shell aviation officer. The report was favourable but the abandoned RAF wartime station had to be built up again.

The establishment of a base on Cocos Islands was reminiscent of the establishment of the Pan American bases on Wake and Midway Islands which opened the way to their flying boat service across the North Pacific. At the derelict West Island, in the Cocos Atoll, it was the Australian Department of Civil Aviation, assisted by the RAAF, which did a splendid job in establishing the base.

In August we received the go-ahead from Arthur Drakeford, and all was ready for a survey flight, Johannesburg being substituted for Durban as the South African terminal. Organization was completed at Mauritius and Johannesburg. Civil Aviation had secured official sanctions from overseas for the survey, organized radio communications, air sea rescue, and the emergency facilities at Cocos.

The crew of the Lancastrian VH-EAS which made the survey flight, consisted of:

| | |
|---|---|
| Flight Superintendent | L. R. Ambrose, In Command |
| Captain | A. R. H. Morris, Deputy Captain |
| First Officer | G. Jakimov |
| Senior Navigation Officer | J. L. B. Cowan |

| Radio Officer | W. R. Clarke |
| Flight Engineer Officer | G. H. Hebron |
| Ground Engineer | R. F. Gross |

The survey personnel were Captain W. H. Crowther, operations manager in charge of survey, D. Maitland, traffic representative, G. O'Mahoney, representative of directorate of Commonwealth Meteorological Services, F. Wright, aviation manager Shell Company of Australia, E. V. Read, airways surveyor, Department of Civil Aviation, and R. Walton and R. N. Buzzacott, Department of Civil Aviation representatives who stayed at Cocos Islands.

At eight minutes before midnight on Sunday, 14th November 1948, Captain Ambrose opened up the throttles and the Lancastrian was off Mascot Airport, Sydney and on its way to Perth, the first stop. A day in Perth was spent in final discussions before the flight to Cocos Islands. On the 18th the long ocean crossing to Mauritius was flown by night to take advantage of celestial observations. During this flight Cowan, the old Indian Ocean wartime crossing navigator, was again in his element, shooting the stars. Ambrose, also an old Indian Ocean hand, was at the controls as his four big Rolls Royce Merlin engines purred on hour after hour until, at break of day, Rodriguez Island was flown over dead on course for Mauritius, where a landing was made at 0731 L.S.T., 12 hours 40 minutes out of Cocos.

On the 20th, the last leg was flown from Mauritius to Palmeitfontein, the airport of Johannesburg, passing over the French island of Reunion where an examination from the air was made of the air-strip. The touch-down on South African soil occurred at 1521 L.S.T. on 20th November 1948, concluding the first flight from Australia to South Africa over the South Indian Ocean. Well organized, well operated by a highly efficient and experienced crew under Captain Ambrose, the crossing had gone off entirely without unforeseen incident. The return trip, commencing on 27th November and concluding in Sydney on 1st December, was equally successful.

On arrival at Palmeitfontein Airport, the survey party was welcomed by South African dignitaries, including General Christopher Venter, general manager of South African Airways, the Australian High Commissioner, Alfred Stirling, and the Australian Trade Commissioner, G. R. B. Patterson. Later, the party met the Hon. D. F. Malan, Prime Minister of South Africa, and Cabinet Ministers, including the Hon. Paul O. Sauer, Minister for Transport. Letters of greeting were delivered from the Prime Minister of Australia and the Minister for Civil Aviation.

An interesting aside was a letter received at this time from an official in Johannesburg, revealing that KLM were planning a similar survey flight with the view to opening a regular service. To Crowther in Johannesburg I cabled the congratulations of the QEA board to him, Captain Ambrose and the crew:

> Flight crew deserve a bar to long range Indian Ocean Star. Flight is in best traditions Qantas.

From the Hon. F. Jones, New Zealand Minister for Defence, who was then chairing the South Pacific Air Transport Council in Wellington, I received a lengthy and very kind cable:

> South Africa Survey flight constitutes another fine feat in aviation. . . . The Council feels that the flight will do much to foster and further develop the good feeling and close relationship already existing between members of the British Commonwealth of Nations. Qantas Airways have played a notable part.

Cocos was now the centre of interest, its rehabilitation the key to establishment of a trans-Indian Ocean service to South Africa. This lonely atoll was also recognized as of strategic importance as a staging post in the ferrying of military aircraft from the United Kingdom, and for possible civil operations through India and Ceylon. Both the RAAF and the Civil Aviation Department were interested in acquisition, and the new Prime Minister, R. G. Menzies, instituted negotiations for taking over the islands from Great Britain, the transfer of control of Cocos taking place in 1955 and of the nearby phosphate producing Christmas Island in 1958.

The Cocos atoll consisted of three main islands, Home Island where Clunies-Ross was established, Direction Island on which was stationed the relay cable station since 1901, and West Keeling Island. Copra was the main export, and there was a first-class row over the 20,000 palm trees cut down by the RAF during the war, though I never knew how it was finally settled. The Australian government bought West Keeling Island from the Clunies-Ross family, and the surplus native population were shipped off to North Borneo, one thousand of them, where they led a happy, less isolated life. During all these negotiations and adjustments, B. de Burgh-Thomas, the Clunies-Ross manager on the island, was of great assistance.

To ascertain the amount of work needed to be done on West Keeling Island, we made a Catalina available to fly up a survey party, led by Group Captain W. Dales of the RAAF and V. Davies, a Civil Aviation Department engineer. Captain Len Grey skippered the flying boat, but before he left we had difficulty getting a special permit to fly the Catalina at an all-up weight of 32,000 lb. The new civil limit was 28,000 lb., though we had successfully operated the Indian Ocean service during wartime at 35,000 lb. The technical head of the Department, C. S. Wiggins, would not give in until Air Marshal Williams gave a special dispensation for us to fly at the desired all-up weight. Hudson Shaw, head of our property section, accompanied the survey and submitted a valuable and encouraging report. The survey party was on the island between 30th May and 12th June 1951.

Some real action now took place. On 23rd November I received from Captain Crowther this memo:

> First ship *Dongala* has arrived at Cocos Islands. Second ship *Canara* sails from Fremantle today. Third ship *Ranghi* sails from Fremantle on Sunday and the Civil Aviation Director of Airports A. Hepburn will be on board.

These were ships of light enough draught to enter the lagoon at Cocos. They conveyed the equipment to build a new airstrip made of crushed coral and the material to erect and repair amenities until the twenty Swedish houses ordered should arrive to house properly the CAD and QEA staff who would operate the station. The RAAF's No. 2 Airfield Construction Squadron team were also aboard, and a magnificent job they did, working in shifts right round the clock to have the 8,000-foot strip ready for us.

In July 1951 we made a final firm proposal for the coming operation to South Africa, and in January 1952 received a letter from Air Marshal Williams advising that his Department had successfully negotiated traffic rights for the new route. After final consultation with our new Minister, the Hon. H. L. Anthony, the opening date for the service was fixed for 1st September 1952.

At this stage H. H. Harman, our general manager, after seventeen years of loyal and distinguished service since the inception of QEA, reached the retiring age. His work for the new route to South Africa had been outstanding and it was a fitting termination to the long list of QEA enterprises in which he had so ably shared. On 1st July 1951 his place was taken as general manager by his assistant, C. O. Turner, while I continued as chairman and managing director.

The proving flight to South Africa was uneventful, as all well organized air journeys are, the Constellation *Charles Kingsford Smith* leaving Sydney on 25th January 1952, with Captain K. G. Jackson in command. Along with him in the ample crew were Captains A. Wharton, J. J. Connolly, P. J. R. Shields and H. W. Radford, with First Officer J. R. Carroll, Navigation Officer J. L. B. Cowan, Radio Officer A. M. Saxby and Engin-

eering Officers N. V. St Leon and E. Manning. Purser A. Wallace accompanied the flight, as did the Cabin Services Superintendent L. H. Avis
and Flight Steward H. Smith.

Among the passengers were our operations manager, W. H. Crowther,
the South African line manager, R. B. Tapp, the chief maintenance
engineer, E. H. Aldis, the QEA press officer, Miss M. McGrath, two Shell
Company officials, two Fox Film representatives and two officers from
the Civil Aviation Department.

On the return of the party to Sydney all was in readiness for the
official commencement of the service, which took place at Mascot Airport
on 1st September 1952. There was martial music that night as the band
we had hired struck up and guests arrived. In his *Qantas Aeriana*, E. A.
Crome described the events:

> At the airport ceremony, prior to the departure of the inaugural flight,
> Air Vice Marshal R. Williams, Director-General of Civil Aviation, intro-
> duced the speakers:

| | |
|---|---|
| Mr H. L. Anthony | Postmaster General and Minister for Civil Avia-tion. |
| Mr Hudson Fysh | Chairman and Managing Director of Qantas Em-pire Airways Ltd. |
| Mr G. C. Nel | Acting High Commissioner for South Africa in Australia. |
| Mr R. R. Downing | Representing the N.S.W. Premier, Mr J. J. Cahill. |
| Alderman E. C. O'Dea | Lord Mayor of Sydney. |
| Mr P. E. R. Vanthoff | Acting Director-General of Posts and Telegraphs. |

> Mrs H. L. Anthony officially opened the service, when Mr P. E. R. Van-
> thoff handed a small bag of mail to the Captain of the aircraft. Mr and Mrs
> Anthony travelled by this service, as guests of the South African Government,
> and Mr and Mrs Hudson Fysh as passengers. The aircraft arrived at Johan-
> nesburg on the 4th September.

| Flight stages: | | *Miles* | *Flying Time* |
|---|---|---|---|
| 1.9.52 | Sydney-Melbourne | 458 | 2.23 |
| 2.9.52 | Melbourne-Perth | 1,814 | 9.29 |
| 2.9.52 | Perth-Cocos | 1,832 | 7.58 |
| 2-3.9.52 | Cocos-Mauritius | 2,680 | 11.36 |
| 4.9.52 | Mauritius-Johannesburg | 1,921 | 7.51 |
| | | 8,705 | 39.17 |

Flight Personnel:

| *SYDNEY-PERTH* | *PERTH-JOHANNESBURG* |
|---|---|
| Capt. J. Connolly, Commander | Capt. K. Jackson, Commander |
| F/O J. Carroll | Capt. R. Uren |
| N/O H. Seymour | C/O H. Shaw |
| E/O S. Rowe | N/O G. Parsons |

| | |
|---|---|
| E/O  B. Lawrence | R/O J. Delaney |
| F/S  B. Sewell | E/O  E. Manning |
| F/S  F. Bartz | E/O  B. Lawrence |
| F/H  H. Lamb | F/S  H. Smith |
| F/S  H. Thibou | F/S  C. Fisher |
| G/E  S. Smith | F/H  M. de Tracy |

The first regular direct air service from South Africa to Australia, across the Indian Ocean, was inaugurated with the departure of the Lockheed Constellation VH-EAD "Charles Kingsford Smith" from Johannesburg on 6th September 1952, arriving in Sydney on the 9th.

When the speeches at Mascot were over and the band gave a final salute, we had set off to Essendon, Melbourne, where the Hon. Paul Hasluck, Minister for the Territories, joined us with Air Marshal Williams, both bound for Perth.

After flying through the night, a landing was made at Guildford Airport, Perth. There were more speeches, by J. Totterdell (afterwards Sir Joseph), the Lord Mayor of Perth, and by Mr Anthony who declared Perth an international airport.

After a fast run to Cocos during which we regained lost time, and a landing on the new 8,000 feet pressed-coral strip, there were still more speeches, one by John Clunies-Ross, the master of the islands, having its amusing side, for Roy Sneddon, our liaison officer, had great difficulty in getting this proud "King" of Cocos to put on his shoes, shoes not usually being worn. There was only one woman resident on West Island at that time, a nursing sister, and some of our lady passengers were startled to see a line of RAAF construction men in the evening going naked to their shower.

Glowing reference was made to the work of Wing Commander P. G. Lings of Perth and his men who, in an incredibly short time, had not only built the airstrip but ten miles of roads, a jetty, slipway, and erected staff houses, passenger houses and lounges and other installations.

We had fourteen staff at Cocos under Roy Sneddon, and there were twenty-eight Civil Aviation, Department of the Interior and Shell Oil men. Connection was being made with our new DC4 service from Singapore.

That evening we took off for Mauritius, the longest civil regular hop at that time. After the long night journey we came uneventfully down at Plaisance, the airport of Mauritius. An interesting day was spent at this ancient, one-time home of the Dodo—a British possession, clothed in vast fields of sugar cane, tilled by Indians, and where French is spoken; the *Fleur de Lis* emblem still on the entrance mantel at Government House.

At Johannesburg we arrived on time to be greeted by the South

African Minister for Transport, the Hon. P. Sauer, and Colonel J. Low, the Chief Superintendent of South African Airways. Our party was introduced by the Australian High Commissioner, Lieutenant Colonel W. R. Hodgson.

After a brief rest at the Carlton Hotel, we were entertained at lunch by the Mayor of Johannesburg, Councillor I. E. B. Attwell. I remember how at this lunch I was placed next to a lady of Dutch extraction, the wife of a high dignitary, but who shall remain nameless. She asked me where I came from. "Australia," I replied. The lady looked at me and then solemnly said, "Australia? You were fighting us in 1900." I was too flabbergasted to reply. Some South Africans have long memories.

At Pretoria a most interesting dinner party was given by Dr Malan which my wife and I attended. I remember how our Minister, Mr Anthony, made in his speech some sympathetic reference to South Africa's racial problem. Dr Malan, in his reply, retorted. "Mr Anthony, you have referred to our racial problem. I would like to remind you that you have a similar problem, but, in your case, it is just outside Australia!"

We were searching for a suitable name for our new service, and while I was in Johannesburg, my friend Chris Venter, the head of South African Airways, a Rugby fan and supporter of the Springboks, suggested "Wallaby" after the Australian football team, and this name we adopted.

It was strange that, after crossing the great ocean without incident, adventure came the way of the Press party who had flown with us and were under the charge of E. Bennett-Bremner, our publicity and public relations chief. As the party flew back from Livingstone to Johannesburg late one afternoon, the pilot of their local DC3 took them down to skim over the elephants, lions and other animals of the district, only to realize, after the fun was over, that the direction-finder was dead. They were lost in darkness and with petrol failing. At last they recognized a small town which they buzzed until the locals lined up their cars on the small strip and, with headlights ablaze, showed the way in. Coming in to land, the pilot clipped the top of a low hill, wiping off his undercarriage and nearly removing an engine. They glided on, to end more or less in a heap on the strip, but with no one injured.

My wife and I had a rushed but fascinating visit to the commercial centres of Capetown and Durban, being accompanied by G. W. Ward, our South African head man. We fell in love with Capetown, full of history and old world charm. Then, exhausted and travel worn, we were put aboard a BOAC Comet for London. Up in the high clouds in the Comet, in a new jet-made world, I made this note in my diary:

110

After many decades of help from the United Kingdom, Australia has at last had the privilege of making some repayment, by the establishment of Cocos Islands Air Base. The Indian Ocean Route to South Africa and Rhodesia forms a valuable new connection, and establishes a reserve and second stage route between the U.K. and Australia in the event of emergency.

Cocos was to cost the Australian government little short of a cool million pounds.

The deputy general manager commercial, Bill Nielson and his department, who have been all too little mentioned in this account of launching the service to South Africa, have provided me with a summary of developments since the service opened, on a fortnightly basis, with Constellation 749 aircraft. The new service, from the opening date of 1st September 1952, attracted low traffic density, and in the early days we had to be content with a low and uneconomic frequency. We were operating without subsidy on the prevailing mail rate, and losses were regularly sustained. But the service was both politically and strategically important, and confidence was eventually expressed in a satisfactory build-up in patronage. In 1957 South African Airways commenced operating in pool with QEA, each partner making a flight once weekly. The aircraft used was the DC7B, the Australian terminal being Perth. Frequency was reduced, and restored again.

Changes came when QEA put on Super Constellations, and in 1963 replaced this type with Lockheed Electras, which greatly speeded up the service. On 29th March 1967 a great change came when South African Airways commenced using Boeing 707 aircraft, omitting the Cocos Islands call and flying right through to Sydney. Qantas followed on 2nd April 1967. Both Qantas and South African Airways now operated once weekly, and a high grade service was provided.

The omission of the Cocos Islands call entailed a direct flight of 3,222 nautical miles between Perth and Mauritius, thus greatly reducing the old route mileage and the time taken in the crossing. The Boeing 707 service took 18 hours 30 minutes elapsed time between Sydney and Johannesburg, against 66 hours 35 minutes when we opened in 1952. The route was now well on its feet, attracting much business and tourist traffic, a promising tourist itinerary, Australia—South Africa—Europe, being now available.

For fifteen years the Cocos Islands Civil Aviation community had led an interesting existence, and supplied a vital link enabling the service to South Africa to operate. Many had become fond of their tropical atoll with its dazzling white coral, golden sands and pounding surf on the ocean side, while on the other they could look out over the palm-tree-girt lagoon, with its moods changing with the daylight hour, and reflected scudding clouds. There was excellent fishing, rare sea-shells abounded, and a fascinating bird life. It was a wonderful haven for those with a leaning towards solitude, and for the naturalist. Our little group at Cocos, to whom I used to send my spare magazines and reading matter, was ably run by R. N. Sneddon, R. W. T. Wallace, C. F. Tapsell and, finally, R. P. Brady.

When our Boeing 707 aircraft were introduced for the South African run in 1967, the staff and equipment had to be flown out of the islands. This was done by two DC4 aircraft flights. The staff had done a good job at their lonely outpost. As in Queensland, and then in New Guinea, the Qantas flag had been raised, the mission had been successfully accomplished, and the flag was lowered, in this case through the coming of modern, long-range jet aircraft.

## ⇛ 13 ⇚

## Coming of the Jets

FAST ON THE HEELS of the Lockheed Constellations and DC6 came the
commercial jet aircraft which were again to revolutionize air transport. As was usual, the development originated to meet military
needs. Germany had her jet fighters up towards the end of the war. In
England, Frank Whittle was working on the jet engine to be taken up by
Havilland and Rolls Royce. Following the recommendation of the Brabazon Committee, de Havilland commenced to build commercial jet aircraft. The U.S.A. was strangely away behind.

De Havilland's first moves were with the DH108 and 110, swept-back-
wing, tail-less types. The 108, powered by the DH Goblin jet engine, was
flown by the de Havilland chief test pilot, Geoffrey de Havilland in 1946.
Later, when going for the world's speed record, he was killed in this type.
Then came the disastrous Farnborough Air Display crash of 1952 when
test pilot John Derry was killed in the 110. It was Geoffrey de Havilland
who had taken me for an interesting flip in the Mosquito during the war.
His death was a great blow for Sir Geoffrey de Havilland, as his other
son, John, had been killed in an air crash in 1943.

The new D.H. Ghost engine, following on from the Goblin, received
its type certificate on 28th June 1948, and from the experience of the
108 and 110 and other experiments, the Comet I aeroplane was evolved
and then built around the Ghost. The Comet I, more conventional than
the earlier experimental types, was first flown by the D.H. chief test
pilot, John (Cats-eyes) Cunningham on 27th July 1949. The Comet I was
a jet aircraft of some 105,000 lb. all-up weight, carrying 36 passengers over
1,500 mile stages at just under 500 m.p.h. The flight caused a terrific sensation, as well it might. There was nothing like the Comet in the world.

I first saw the Comet I fly at the Farnborough Air Display in September 1949. What a thing of beauty it was! I was terribly impressed. When
I returned to Australia, I wrote:

> I think it is reasonably true to say that the difference between the con-
> ventional aeroplane driven by a piston engine and a propellor, and a jet
> aeroplane, is going to be as great as that between a horse and cart and a
> motor car. From the clip clop of a horse, the purr of a motor car, and the
> roar of a piston driven aeroplane engine, we now have the high pitched
> whine of the jet engine, which marks the development we are entering into.

113

At the Farnborough Air Display, just outside London on 7th September 1949, the Society of British Aircraft Constructors showed to the world what Britain had; and the spectators were certainly treated to an astonishing display, the predominant factor being that high pitched singing whine of the jets sung in many keys—it was the aerodrome noise of the future.

U.S.A. aviation authorities pricked up their ears at the sound and became alarmed at the long lead in jet air transport stolen from them by Britain. At the 1950 Farnborough Display, Bill Allen, head of the Boeing Company, was greatly impressed by the Comet I. In October, I flew in the Comet I at Hatfield: a wonderful sensation, eighteen years ago, to be over England at 40,000 feet. The Channel seemed a ditch, and France just away at an angle, and we passed from country to country in minutes, in "motionless" flight, aerially uniting the nations.

However, a sober look at the Comet I figures showed that, with its short range and lack of volumetric capacity for mails and freight and leg room, even if it successfully negotiated its inevitable teething troubles stage, it would not be suitable for our long routes; but BOAC had ordered and the new aeroplane was away.

Though I had been impressed, I wrote in my diary:

No help at all on cost and range. BOAC will lose a packet.

It was on this visit to Hatfield that I was first introduced to the "egg trick". I wanted my son John to meet that famous and lovable old pioneer, Sir Geoffrey de Havilland, and we were told we would find him on the lawn. There he was performing some strange rite, looking up to heaven and then down again. We thought he was playing two-up but he was throwing an egg far up in the air, to let it come back and bounce on the lawn, where it came to rest without breaking. He was interested in the design of the egg. We tried it out, and it worked. I performed the trick many times before incredulous audiences and usually with success; but what a fool one looked when the egg broke, as it occasionally did. The egg must be fresh and the lawn well chosen.

Sir Miles Thomas, now chairman of BOAC, was enthusiastic about the Comet I. If it could be made to work, they indeed had a world beater, with world leadership for the Comet and great prestige for BOAC. Following an intensive pilots' training programme, BOAC on 2nd May 1952 put the Comet I into service on the London-Johannesburg run, where it went on to operate without serious trouble in the hands of these very experienced pilots.

Following the inauguration of our service from Australia to South Africa, my wife and I found ourselves on board a Comet I at Johannes-

114

burg ready to take off for London. My wife remarked that through Qantas history we had always tried the new types out on her, but, as usual, she was game. In my diary I noted the shortcomings:

> We did the last 608 miles stage in 1 hour 55 minutes, much too short a stage to be impressive as to speed, we recording 300 m.p.h. block to block.
> We took 45 seconds to lift off at Livingstone, and then came the clean climb, the noise in the cabin under climb power being akin to a vacuum cleaner at work.
> Now we reach cruising height, the vacuum cleaner packs up and two new sounds mingle, the rush of the Comet through the air and an undulating engine hum. The air "bumps", all in the space of writing, have been completely broken through, and the journey carries on with complete stability in the cabin.

At Entebbe, which had some height, our pilot manoeuvred in to avail himself of every foot of the runway, and then touching down the Comet I ran on and on, down that runway before coming to rest right at the far end. The take-off was equally hair-raising for an old piston engine pilot, and I felt that this type of operation had its limits and was only made possible by the wonderful "Battle of Britain"-like training of the BOAC crews. At Beirut, after a night landing at Khartoum, we were stuck with undercarriage trouble, the poor passengers caught up in one of those creeping delays, spending two nights in the lounge or rooms of a small hotel while our luggage and overnight bags remained out at the airport. An impatient influential passenger frantically rang members of parliament at Westminster, and the hapless Sir Miles Thomas, to the grim amusement of the rest of us as we whiled away the hours draped across or dozing on chairs in the hotel lounge.

When we did reach London, I heard with renewed interest that plans for production of an improved Comet, the Comet II and Comet III, were being considered by BOAC and de Havilland. This new series was virtually a Comet I with Rolls Royce Avon engines, the greater power enabling an increase of all-up weight to 120,000 lb. The fuselage was three feet longer and the performance, range, and payload went up. However, our experts still felt that this was not the aircraft for our long routes.

Scotty Allan was still our controller of technical development, doing an excellent job on the looming problem of replacing our Lockheed 1049 fleet. Then he became assistant general manager, handing over to Bert Ritchie who became technical manager. Together with the board and C. O. Turner, the general manager, we were concerned with the need for fleet replacement, and all thought alike.

BCPA had ordered two Comet II aircraft. Pan American Airways and others were planning to replace their fleet, and we felt we were getting jostled. How could we compete with the speed of the Comet with our fast obsolescing piston aircraft? We had pressure put on us to order, but we played for time.

Then came the dramatic series of Comet I crashes, the first on 26th October 1952 at Rome, when a BOAC aircraft failed to get into the air properly and crashed off the end of the runway. On 2nd March 1953 at Karachi a Canadian Pacific Airlines Comet IA, on its delivery flight to Sydney, also failed to get into the air properly and all were killed. Clearly, take-off characteristics were under suspicion.

These two accidents were quickly followed by a BOAC Comet I breaking up in the air on 2nd May 1953, in bad turbulence, soon after take-off from Calcutta airport. All aboard were killed. There were eight months of satisfactory operation until 10th January 1954 when a BOAC Comet I crashed into the sea off the island of Elba. This was followed by a similar loss near Naples on 8th April 1954. All were lost in both accidents. In four fatal accidents, 24 crew and 85 passengers had been killed.

The certificates of airworthiness were withdrawn, and an intensive investigation made, following the recovery from the bottom of the sea of most of the remains of the Comet I off Naples. It was deduced from these examinations that the cabin of the aircraft had burst, and that the likelihood of fatigue resistance properties of a pressured cabin had not been realised. Further precautions were necessary, either in design or the test then provided by the static strength requirements. These matters were tightened up with the result that further versions of the Comet proved satisfactory after the Comet II aircraft then going through the shops were all modified.

The Comet II, even with its more powerful Avon engines, still did not fill the bill for a main fleet airliner on long world routes, or indeed for trans-Atlantic crossings. Meanwhile, de Havilland, undefeated, had been working on a virtually new type. This was evolved out of the experience of the earlier Comets, and resulted in the Comet IV, an aircraft which had the full Comet beauty of appearance, but now had a 158,000 lb. all-up weight, more engine power in development of the Avon engine, more volumetric capacity, more speed, better economics and greater range.

The Comet IV was first flown by John Cunningham on 27th April 1958, and BOAC put it into service on the North Atlantic on 4th October 1958, the first jet aircraft to operate on that route. The Comet IV went on to prove itself a most satisfactory aircraft in its class, and in this year of 1968 its graceful form is still seen in the air on a number of

At the BOAC-QEA 21st anniversary dinner. *Left to right*—Sir Thomas White, Sir Miles Thomas, H.R.H. the Duke of Gloucester, a BOAC captain, Sir Hudson Fysh (*Photo*: BOAC)

Inauguration of QEA round-the-world service. Two aircraft were dispatched from Essendon aerodrome, Melbourne, each flying in a different direction. Mrs Bolte cuts one ribbon, and Mrs Paltridge prepares to cut the other. The Hon. C. W. Davidson (later Sir Charles) in rear

Our first Boeing 707 takes to the air (*Photo*: *Sydney Morning Herald*)

QEA service aboard (*Photo*: Qantas)

routes, a reminder of the de Havilland drama, of their magnificent contribution to world commercial jet aircraft development in its critical infancy, and of how nearly Great Britain swept the world's markets with Comets.

However, in the long interval of six years between the appearance of Comet I and Comet IV, the important time advantage had been lost. Boeing and Douglas and Pratt & Whitney, benefiting from the de Havilland experience, had now raced ahead. Work started on the Boeing 707 prototype conception on 24th April 1952, the first aircraft being rolled out in Seattle for taxiing tests on 15th May 1954, when it promptly sat down on its undercarriage and six weeks were lost in repairs. Boeings had their troubles, too. I was in Seattle for the roll out and, like everyone who saw this new wonder, the Boeing 707, was greatly impressed.

On 15th July 1954, Boeing test pilot Tex Johnston took the 707 into the air for the first time, but the economics of production remained a problem. Could the world's airlines pay for such an expensive aircraft? And for operators like ourselves, it was not only could we pay for it, but was it too large in carrying capacity for the traffic available on our routes?

The Boeing problem was solved for Bill Allen when the U.S. Air Force, in March 1955, placed a large order for 707 tankers for refuelling in the air the big Boeing B-52 bombers, enabling them to "reach any target on the globe". Such an order, something unattainable in similar United Kingdom ventures, was of enormous advantage. Boeing could now go ahead with confidence on the civil version of the 707.

At Seattle, I flew in the prototype 707 in 1956 and was enthusiastic about this wonderful new type, seven of which we ordered for delivery to us in May 1959. In October 1958 the first version of the Boeing 707 went into service across the North Atlantic and on U.S.A. domestic services, almost at the same time as the Comet IV which it had superseded on long distance, high density routes.

It is fitting to mention a third competitor, the Russian TU104 (Camel), a development of the TU-20 bomber, which first flew on 17th June 1955, then went into service with Aeroflot on 15th September 1956. The Camel was the first commercial jetliner to go into service and stay in service. More than 150 of these jets were to be operated by the Russian national operator. The aircraft carried a maximum of a hundred passengers at some 500 m.p.h. over stages up to 1,260 miles, fully loaded.

In November 1958 my wife and I flew with Aeroflot in a TU104 between Delhi and Moscow, a visit of amazing interest described in my pamphlet "Visit to Moscow". We wondered how we would be received and before we left Delhi removed from our luggage anything we thought

I

might anger our hosts. What I endeavoured to convey in my pamphlet was indicated in my first impression when we landed at Tashkent:

> I will always remember my first impression of Russia. As the engines of the TU104 Russian jet plane stopped and we walked out on the landing step, a train in the distance whistled loud and long. The sound was not a special Russian sort of whistle, something that could not be understood. It was identical with our New South Wales train whistles! What, the same train whistles that we have? How strange!

We thought the TU104 was rather crude and utilitarian. The interior was decorated in old-world railway carriage style. In the washroom, we were amused to note the installation of a pull-the-chain lavatory. Of course, there was no plug in the wash basin, as was the case with all Russian aircraft. In our hotel room in Moscow we had to use a handkerchief as a plug in order to have a bath. So, perhaps, after all, Russia was different.

The TU104, although there were a number of crashes, and though it was an aircraft which I would say was most uneconomic, went on to do a good job and is still, I believe, in service with Aeroflot.

In 1968 we see the aviation world poised in anticipation of the promised flights of the Russian commercial supersonic aircraft, and the British-French Concorde, with the U.S.A. again bringing up the rear in the production of the Boeing supersonic aircraft. Will history repeat itself?

Commercial jets employing an entirely new means of propulsion and blown up inside at 40,000 feet present many problems to be overcome. External noises from the big Pratt & Whitney engines on the airports and in take-off were so disturbing that doubt was expressed whether the 707 would be acceptable. Airport buildings tended to be sealed behind protective glass; blast barriers went up, and ground engineers wore ear mufflers. It was thought that, because of the noise problem and to economize on the use of fuel when taxiing, the aircraft would be towed to and from the end of runways, passenger handling being carried out by means of buses to and from the airport buildings.

The noise problem was overcome in the bigger jets by the fitting of silencer systems which, after much trial and anxiety, were made to operate without significant loss of power. This took time to develop, as did the "reversible thrust", that miraculous, simple attachment to the rear of jet engines which reverses the blast flow, effectively retarding that long, sleek, gliding never-ending roll down the runway which we had experienced on our Comet I journey through Africa.

During the years of straight jet development, the ever busy aircraft manufacturers had been equally active in producing a prop-jet engine, that is, a jet engine which turned a propeller. As in the Comet, Britain again led the world, Rolls Royce and Vickers being first in the field. The Vickers Viscount, powered with the Rolls Royce Dart turbo-prop engine, first flew away back on 16th July 1948. Much development took place before 20th August 1952 when the first production aircraft for British European Airways was flown, and then went into service.

Two hundred and eighty-seven Viscounts were built, some of which are still in service. The Viscount carried 53 passengers at some 324 m.p.h. over stages exceeding 1,000 miles, an ideal European type.

Work also proceeded on the Bristol 175 "Britannia", a much larger aircraft designed for work on world routes. Powered by four Bristol Siddeley Proteus turbo-prop engines, the "Britannia" cruised at some 355 m.p.h. over stages up to 4,000 miles, carrying 133 passengers. The prototype first flew on 16th August 1952, and the new type, after many teething troubles, first came into service with BOAC on 1st February 1957. It was unfortunate that the many delays in getting this promising aircraft in a satisfactory condition had frittered away the time advantage and the Boeing 707 was now on the verge of going into service. The great virtue of the Britannia, vociferously extolled by many British experts, was its alleged marked economy in comparison with the Boeing 707, all straight jet aircraft being considered uncompetitive in this respect with a good turbo-prop.

It was always possible to raise an argument on this issue and I was involved in quite a few. We continued to believe the performance figures put out by Boeing which we later knew were amply realized. The wonderful thing about the Boeing 707 and the DC8 was that they were not only able to supply great extra speed, that first essential in any progressive aircraft, but at a lower cost per seat mile and with greater reliability. That is why the new straight jet types came to sweep the world's air routes and revolutionize air transport, while the Vickers Viscount and its successors held their own for shorter operations.

Lockheed made a final effort with piston engined aircraft in the Lockheed L1649A Starliner, which cruised at some 342 m.p.h. over stages exceeding 6,000 miles, but only a few were sold. The jets had come for good. Lockheed then turned to the Electra, powered by four Allison turbo-prop engines, and deliveries to the airlines commenced in October 1958. This aircraft filled a great need on medium range routes, and did good work despite two disastrous crashes through structural design faults. Over 175 of the type were built and many are still operating.

Scotty Allan, as our technical head, had for many years played an important part in advising the QEA board on new aircraft, and I felt

I was a good judge myself through long experience. It had been once a case of marshalling a few facts, walking round the aerial beast as we would a horse, admiring his good points and looking out for broken knees. Then, in the 1950s and on, the game became highly technical requiring close and expert examination, both technical and economic.

During this jet introduction period, which began with H. H. Harman as general manager and then C. O. Turner, but with Scotty Allan and Bert Ritchie coming forward as the chief technical experts, a very strong team was built up to evaluate the new types. The technical, operational, economic and traffic leaders of the company made up the important committees which later, with additional complications, became wider in scope. The QEA record, untrammelled by politics as we were, stood high for being good choosers of new aircraft.

# ⇒ III ⇐

*As the pioneers depart, and death and change take their toll of the old, new and brilliant horizons open up.*

*Destiny sees the Qantas flag fly the South Pacific ocean, marking the realization of a long-fought policy, and making possible the new achievements which lie ahead.*

## ✦ 14 ✦

## *Death of the Pioneers, and a Dobell Portrait*

I N PRECEDING CHAPTERS I have specifically dealt with some important
ventures, the stories of which I felt should be carried through to a
conclusion. By doing this, I have, in point of time, passed over some
events which should be included in the history of the company; some
marked the beginning of changes in our make-up; and there were political changes which were to carry us on into a new phase. Also, time was
passing on and some of the old Qantas pioneers were to end their days. I
never cease to wonder how I have been spared for so long.

In Brisbane on 2nd April 1949 Arthur Coles, chairman of TAA, and
Lester Brain, the general manager, took over our Queensland and Northern Territory services and Flying Doctor operations from our then
Queensland manager, N. A. Black. This was in conformity with the government policy of confining QEA to overseas services, TAA, our sister
organization, being responsible for Australian inland services, but still in
competition with ANA.

There was little to take over: some obsolescent hangars for which the
government offered us £A13,070, and four D.H. Dragon aircraft, various
odds and ends which went to TAA for £A13,000. We had disposed of the
rest, keeping some items for our New Guinea services. We had no rights
or goodwill value. There was just the carrying out of an edict. Perhaps
the most important take-over by TAA was the old Qantas man, Lester
Brain, and 41 of our Queensland staff—an important contribution to our
sister organization.

On 30th June Arthur Baird, head of our engineering section, retired
after a wonderful service dating back to the old fighting days at Longreach. He was one of the original staff of three and had served for 28
years. His place was taken by D. H. Wright as chief engineer, another
Australian aircraft engineering pioneer. After serving in a consultative
capacity, Arthur Baird died on 7th May 1954, at the age of 63 years. I
wrote this of him:

> I cannot think of anyone who has done more in laying the foundations
> of Australian air transport engineering, both in regard to the work he did
> himself and what he initiated; and also in regard to his choice of staff, the
> character he put into everything he did, and the principles which he im-
> parted to others.

The Menzies Government came into power on 19th December 1949; and though, beginning with T. W. White, we had a long succession of Ministers, Sir Robert himself until he retired on 26th January 1966, well understood the significance of our role as Australian overseas operator and gave us strong support.

When the new government took up office, Arthur Coles on 10th May 1950 announced his resignation as chairman of TAA, and his place was taken by G. P. N. Watt, an original member of the TAA board and of QEA since 1947. This was an important change, for Watt, secretary of the Commonwealth Treasury, continued the policy of Treasury representation on the boards of government air transport instrumentalities and, in some degree, the interlocking of directorships.

On 8th August of the same year we lost Sir Fergus McMaster—"The Farmer who pioneered a Famous Airline"—when he died in Brisbane after a long illness at the age of 71 years. I wrote of him:

> Sir Fergus' friends, and all who knew his worth, will feel a great sense of loss in his passing. A man of rugged character, he possessed great tenacity of purpose. This, plus a code of personal integrity and public duty which set a very high ethical standard, was the spirit which for so many years had inspired Qantas, then QEA.

Later in the year Qantas celebrated its thirtieth anniversary. We had an Anniversary Exhibition and other publicity about the doings of the company, and some of the QEA staff in their usual kindly way decided to make me a presentation. It was to be a portrait, but who was to paint it? Scotty Allan said, "Bill Dobell, of course," and so Bennett-Bremner and a committee arranged with this great painter to do the job. The result was presented to me at a function in the old Wentworth Hotel. When the portrait was unveiled, it was rather a shock to some people; but my wife and I were very pleased with it, even if it was in Bill's usual controversial style.

I felt it a great honour to be painted by Bill (later Sir William) Dobell. His landscapes and similar work can only be described as magnificent, and this is also true of his portraits; but they are unusual and controversial, and have never been known to flatter his subjects. I had become another Dobell victim, but perhaps one of the first to express in print his feelings.

Dobell never wished to undertake a commission to paint a portrait and usually had to be persuaded into it, often with disastrous results for his own, ever sensitive feelings. What he loved to paint was some character of his own choosing who appealed to him as having out of the ordinary characteristics: "The Dead Landlord", "The Duchess Disrobes", "The

Burglar", "The Sleeping Greek", "The Red Lady", "Billy Boy", and so on. Goya, El Greco and Velasquez had great influence on Dobell as he probed the hidden surface and seized on features, expression and peculiarities, and accentuated them sometimes to the point of caricature. He loved to lampoon, not deliberately; it was just that out it came.

If you sit for a great artist you should watch yourself carefully because, as he paints, he will bring out what he sees. Bill's method is to do a number of pencil sketches of his subject's features, then do a small sketch in colour. The sittings are soon over and he returns to his retreat at Wangi Wangi to work out his treatment, often in some agony of despair, lashing himself for inspiration.

In his little studio at King's Cross, I sat for Bill after a heavy day's work, tired out. The studio was hot and drowsy as the late summer's sun streamed in. Bill gave me two whiskies. I always wore glasses but was induced to take them off to be painted. This produced an inevitable squint. The finished portrait could well have been entitled "Man Without Glasses". He painted what he saw.

Most penetrating, Bill, true to his art, never flattered his subjects, and carried on, interested in the bizarre, the unusual, the hidden quirks of character, and the all too human frailties of feature and expression. The pretty, the self-imagined nobility, the great business tycoon, never went into Bill's portraits. Yet he produced magnificently painted, unmatched portraits. Dame Mary Gilmore, Margaret Olley, Elaine Haxton, Brian Penton and others are so striking in unusual, magnificent technique and colour that when you enter a gallery and see one hanging, it becomes immediately the focus of your attention. It is the only picture in the room.

My portrait was a magnificent piece of work of a great master; but the treatment of the face, which was somewhat in the style of the Dame Mary Gilmore, Billy Boy, Mrs South Kensington or Joshua Smith paintings, made me look so dissipated and haggard as to cause me to remark that if someone in fifty years' time were told that the subject was a founder of the great airline Qantas, he would refuse to believe it.

With the help of Frank Clune who brought the painting from Wangi Wangi on top of his car, it was duly presented and hung in my home. One of my sisters, on seeing it, indignantly exclaimed, "If I had a knife I would slash it. All the evils of our ancestors come out in that portrait!"

But I would have hated to be painted in a grandiose manner, or flattered. Dobell anticipated the future because, as I grow older, the portrait looks more like me every day, and it is a foil to one painted by Mary

Allen of me in my twenties in uniform. Have you ever seen Goya's famous portrait of Queen Maria Lucia?

Bill Dobell entered the portrait for the Archibald Prize at the end of 1950. The prize was won by a very good but quite conventional painting by William Dargie, a likeness of Sir Leslie McConnan, very suitable to hang in a board room, as was the excellent portrait of Sir Fergus Mc-Master which I had Dargie do for the QEA board room. The art critics came down heavily on the side of Dobell, as did the public. Said the Sydney *Sun*:

> With few exceptions, people interviewed at the Art Gallery claimed that William Dobell, with his portrait of Hudson Fysh, should have got the prize.

Some of the remarks of the critics were interesting.

Mr J. McDonald:

> Dobell's portrait lives. . . . It's not like something that your grandson would hang in the attic!

Miss A. E. Hall:

> I hate Dobell's painting—and that horrible narrow faced man.

Perhaps the Sydney *Bulletin's* brilliant description was best:

> It is ugly. But yet it is alive. There is something genuinely memorable in the negligent ease of the portrait, with so much alert vitality, both of sitter and painter, underlying the surface of polite humour.

An important, but almost unrecorded, exploratory flight was that carried out in 1950 through the vast, scattered island areas to the north-east and east of Australia, but primarily to the Fijian Islands group at the instigation of the Fijian government, as a forerunner for the establishment of regular services. It was then decided to go farther east as far as Tahiti to explore for information which might assist towards the extension of our services there and on to the South American mainland.

Our Catalina, aptly named *Island Voyager*, left Rose Bay on 22nd July 1950 with Captain W. H. Crowther in charge of the survey, Captain H. M. Birch in command of the Catalina, his crew consisting of First Officer M. Burgess, Navigator J. W. Keith, Radio Operator A. M. Saxby, Flight Engineer B. G. Costello, and Ground Engineer T. B. Mitchell.

In his interesting and informative report, Captain Birch described the start of the trip:

> It was 9 p.m. when the Catalina *Island Voyager* commenced her run down the flare path at Rose Bay into a cold southerly night. The beginning of a journey which was to cover more than 8,000 miles of fascinating flying over the routes of the early explorers from Quiros to Captain Cook. . . . Eight hours later, with the dawn breaking, New Caledonia came into sight.

The main route followed was Sydney-Noumea-Suva-Tonga-Tahiti, visiting many islands and gathering valuable information. We were not able to benefit from Captain Crowther's report of his 8,523 mile survey until the purchase of Fiji Airways in 1958 and, in 1964, the long hop was made through Tahiti to Mexico City and on to London.

Our offer in 1950 to operate a local islands service was not accepted, the Fijian government making an agreement with Harold Gatty, the pioneer Tasmanian and U.S. airman, to form Fiji Airways. In pursuance of the arrangement between the Australian and New Zealand governments that the latter had responsibility for areas east of the 180th longitude cutting through the Fijian group, TEAL on 6th June 1950 extended its Solent flying boat service from Auckland to Suva. On 27th December 1951 this service was extended via Aitutaki in the Cook Islands to Papeete in Tahiti. This was christened the "Coral Route" and first ran on a monthly basis, developing into an interesting and important route.

Incidentally, in 1950 TEAL had completed ten years of operations, their flying boats having flown 5,859,673 miles as at 31st March and having completed 4,370 crossings of the Tasman Sea without any injuries to passengers. This was a grand record, and the company was awarded the Cumberbatch Trophy by the British Guild of Air Pilots and Air Navigators for an "outstanding contribution towards the maintenance of safety in the air." In after years, TEAL were to lose a DC8 with crew casualties, on a training flight, but went on to have flown 54,535,985 miles by 31st March 1967 without injuries to passengers during the 27 years of the company.

P. G. Taylor was interested in being the first to conquer yet another great ocean, and in March 1951 this great pioneer airman took off in his Catalina *Frigate Bird II* from Rose Bay to Valparaiso, via Tahiti and Easter Island. With Taylor on this historic flight were Captain G. H. Purvis as first officer, L. L'Huillier, engineer, A. Allison, radio officer, and Jack Percival, executive officer and correspondent, who had become a seasoned member of P. G. Taylor's great flights.

We had completed our commercial survey as far as Tahiti in August 1950 but had deliberately refrained from proceeding to Valparaiso because of the necessity to refuel at Easter Island which was surrounded by the open sea. It was not a risk which we should take in our business, and there was no information of possible early use to be gained. We doubted, anyway, whether a heavily loaded Catalina could take off on the open sea. We, unfortunately, did not seem to be on the best of terms with P. G. Taylor and were not in favour of his flight.

P. G. Taylor has something to say about this in his book, *The Sky*

*Beyond*, in which he describes this and other flights. Easter Island was the snag for the South Pacific crossing. The take-off was one of extreme hazard, and it was only made possible by the skill of Taylor and his crew, and the use of Jato rockets, which were attached to the side of the aircraft and fired at a critical take-off moment to shoot the aircraft into the air.

The accounts in Taylor's books *Frigate Bird* and *The Sky Beyond* are a thrilling description of one of the most difficult operations. Then, not only did *Frigate Bird II* reach Valparaiso, but turned back and flew to Australia, again successfully overcoming the dread Easter Island landing and take-off.

The navigational skill needed makes the flight, I feel, rank as one of the greatest pioneer flights in the world's history of aviation. It will rank as a great Australia first, but not for commercial reasons. The flight was sponsored by the Australian Government, T. W. White, R. G. Casey and the Prime Minister himself, leading in advocacy. *Frigate Bird II* was presented to P. G. Taylor before the commencement of the flight, perhaps his only reward, except the glory of achievement.

In May 1951 John Flynn, "Flynn of the Inland", of Flying Doctor fame, died and then in June Ben Chifley who had created the new Australian air transport set-up. The old pioneers were passing on, and on 4th February 1952, Paul "Ginty" McGinness, my old partner, died in Perth. I wrote of him:

> The death of P. J. McGinness, D.F.C., D.C.M., recalls to mind the part he played in the 1914-18 war days, and in the early days of Qantas. . . . Paul McGinness, who was always essentially an adventurous spirit, not given to the humdrum and everyday aspects of life, drifted off into other occupations and adventures, and was lost to aviation in his latter years.
>
> A staunch wartime friend, with lots of guts . . . in those hazardous days of Civil Aviation in Australia, helped to ignite other minds into founding Qantas.

My old friend C. G. Grey, the great aviation journalist, died in December 1953, and almost at the same time Albert Plesman, the head of KLM, universally recognized as the world's No. 1 air transport executive. I wrote of Plesman:

> A man full of advanced ideas and ideals for the furtherance of air transport. He poured these out during his 33 years of service. He was full of chafing impatience and intolerance for the limitations imposed on progress. In KLM he set a standard of competition which was of value to the Airways of the world.

At this time I received my K.B.E. in the Queen's Coronation Honours List. The QEA staff tendered me a memorable dinner at the old Wentworth. In March 1954 I personally received the accolade during the Queen's visit to Australia. Sir Daniel McVey was honoured at the same ceremony in Government House, Sydney. He had long deserved the distinction. Of the honour paid me I wrote:

> As head of QEA I am grateful for this great honour . . . which carries with it a "Qantas" tradition. I have been personally fortunate in my associates in QEA. . . . This honour is a recognition of the work done by Qantas over the whole life of civil aviation in Australia.

Some time later I was chatting with Bob Menzies in his Canberra office. He was under attack, as he was so often. I said I appreciated the distinction, and he replied, "Hudson, I hear it is my one good deed!"

In March 1954 we undertook the first of a series of flights when Her Majesty and the Duke of Edinburgh were flown more than 4,000 miles on their tour of Australia. Our Constellation 749 *Horace Brinsmead* was attractively fitted with special cabin arrangements. It was commanded by Captain D. F. MacMaster, backed by our most experienced cockpit and cabin crews. Flight Stewards Harold Smith, K. W. O'Flaherty and Sydney Preece and our head hostess, Marjorie de Tracy, gave personal attention.

An innovation was begun on 1st April when tourist class services were introduced between London and Sydney at 20% off the regular first class fare. This was made economically possible by reducing the amount of "leg room" between seats and catering services aboard. These lower fare tourist arrangements began with specially scheduled all-tourist flights, and, with the coming of larger aircraft, went on to the present practice of dividing the cabin into tourist and first class compartments. With the saving of £135 on the return Sydney-London fare, tourist traffic soon became a great success. The principle was first introduced on the North Atlantic runs, with the blessing of IATA. The reduced fares were proof that one of the basic objectives of the world's airlines was to prevent rises in fares and to extend the benefits of air travel.

Air tourism has made enormous progress, and in 1957, as deputy president of the Australian National Travel Association, in a speech at Canberra on "Tourism as a business and a human need", I summed up the values:

> It has been said that finance-wise a tourist brings something to a country and takes nothing out; but spiritually both export and import countries benefit. The world today is full of budding Marco Polos who wish to explore the wonders and mystery of life in countries they do not know. It is easy to do this today; in the year 1260 there were no travel agents.
>
> Consider the poor immobile jellyfish drifting along, the oyster, then turn to the flashing swifts, winging their way in countless numbers each season, between Siberia, Japan and Australia; then returning.
>
> The swift should be the emblem of international air transport.

## ✣ 15 ✣

## *The BCPA Takeover*

ALTHOUGH frustrated and impatient at times we continued to reach out to fulfil our destiny as Australia's overseas airline. The take-over of British Commonwealth Pacific Airways, and our establishment on the South Pacific route to the U.S.A. and Canada, was one of the most significant events in our history. It paved the way for further great expansion.

As told, BCPA commenced operations in 1946 by chartering ANA DC4 aircraft, QEA having only the unsuitable Lancastrians to offer. BCPA then purchased four DC6 aircraft and prepared to operate, but first had to conclude arrangements with ANA. This was difficult as the company felt they were established on the route. Many obstacles were raised, but Arthur Coles, chairman of BCPA, and the Australian government, were determined on the take-over.

The story is told that, by a certain date, a cheque in the region of £A1,000,000 had to go to ANA in payment for equipment. On the eve of payment being due, Arthur Coles went to ANA with the required cheque, drawn on the Commonwealth Bank. The cheque was refused as it was not guaranteed by the bank. Coles, not to be outdone, rushed to his own bank, the E. S. & A., where a cheque was drawn and guaranteed by the bank. This was presented to ANA and accepted. How true the story is in detail I do not know, but it sounds like Arthur Coles, and illustrates the difficulties of the time.

BCPA had been formed during the chasing of that dream of joint British Commonwealth operations, despite the deficiencies of TEAL. It was also to be the means of getting going a South Pacific service in competition with Pan American Airways and CPAL who were preparing to operate from Canada to Australia. With Canada out, the three other Empire parties were Australia, New Zealand and Great Britain, all with bargaining rights. One could hardly start the service without the other two agreeing. The U.K. was too far away, and Australia and New Zealand would not let her start on her own. New Zealand was short of capital, and also of know-how at this stage, while Australia too was not prepared or able to go it alone. So BCPA was formed and went on to carry out a valuable service for seven and a half years, holding its own with Pan American Airways in traffic carried, and well exceeding CPAL.

As the BCPA service continued, however, it became increasingly evident that the trend was getting farther and farther away from its type of operation. Dollar restrictions were a restraint on travel, there was no heavy mail carriage as on the Kangaroo route, selling was difficult, and the company was debarred expansion, either westward or eastward, because of BOAC and QEA interests; BCPA stood in the way of their progress. In the years of its operation the cumulative profit of the BCPA company amounted only to £29,718, despite special grants from the three shareholding governments to the total of £1,216,425.

On 20th April 1950 the QEA board made a well worded submission to our Minister, T. W. White, proposing to take-over BCPA, and setting out our views for expansion, which entailed:

1. An extension from Vancouver across Canada, and linking with BOAC at New York.

2. A service from Sydney to Johannesburg linking there with BOAC.

3. A future service from Sydney to Valparaiso linking there with BOAC.

On 13th November 1951 I wrote a memorandum entitled "The Unsatisfactory Position in the Relationship of QEA and BCPA". I doubt if it ever was officially recognized, but I believe it well expressed the position of that time, and foreshadowed the QEA Round the World service which was to come:

1. The direct divergence of interests between BCPA and the QEA/BOAC partnership interests, in that BCPA are openly competing for London-Australia traffic, has now reached a stage where action should be taken.

   Sir Miles Thomas, with whom the problem has been discussed, recognizes the present difficulties which are now at a stage where BOAC are constantly embarrassed by having to judge between two interests. He strongly advocates application of the BOAC/QEA parallel partnership arrangements to the Pacific, and any extension of the Pacific service.

   The first step to secure this would be the purchase by QEA of the Commonwealth Government shares in BCPA, thus placing QEA on the same footing as BOAC in BCPA. At the same time reconsideration of the shareholdings should be considered.

   Present holdings are as follows:

| Route | Company | Capital Interest |
|---|---|---|
| Australia/U.K. via India | QEA | 100% Australian capital |
| | BOAC | 100% U.K. capital |
| Australia/U.S.A. | BCPA | 50% Australian |
| | | 30% New Zealand |
| | | 20% U.K. |

2. At the present time both the British Government and the Australian are competing against themselves for the London-Australia traffic.

3. It is out of the question for QEA, BOAC and BCPA to come to any effective agreement in regard to co-operation and selling because, owing to the balance of interest, QEA and BOAC must sell against BCPA and the trans U.S.A. airlines.

   In any event, QEA and BOAC must continue to sell against PAWA and CPA, competing via the Pacific for Sydney-London traffic. This automatically means selling against BCPA.

4. In these circumstances, it is embarrassing to QEA to have on its board two members of the BCPA board, who derive information from QEA which can be passed on to BCPA (especially as one is chairman of BCPA) while QEA gets no like benefits from BCPA, as this is a subject not discussed by the mixed board members, and it is obviously too embarrassing to discuss if the board is to remain effective and in a proper degree of harmony and unity of interests.

5. Round the world operation for large operators is now an absolute essential in planning. At present day speeds of 265 m.p.h. to go half-way round the world and then return the same way, when the complete circle could be flown without any addition in mileage, is obviously poor and ineffective competitive operation. How much more so at the speeds to come!

6. In short the present set-up, as described above, is untidy and alleviation should be planned.

   The position can be rationalized by—
   A decision to aim for, and accomplish as soon as possible, BOAC/QEA parallel partnership round the world services, the main principle of which would be pooling of revenue. The first step in accomplishing this would be the purchase by QEA of the Commonwealth Government shares in BCPA.

New Zealand was unhappy, not, at this stage, being prepared to operate her own longer international services; Australia and the U.K., however, saw the great need for some drastic change. When representatives of the three governments met in Canberra in August 1952, among other important matters, it was recorded:

> The most effective way of promoting community of interests between the Kangaroo Route and the Pacific Atlantic route operations, would be to entrust the responsibility to one operator. It seemed logical therefore that QEA should assume both operational and financial responsibility for the Pacific section of the Pacific/Atlantic route, thereby obviating government grants to this operation.

Things began to move and, in anticipation of changes, after correspondence with my Minister, L. Anthony, I accepted a seat on the BCPA board, the other members of which were G. P. N. Watt, chairman, Sir Leonard Isitt, E. L. Greensmith, and Lionel Hooke as alternate for Sir

William M. Allen, chairman of Boeings, and Mrs Allen enjoy their trip (*Photo*: Qantas)

Honolulu—our fabulous airport reception (*Photo*: Qantas)

Boeing 707 taking off at Mascot, using water injection (*Photo: Daily Mirror*)

Boeing 707 taking off at Mascot—"Pardon my dust" (*Photo: Daily Mirror*)

Miles Thomas. At that time G. P. N. Watt was also chairman of TAA, while I was also chairman of QEA and on the TEAL board. It was rather a mix-up which sorted itself out well in the end, though not for all.

The ANA camp, led by Sir Ivan Holyman, was most unhappy and, I am afraid, missed the chance of becoming the permanent second operator in the two domestic airlines system. They had taken some terrific beatings over the years. In July 1953 this startling headline appeared in the Sydney *Sun*: "ANA move for Airline Merger shocks officials". The merger was to include the amalgamation of all Australian major airline activities, including QEA. This was in spite of a fifteen-year agreement with the Australian government to have TAA and ANA on an equal basis. ANA threatened to close its doors if the merger proposals failed. They did fail. ANA decided to close operations, with the result that Reg Ansett, coming to the assistance of an acutely embarrassed government, formed Ansett-ANA by buying out ANA.

As could be expected, some of the interests involved were not pleased about the way things were going for BCPA. There was a move for a merger between BCPA and TEAL, but it did not come to anything.

On 14th and 15th October 1953 representatives of the U.K., Australian and New Zealand governments met in Christchurch, New Zealand, the leaders being Mr A. Lennox-Boyd for Great Britain, H. L. Anthony for Australia, and Sir Thomas MacDonald for New Zealand, and settled arrangements for the South Pacific services. It was announced:

> Under the new arrangement QEA and BOAC will continue in parallel partnership on the Kangaroo route. QEA will operate services to the United States and Canada, connecting with BOAC at San Francisco when BOAC extend their North Atlantic service to that point. Tasman Empire Airways will connect with these world routes at both Sydney and Nadi (Fiji), thus continuing in a different form the partnership in which the Governments have been associated for many years.

Another important decision affecting TEAL was taken at the conference, the Australian government having taken over the QEA shareholding in that company. It was decided:

> Under the new arrangement Tasman Empire Airways will be owned equally by New Zealand and Australia, the aircraft being based in New Zealand.

TEAL was also to take over the four BCPA DC6 aircraft and to operate them on the Sydney, Auckland, Nadi run.

The number of aircraft dramatically came down to three when, two weeks after the Christchurch conference, the BCPA DC6 *R.M.A. Resolution* crashed into the hills when making its approach to San Francisco airport. The aircraft was a total loss, and Captain B. N. Dickson, his

K

seven crew members and eleven passengers were killed. A long litigation ensued in the U.S.A. courts over damages for some of the passengers. In the case of William Kapell, the famous pianist, the proceedings continued in trial after trial until it all ended with the award of no damages, for it was extremely difficult to prove "wilful misconduct" and, in this case, impossible, as all aboard the aircraft died at once. QEA had inherited the liabilities of BCPA and the cost of these proceedings totalled $A306,103.

The take-over of BCPA involved much discussion between the governments, QEA and BCPA, especially about the merging of BCPA staff with QEA. Finally the Christchurch Agreement was ratified by the governments and I telegraphed Robert Menzies, thanking him on behalf of the QEA board. He replied on 31st March 1954:

> My dear Hudson Fysh. Your telegram of congratulations upon the outcome of the Pacific and Tasman negotiations is most heartening, and I am delighted to think such a happy result was achieved.

Our planning had gone well. On 29th March 1954, in San Francisco, Mrs Spender (later Lady) wife of the Hon. Percy Spender (later Sir Percy), Australian Ambassador to the U.S.A., christened our first grand new Super Constellation *Southern Constellation* and on 15th May the same aircraft left Sydney inaugurating our new South Pacific service.

There was an impressive ceremony at Mascot, our Minister, the Hon. H. L. Anthony, speaking, and Mrs Anthony cutting the ribbon releasing the gleaming *Southern Constellation* for its long inaugural flight.

The crew were:

| | |
|---|---|
| Captain | K. G. Jackson |
| Captain | J. J. Connolly |
| First Officer | R. Chasney |
| Navigation Officer | H. A. Seymour |
| Radio Officer | H. W. Taylor |
| Engineer Officer | H. W. Strangward |
| Engineer Officer | D. E. Brown |

From Honolulu the aircraft was taken on by:

| | |
|---|---|
| Captain | P. J. R. Shields |
| Captain | P. J. Miller |
| Captain | J. B. Fawcett |
| Navigation Officer | D. N. Bain |
| Radio Officer | K. A. O'Dwyer |
| Engineer Officer | J. R. Silver |
| Engineer Officer | A. J. Forsythe |

G. P. N. Watt, former chairman of BCPA and a director of QEA, my wife and I, accompanied the flight.

As I have only brief records of the many speeches made, I quote short extracts from my own comments *en route*:

At Mascot:

> It is good to see Australian overseas transport keeping to the forefront. Qantas, as the chosen instrument of the Commonwealth Government, realizes its great responsibilities and we are all out to provide services which will add to Australia's good name among the nations.

At Fiji:

> It is good too, to see Mr Tom Barrow, a director of TEAL, who has brought along their DC6, inaugurating their new service.

At Honolulu:

> We have done a lot of pioneering, but we, or even BCPA, did not pioneer the Pacific. That was done by Sir Charles Kingsford Smith and Charles Ulm, Warner and Lyons, and P. G. Taylor.

At San Francisco:

> As an old flying man who has put away his wings, I feel I am standing on hallowed ground here this morning. . . .
>
> PAWA pioneered the Pacific Ocean for air transport from here in the old flying boat days. It was an epic. BCPA and CPAL followed on, and if we can do as well as BCPA whom we follow, we will be doing very well indeed.

At Vancouver:

> Early Civil Aviation in Australia took much the same form as in your early Canadian pioneering days, and your bush flyers correspond to our pilots of the Never-Never.
>
> Air transport nowadays forms the spearhead of trade, commerce and human relationship. We bring you the new Super Constellation on this opening service.

The new Trans Pacific service was off to a good start and never looked back. BCPA staff who came over to us, numbered 264, and formed an excellent, knowledgeable nucleus in running the new service, under Alec Barlow, the former BCPA general manager. Also we had back with us our one-time board secretary, Ivan Lawson, who now wrestles mightily as chief property development manager, dealing with almost unbelievable expansion of Qantas Airways in properties. Of course there were difficulties in such a merger of staff, and I remember C. O. Turner saying it would take ten years to level things out. This was more or less correct.

A. C. Joyce, the hard working liquidator of BCPA, continued to deal with complications arising from the merger, and, indeed, did not present his final report and accounts until April 1967, some thirteen years after QEA commenced to operate across the Pacific. The final accounting then was not completed by 30th June 1966 beyond which date this book does not deal; but an entry in our balance sheet, which was an account of the BCPA purchase, read: "Capital advance, pending allotment of shares— £A1,958,823."

On 2nd April 1957 the first BOAC flight left London for San Francisco, thus providing a thorough BOAC-QEA connecting partnership service and realizing the objective of a round-the-world connection.

## ⁂ 16 ⁂

## Time and Change—from Managing Director
## to Whole-time Chairman

THE TAKING OVER of BCPA in 1954 ushered in a new and advanced state of existence for Qantas. We had survived a change of government, crisis after crisis had been weathered, QEA was established as the country's national overseas operator. We believed wholly in the Australian international and domestic airlines system, and against the ANA, and then Ansett-ANA effort to enter our domain, we had kept the Government on the rails. We ourselves had no desire to enter into domestic operation in Australia, the affair of TAA, Ansett-ANA and the smaller feeder services.

The QEA directorate in 1955 were busy coping with the general rapid advancement in our own sphere. By that year our staff had jumped to 5,387 and head office in Shell House was overflowing. It was time we had our own building. As far back as 1949 we had purchased land at the corner of Hunter and Elizabeth Streets for this purpose, and now plans were made for a modern building, which was to be our sixth home in a series of moves over the years. This valuable and strategically placed piece of land was purchased from Modern (non licensed) Hotels Ltd for £87,000, the land today, no doubt, being worth in the vicinity of £A1,000,000.

As our business grew and tended to become most wide-spread, involving continual acquisition and re-organization, Turner as general manager, took an increasing responsibility, while I as chairman and managing director was also fully taxed. An additional part of my work entailed an overseas trip twice a year to attend executive committee and annual general meetings of the International Air Transport Association. This also gave me a valuable opportunity to keep in touch with our own operations overseas. I found rubbing shoulders twice a year with the top air transport people of the world was of incalculable importance in those days of our struggle for emergence. I also continued to serve on the TEAL board, becoming vice chairman; on the Wentworth Hotel board as chairman, and as deputy chairman of the Australian National Travel Association.

I found I was getting jumpy under the pressure of it all. Difficulties in the board room grew up. More executive work was being taken over by Turner, and so on. I wrote to my Minister, Athol Townley, on 7th December 1954 suggesting that I should relinquish my duties as chief executive on 30th June 1955, when I would be sixty, and continue as whole-time chairman of the Board.

The position was discussed with the Minister and with the Director-General of Civil Aviation, Sir Richard Williams. Both were rather surprised and let me understand that, as far as they were concerned, there was no need for the change to come about. However, I realized I had too much on my hands to give the close attention to detail I wished to give, and I think my decision was a wise one. The change came about as from 1st July 1955, Turner taking over as chief executive and general manager. I had held the position of managing director with Qantas, and then with QEA, for thirty-two years.

I was now under a new directive as whole-time chairman, responsible for contacts and correspondence with the Minister and top contacts with the Director-General of Civil Aviation, and not able to accept any other business activities, such as directorships, without the express permission of the Minister. The QEA organization had always been rather peculiar and I was now a full-time chairman but with important executive duties. This was very different from the position of other Federal government instrumentalities where part-time chairmen headed the boards, there being no managing directors. General managers ran the organizations.

Sir Keith Smith, who had served as a director on our board since the inception of QEA, died on 19th December 1955, and the board recorded their appreciation of his services:

> Sir Keith, who was one of the great pioneers of aviation, as well as a man of considerable business standing, has been a director of Qantas since 1945. His colleagues on the board desire to record their sincere appreciation of the valuable service he rendered to the company for so many years.

On 21st May 1956 R. R. Law-Smith was appointed to the board. It was an appointment in which the Prime Minister and our Minister, Senator Paltridge, were very interested, introducing to the board new young blood, but with an atmosphere of aviation and business experience gained from the World War II era. Bob Law-Smith was forty-one when he took his seat on the board. An active private aircraft owner, with a first class instrument rating, he had obtained his pilot's licence in 1939, and had gone on to serve in Nos. 2 and 100 Squadrons, and Transport Squadrons, finishing up with the rank of RAAF Squadron Leader when he was Director of Postings. Bob Law-Smith gave valuable and unsparing service on the QEA board and became vice chairman. He joined the

B.H.P. board in 1961 and, as could be expected, had to face many smiling queries about the activities of that great company, but kept a poker face and tight lips. He was appointed to the TAA Commission in 1962.

The QEA board, as organized in 1956, consisted of myself as chairman, W. C. Taylor, vice chairman, G. P. N. Watt, Sir Daniel McVey, Sir Roland Wilson and R. R. Law-Smith. F. C. Derham was the company secretary, and also finance manager.

C. O. Turner, in his new position as chief executive, had organized a strong management group, which he called the "Head Office Executive". Besides himself, they consisted of G. U. Allan, assistant general manager, A. A. Barlow, manager Eastern Division, W. H. Crowther, manager Western Division, F. C. Derham, finance manager, C. W. Nielson, commercial manager, and R. J. Ritchie, technical manager. This top group was then backed up by "other Executives" in L. R. Ambrose, Dr E. H. Anderson, P. J. Booth, W. L. Harding, N. H. Hay, P. W. Howson, D. B. Hudson, E. C. Johnston (who had joined us as international adviser), I. O. Lawson and V. C. Sommerlad.

At Sydney, the base and nerve centre of our operations, we were reorganized, and there great activity prevailed. Our work and interest were predominantly overseas and, in addition to our now important contact with IATA, the welfare of our partnership with BOAC was not to be neglected. We regarded this as basic. The association during the years ahead was to have interesting developments. Keeping the peace was a responsibility in which I felt I had much success. Crises occurred, and differences had to be patched up with expressions and actions of good will.

Sir Miles Thomas, a World War I pilot and journalist, had an impressive business record which led to his appointment as managing director of the Nuffield organization. He was induced to become chairman of BOAC where heavy losses were being recorded and undertake a clean-up. We both recognized the importance of the BOAC/QEA partnership and together arranged for 21st anniversary celebrations, the main function being a dinner held at the Dorchester Hotel, London, on 5th December 1955.

The dinner was a memorable occasion attended by the Duke of Gloucester and an imposing array of air transport identities with records going back to the early pioneering days. Some of those present were J. A. Boyd Carpenter, U.K. Minister for Transport and Civil Aviation, Sir Thomas White, the Australian High Commissioner, Lord Bruce, Sir John Salmond, Sir Frederick Handley Page, F. E. N. St Barbe, Sir Alan Cobham, George Woods Humphery, George Cribbett, Sir William Hildred, Lord Tweedsmuir, Lord Burley, Lord Rennell of Rodd, General Critchley, Captain O. P. Jones, Captain Jerry Shaw, Captain "Buddy" Messenger, Sir Victor Tate, Dennis Handover.

"Wren", the famous aviation cartoonist, was there and made an amusing recording. Sir Miles had done a good job. The speeches were good. A presentation was made to me by BOAC. I tried to make a few points, and much goodwill resulted from the occasion.

The last day of 1955 saw the retirement of Sir Richard Williams who had passed his sixty-fifth year, his place as Director-General of Civil Aviation being taken by D. G. Anderson. With the going of Sir Richard, departed our oldest pioneer airman administrator, one with perhaps the greatest record of service in the air performed for Australia by any Australian. It had been fitting that his brilliant career in the Australian Flying Corps and RAAF had been followed by his nine years' leadership as head of Civil Aviation. It had been a period of amazing development in which he played a great part in laying the permanent foundations for civil aviation of today.

To make the break with the past even more sharp, Captain E. C. Johnston, the Assistant Director-General of Civil Aviation, was retired on 30th April 1956, after having served for thirty-five years. He had a long and dogged innings in top positions where he fought hard for the advancement of civil aviation and for the protection of Australian air transport rights abroad, a subject in which his knowledge was unequalled.

As a parallel to the appointment of Bob Law-Smith to our board at the age of forty-one, came the appointment of Don Anderson at the age of thirty-eight as head of the Department of Civil Aviation. A new generation was facing the problems of the future. Don Anderson was an experienced airman, having logged some 3,000 hours as a transport pilot in World War II for the RAAF and the U.S. Air Corps. He ended his war service as a test and acceptance pilot with Ferry Command in the United States.

He joined the Civil Aviation Department in 1946 as Examiner of Airmen, and experienced a quick rise to senior positions, being appointed Assistant Director-General in 1952. During the developments of the 1950s he played an important role, leading Civil Aviation delegations on overseas missions. A keen sportsman, he was an opening batsman and bowler for Essendon in the Melbourne district cricket competitions. He and I played against one another for some years when we organized the annual Civil Aviation *versus* QEA cricket match for the Shane Paltridge Cup.

140

The only acceptable foundation for a good airline, for the attaining of competitive traffic appeal and successful financial operation, lies in securing aircraft fully competitive with the world's best, and in limiting the types operated to a minimum, phasing out the old as the new come in. It might be added that the superseded aircraft, if well chosen in the first place, usually have a handsome re-sale or trade-in value.

Following these principles, from the end of 1954, through 1955 and on into 1956, QEA phased out its Constellation 749 fleet and introduced the improved Super Constellations. Of this type we came to own sixteen aircraft which carried on very effectively until the Boeing 707 jet fleet was delivered in 1959 and the Super Constellations were disposed of, many to U.S.A. buyers.

The Boeing order was made in September 1956, after an exhaustive investigation by C. O. Turner and his technical and economical experts. These aircraft began an entirely new era of air transport. The initial order was for seven jets.

The increased work capacity offered by the Boeing 707 pointed to great opportunities for expansion of the company. Forward planning and budgeting engaged the attention of our experts. In such circumstances, it seemed appropriate to make our position clear to our partners, BOAC, and in September 1956 I read in London to Gerald d'Erlanger, chairman of BOAC, and to George Cribbett, deputy chairman, the following note, which is in my handwriting:

## QANTAS PRINCIPLES

1. Maintenance of an independent Australian international airline.
2. Maintenance of vigorous competitive element with foreign airlines and co-operation with BOAC to make this as effective as possible. Inversely, BOAC to co-operate with QEA to same end.
3. Development of round the world service made essential to QEA by the challenge of the major international airlines.
   Extension of the parallel partnership principle on a round the world basis, as already agreed.
   Australia's geographical position in relation to Europe, and because of the unstable political position along two-thirds of the whole Kangaroo route, makes it urgent for QEA to secure rights across North America to Europe and to organize such a route commercially.
4. The development of an effective sales force in Europe.
5. Recognition that countries adjacent to Australia are of close interest to her politically, and in regard to air communications; countries such as Indonesia, Malaya, New Zealand and Hong Kong.
6. Tasman Empire Airways is owned 50/50 by New Zealand and Australia, and out of that partnership will be developed by the two countries the part to be played by New Zealand in the future.

141

7. In regard to equipment, QEA must choose the most highly competitive available, and out of such a policy has resulted, and will continue to result, an enormous advantage to the partnership.
The same policy is essential to BOAC, if QEA is to be effectively supported.

The year 1957, another eventful year, opened with a disaster when our great new hangar at Mascot collapsed, on 12th January, with a low grinding rumble. Fortunately, there were no aircraft in the hangar at the time and thus any loss of a catastrophic nature was avoided. The steel for the job had been designed and fabricated in Europe and assembled and erected on the site.

In the protracted negotiations to secure a settlement, claim and counter-claim went on for months. The architects, Rudder, Littlemore and Rudder, denied all responsibility, as did the builders, E. T. Eastment and Sons; so did the suppliers of the Italian steel. QEA denied all blame. We were insured, but not sufficiently to cover the cost of repair and re-erection of the building. The affair ended in a compromise settlement. The new Qantas House was then nearing completion, and there was some satirical speculation as to whether it would also fall in on us.

In April came the direct action and strike of our pilots. Then in May came brighter happenings when the historic negotiations in Washington commenced, which resulted in the U.S.A. granting us rights to operate from San Francisco to New York and on to London. This gave us the essential framework of our world operations, a backbone which encircled the earth through the U.S.A. and the United Kingdom.

Negotiations of air route rights had become one of the vital functions of the Civil Aviation Department and, prior to the Washington talks, nearly thirty of these had been negotiated by the Australian Government. On the outcome depended the viability of Australia's international operator. At the same time there must be agreement for foreign organization to operate to and through Australia. This was essential for international good relations, trade, and that new and modern gold—tourism.

The agreements varied in almost every case, but all were based primarily on third and fourth freedom rights between the two negotiating countries. This was traffic in which each obviously had an equal share. If there was no traffic between the two countries, there could be no agreement. Australia, in enforcing this principle, protected that growing share in the national economy which was bound up in its international airline. A foreign airline booking a passenger in Australia exported the fare overseas. An Australian airline booking a passenger overseas imported the fare. In the long and difficult negotiations the Department of Civil Aviation sought to preserve a correct balance of the economic factors.

The negotiations which opened in Washington on 15th May 1957 sought an up-dating of the existing U.S.A.-Australia Agreement and examined the claim of Australia to extend QEA service from San Francisco to New York and on to London. Success was imperative for the future of QEA. Our prospects of crossing Canada were about nil; a service via Mexico was premature, besides being barred by the long Tahiti-Mexico City stage of 4,350 statute miles. Air traffic between the U.K. and Europe via the U.S.A. was growing at a great rate, as political and other difficulties increased along the old Kangaroo route via India. Businessmen and tourists travelling between the U.K. and Australia wanted to stop off at New York and San Francisco; and this end-to-end traffic was owned by the two countries, both wanting permission to fly over the U.S.A. and pick up some extra traffic on the way. There was growing political association between the U.S.A. and Australia, the U.S.A. also wanting new rights for its service to Australia by Pan American Airways and permission to operate through and beyond Australia.

The conference opened in high hopes, perhaps the main snag being Australia's desire to operate across the U.S.A., a right which no other country had. Even Pan American Airways had no such right, the trans-U.S.A. services being in the firm hands of domestic operators.

Howard Beale (later Sir Howard) was Australian Ambassador in Washington, and the Australian Civil Aviation team was led by Donald Anderson. With him in an advisory capacity was a strong QEA team led by C. O. Turner.

It was reported as an American-style negotiation. From the outset protracted discussions took place on the measurement and extent of Australian third and fourth freedom traffic moving via the U.S.A. to Europe. The Australian delegation was able to demonstrate strategically the volume and growth of this traffic flow. Sir Donald Anderson pays a tribute to the late R. K. Goodrich whose work in the assembling of these statistics was most notable.

The conference ended with high hopes, though a measure of official opposition remained which ceased with the acquiescence of the State Department, the final authority. Australia was given the necessary rights and, in exchange, the U.S.A. was granted a series of most important rights providing for expansion of operations to and through Australia. Provision was made for services to Sydney, Melbourne, Perth and Darwin, and beyond Australia to South-east Asia and beyond, to Antarctica and beyond, and for a new route to Australia via Japan. Despite these very wide rights granted to the U.S.A., a minor disappointment to us was the refusal to

143

permit us to include Los Angeles. Later came the argument as to whether Tahiti had been included in the Australian rights in flying to the U.S.A.

The price which Australia had to pay was heavy but inevitable, and, I feel, well worth the concession to QEA to operate across the U.S.A. However, perhaps the great price will be justified only if U.S.A. air traffic in and out of Australia can be held to a third and fourth freedom basis, and not full Bermuda type.

The route granted to QEA made it the first airline to operate round the world services, transitting the U.S.A., a unique position of great significance, which prepared the way for our development into one of the major world airlines. Donald Anderson, after this major international negotiation, the first since he had become Director-General, could feel well satisfied when he returned to the acclaim of his Minister, Shane Paltridge, and so also might C. O. Turner.

## ❋ 17 ❋

## New Ventures, and Qantas House Opens

OTHER interesting events in 1957 included our entry into Malayan Airways, later known as Malaysia-Singapore Airlines Ltd, and Fiji Airways. These new ventures assisted the work of air transport in nearby friendly countries and reinforced the position of QEA against growing competition by large operators such as Pan American Airways, TWA and BOAC. A lead had earlier been given by Ivan Holyman's ANA, which had shareholdings in Air Ceylon and Cathay Pacific Airways in Hong Kong, but ANA opposed QEA interests.

Australia was particularly interested in Singapore and Malaya where she had anti-communist forces stationed. Sir William J. McKell had helped with advice on the new Constitution of the Malaysian-Singapore Federation. QEA had for many years been responsible for the Singapore area as part of its Kangaroo route operations and had a strong organization centred there.

BOAC had started off in a big way to take a financial interest in airways domiciled outside the United Kingdom. This was expressed in the Air Corporation Act of 1949. BOAC was to become interested in the West Indies, the Bahamas, Aden, the Persian Gulf, Hong Kong, West Africa, in the Lebanon, in Turkey, and also in Malaya and later in Fiji. No doubt these connections served a useful purpose during the period when rapid competitive development of world airlines was taking place, and in political contact; but participation in these minor companies involved BOAC in heavy financial losses before there was readjustment of the position.

When in London at the end of 1956, I discussed with Sir George Cribbett the desire of QEA to participate with BOAC in Malayan Airways, and the matter was followed up by C. O. Turner in Sydney and with my board. The result was that in 1957 we invested £A339,554 in a reconstructed Malayan Airways Company, this amount representing 32·9% of the capital, and BOAC holding an equal amount. The other shareholders were the Malaysian Federation Government, the Singapore Government, British North Borneo, Sarawak, Brunei, Ocean Steamships, Straits Steamship, and the general public.

The first chairman of the company was Dato Sir Mahmud Bin Mat, the other board members being N. A. Goode, F. L. Lane, P. R. Lewis, Lord Rennell of Rodd, J. A. Vick, managing director; and, nominated by QEA, W. C. Taylor and C. O. Turner. Captain J. W. Solly from QEA was general manager.

When taken over the company was in a very low state, indeed I had never seen anything worse. With the infusion of new capital, direction and management, it pulled round to become a profitable and successful undertaking. C. O. Turner and W. C. Taylor deserve credit for the favourable position reached, and so do our two later appointees to the board, G. U. Allan and E. C. Johnston.

Lord Rennell and his fellow BOAC nominated directors were also active. However, during the difficult early period, it was not a happy association. There were deep differences of opinion, mainly over the types of new aircraft. This was an old argument. Then there was the problem of keeping a balance between BOAC and QEA interests. At one time the QEA board and I were seriously called upon to intervene when the differences of opinion on the operation of this small sideshow threatened the well-being of the whole BOAC/QEA relationship in world routes. BOAC were pushing their Comet aircraft, while QEA pushed their DC4 for use by Malayan Airways. Much correspondence and a near crisis in relations resulted from criticism of the Comet expressed by our chief executive at a Hong Kong party.

During the middle years, Dato Loke Wan Tho became chairman of Malayan Airways and did much to develop a more harmonious directorate. A Singapore Chinese millionaire, business magnate, famous photographer of birds and lover of the arts, he will be remembered as a kindly and efficient personality. The Dato was killed in a tragic air crash in Korea, and Yong Pung How became chairman.

In the years prior to my retirement we were still active with BOAC in Malayan Airways and we shared the responsibility of that difficult stage of Malaysianization of the undertaking when the Malayan and Singapore Governments increased their shareholdings and the holdings of BOAC and QEA were reduced to 13·20% each. Local ambitions were achieved, and we avoided having to share responsibility for heavy capital commitments for new aircraft equipment.

Regular profits had been made, BOAC and QEA had been of great assistance, friendship with the Kuala Lumpur and Singapore authorities had been built up and maintained, and I feel that we could look back with satisfaction to our part in the association which still continues.

Malayan Airways had mainly operated domestic services throughout Malaya and Borneo, and to Bangkok, Indonesia and Hong Kong, in competition with Cathay Pacific, the Hong Kong Company. Malayan Airways were members of IATA and conformed to their rules on fares and rates. Cathay Pacific were not and set their own independent pace. This resulted, unfortunately, in Malayan Airways having to retire from IATA in order to counter the methods of Cathay Pacific.

The latest development of Malaysia-Singapore Airlines has been so pronounced that it will soon be flying its Boeing jets to Australia in pool with BOAC and QEA and kindred operators. South-east Asia is fast emerging from commercial obscurity, and Australia's help and understanding have been important factors in the transformation.

An interesting pattern was formed in the establishment of QEA interests on the Australian perimeter. We had our shareholding in TEAL before it was taken over by the Australian Government. There was our important operation in Papua-New Guinea. Then, in April 1958, the Fijian area was entered when, following the death of Harold Gatty, Fiji Airways was purchased for £A53,675 from his estate, Katafanga Estates Ltd.

The story of aviation in Fiji had begun on 5th June 1928 when Kingsford Smith's *Southern Cross* came out of the skies from the far away Hawaiian Islands to rest under the guidance of that master pilot on the little Suva football ground. In 1932 Fiji Airways Ltd was registered in Adelaide, being underwritten by the New Guinea pioneer operator, Guinea Airways. On 20th March 1933 subsidized passenger and mail services were commenced in the Pacific Islands with two small Genairco float planes piloted by Alan Cross and Captain Fenton. Mishaps occurred, operations were uneconomic with insufficient government support, and operations closed in 1934.

It was not until July 1951 that Fiji Airways was founded by Harold Gatty, and on 1st September 1951 began its first service with DH89 Dragon Rapide aircraft, linking Suva with the new Nadi international airport. The services extended, the Dragon aircraft being kept in use until 1954 when two D.H. Drovers were purchased from QEA. In 1958 came the purchase of the undertaking by us.

Harold Gatty, a great aviation pioneer, was born in Tasmania, later becoming a U.S.A. citizen. He was a keen publicist, and I have hanging in my office a beautifully embellished Fiji Airways life pass, issued to me on 15th June 1953 which states:

> Fiji Airways doth hereby grant to you this life pass entitling you and the members of your immediate family to free passage during your lifetime upon all routes of Fiji Airways.

It was signed by "Harold Gatty, Proprietor", and I have often wondered whether this liability held good for honouring by QEA after its acquisition of Fiji Airways.

In 1959, the year after the purchase by QEA, Fiji Airways had a nominal capital of £F500,000 and a paid up capital of £F180,000, which provided for the purchase of two D.H. Heron aircraft. The board consisted of W. C. Taylor, chairman, C. O. Turner, and R. O. Mant, who was general manager.

Much needed to be done to straighten out our newest overseas venture, and I have found with some amusement an early board minute on insurance:

> Mr Kay pointed out that it is impossible to insure cash in Fiji, and the system of handling cash was explained to the meeting. It was decided that the manager do everything possible to speed up the delivery of the safe for Suva Booking Office.

The desire of the Fijian and New Zealand Governments to share in the company resulted in a reconstruction which meant that on 1st January 1960 there was a paid up capital of £F240,000 subscribed equally by QEA, the Fijian Government, BOAC and Air New Zealand. The directors were W. C. Taylor, chairman nominated by QEA, J. N. M. Weir nominated by BOAC, and G. N. Roberts nominated by Air New Zealand. C. D. Ritchie was general manager, nominated by QEA, and, on the retirement of W. C. Taylor from the board of QEA, G. U. Allan became chairman, and the Fijian Government also had a member on the board. R. S. Kay was secretary. An interesting aspect of the agreement was that QEA should be entirely responsible for the management. The TEAL and BCPA set-up and its deficiencies had been a precedent we wished to avoid.

I always felt that Fiji Airways was run economically and effectively; but to make both ends meet was a constant struggle, profit and loss coming out at about line ball until 1966 when a loss of £F71,605 was recorded.

The chief problem was to secure suitable aircraft to serve a variety of routes, without resorting to an uneconomic diversity of aircraft. The four-engined Herons did a good job locally, but in operating the greater distances of the new services to Tonga, Western Samoa, the New Hebrides, the British Solomon Islands, the Gilbert and Ellice Islands, the number of seats had to be drastically reduced in favour of an increased fuel load. These more ambitious services were instituted at the wish of the Fijian Government as developmental routes. But the subsidy to cover the inevitable losses was not made by the Government as would have been made in Australia or the U.S.A. for similar services. The

Boeing 707 with reconstructed Avro 504K Dyak similar to the original aircraft of 1921
(*Photo*: Qantas)

Notice on Winton airport building (*Photo*: Qantas)

The Winton, Queensland, memorial to Qantas (*Photo*: Qantas)

position of the Fijian Government, that of a small British colony with only shoestring funds, was difficult.

Financially, Fiji Airways Limited proved the most unprofitable of the ventures we owned or took part in. Malayan Airways paid regular dividends, TEAL scraped along although at times we had almost to force dividends out of the New Zealanders. The Wentworth Hotel was a little goldmine of which I felt very proud.

Of our main operations, New Guinea only scraped along, while the South African service was expensive and was profitable only on an extra cost basis. Our early all-cargo services also cost us money, but they had to be supported. In the overall count, Qantas and then QEA made unbroken profits from 1924 to 1966, a period of forty-two years. It was a record of which we could feel proud; we had made progress, sometimes venturesome progress. The pilots' strike at the end of 1966 was financially disastrous and dissipated millions of pounds of profit for that financial year. It may be said that, leaving out our aircraft troubles in the early 1920s, this was the first severe financial setback the company had received. The pilots lost too, but they more than made up the loss over the years in increased salary gains.

To return to a more pleasant topic, on 28th October 1957 Qantas House, at the top of Hunter Street, the new home of QEA, was opened by the Prime Minister, R. G. Menzies. There had been a great deal of planning and hard work by C. O. Turner and his staff, I. O. Lawson as administration manager carrying a heavy burden. In 1957 Qantas House stood as a symbol of Australia's aviation progress. The £1,300,000 building was to be our new headquarters from which would be controlled the operations which made Qantas the seventh largest international airline in the world, with an unduplicated route mileage of 65,597 miles, and, at that time, about the same capacity tonne miles flown per annum.

The striking, curved-fronted building of thirteen floors bordered Chifley Square and, for the first time in many years, brought together the thousand people in our head office organization. Previously they had been scattered throughout no less than fourteen buildings in the city where we were forced to hire space because of the post-war shortage of accommodation and the company's rapid expansion of business. The building won an award for Rudder, Littlemore and Rudder, the architects, and was to become a much admired landmark in the city. It is still that, despite the many lofty buildings erected in the vicinity which have turned the locality into a steel and concrete jungle, though a nerve centre of business, commerce, travel and tourism.

The new building had many interesting features, notably the striking

149

L

passenger booking hall on street level, the display area and theatrette. The 11th floor, with its view over the city, was made a staff diningroom and general assembly area, while on the ninth floor were the executive suites and board room. The board room was, we felt, the best in Sydney, with its large map of the world, display arrangements, lovely walnut table and blue chairs, though these took some getting used to. It was topped off by a small adjacent, circular diningroom, and annexe graced by Dargie's portrait of Sir Fergus McMaster.

On the day of the opening, as chairman of QEA, I had to make the opening speech introducing the Minister, the Hon. Shane Paltridge. I said, among other things:

> We are here for what we feel is a great event, the opening of Qantas House, which, besides representing a great economic and organizational advance for the company—a drawing together of our badly scattered Sydney forces—is a tangible witness to the progress of this pioneer undertaking, which had its humble beginnings in Western Queensland thirty-seven years ago.
>
> There are many people who have shared in this thirty-seven-year effort— our great Prime Ministers from Hughes to Menzies, Ministers responsible for Civil Aviation from Pearce to Paltridge, and Directors of Civil Aviation from Brinsmead to Anderson.
>
> Just as our head office has progressed from a small weatherboard structure at Longreach—Fred O'Rourke's store—to this fine building which is our world headquarters—because we fly to many distant lands, so our technical and operational organization has grown from a small barn-like wooden shelter at the Longreach Showgrounds with Arthur Baird as engineer, to the comprehensive and complex aerodrome establishments which are either in operation at Mascot airport, or pending to cater for our coming fleet of Boeing jet aircraft.
>
> As the Australian international airline, besides acting as a national instrument of prestige and convenience of transport, we also endeavour to make a profit in the usual way, but we have other functions to perform, especially in a young and developing country like Australia. . . .
>
> What we would like to see is the cash registers of Australia ringing merrily throughout the land, on a fair international share of visitors' spending money—this is the new gold.
>
> Our aim is to preserve the spirit and enterprise of Qantas as a power for progress and for good, and to continue to serve Australia in the tradition of the company.

When the time came for Mr Menzies, as he was then, to make his speech and declare Qantas House open, the packed-out great passenger booking hall was privileged to listen to one of the Prime Minister's magnificent addresses, full of colourful humour and meaningful remarks as he paid tribute to the company and its pioneering history. Here are some fragments:

150

There seems to be a well-established superstition that nobody may open a building without making a speech first. The superstition is quite unnecessary today. . . . You have heard my respected colleagues steal every fragment of my thunder.

But, in any event, I have been thinking about this opening and saying to myself, well, why not have a session of silence instead of making a speech? Silence, in which people may do some thinking, because there is so much to think about at this moment, in this building.

What pride those who have been in this enterprise must have, to think that from the most impossible, trifling beginnings, this vast achievement has been brought about.

Quite true that in recent years Governments have been behind Qantas. Quite true. Quite true that the only benevolent moment that Sir Roland Wilson ever enjoys, is when he is sitting on the board of Qantas.

These are happy events, and they are worth thinking about, but there would have been no Government interest, and no benevolent smile on the head of the Treasury if it had not been for the work of these plain men, back in the twenties of this century . . . this is one of the greatest pioneering efforts in the history of Australia.

The day will come, no doubt, when, as well as having a statue to Burke and Wills and some of the ancient explorers, we will be having a statue to people like Hudson Fysh—the only difference is that, artistic ideas have moved on, you can recognize Burke and Wills, but you would not be able to recognize him. But, my dear Hudson, I don't despair of the time coming when a rhythmical movement in fencing wire and stone will be put up, and somebody will say—Look at it, that's superb, don't you see, this is the rich symbol of the soaring bi-plane. You might stand a chance of having one. I won't, because if they put one up to me, they'll find that the estimates have been grossly exceeded.

. . . . quite frankly, when I step into a Qantas plane, I feel that I am coming back home. I'm in my own country, so to speak, and among my own people. That's a great feeling to have. The air hostesses—they have a quality denied to most young women of the same age, I must say. They gaze at old fellows like myself with a benign and, occasionally, quite an affectionate look. . . . But this is, in other words, sir, a great human international airline. It has great quality, and great qualities of humanity . . . this is the whole spirit which we need to preserve. We have it, fortunately, in abundance. There is plenty of it in Australia, and the more there is of it, the more certain will it be that the most remarkable period in our history —the last fifty years—will be as nothing, compared with the next fifty years of our history.

Qantas House was then declared open by our great Prime Minister, who, himself, had done so much through the years in support of the Qantas enterprise. And now Qantas has outgrown Qantas House, staff are again in overflow premises, and the great new building complex is under way up at the old Wentworth Hotel site . . . and so Qantas moves on into that next fifty years which the Prime Minister had spoken about.

151

# ⁂ IV ⁂

*In which Qantas spreads its wings to the world. In 1957 we encircled the globe, and sprang to world prominence, backed by a fine human service, the Qantas staff; and so we prospered.*

*The author bows out. . . .*

# ⇒ 18 ⇐

## Qantas, a Modern Jules Verne—and Enter the Boeings

O NCE the agreement giving us traffic rights across the U.S.A. was signed, organizational work to make this route a reality started in earnest, particularly for John Howell, operations' planning superintendent, and his assistants. On the 14th January, our Minister was able to announce:

> The two flights scheduled to leave Kingsford Smith airport today—one eastbound and one westbound, and both encircling the globe—mark an important step in the development of Australian civil aviation.

Melbourne had been made a regular stopping place on the new global route and had the honour of staging the official inauguration of the service. The Premier (Sir) Henry Bolte, and Senator Paltridge made speeches, and after Mr Bolte cut a ribbon attached to our Super Constellation *Southern Zephyr*, westward bound for London, and Mrs Paltridge did the same for the *Southern Aurora*, eastbound for the same city, the two aircraft made a double-header dispatch.

The one route was via Djakarta, Singapore, Bangkok, Karachi, Athens and Rome, the other via Sydney, Honolulu, San Francisco and New York. The two aircraft were timed to arrive in London within a few hours of one another, and then complete the round-the-world circuit back to Melbourne in about 128 hours. They left Melbourne on Tuesday and met in London on Thursday. A new stamp had been struck by the Australian Post Office depicting a Super Constellation encircling the world, and a heavy philatelic mail was carried.

The crew on the new Southern Cross route via the U.S.A. consisted of:

| | |
|---|---|
| Captain | K. D. Meares |
| First Officer | G. L. Halcrow |
| Second Officer | O. A. Kendall |
| Navigation Officer | R. G. Goodwin |
| Engineer Officer | K. Vickerman |
| Engineer Officer | F. A. Burke |
| Flight Steward | L. Wright |
| Flight Steward | R. Vidler |
| Flight Steward | I. Ross |
| Flight Hostess | M. Sainsbury |

On the Kangaroo route via India:

| | |
|---|---|
| Captain | J. P. Brodie |
| First Officer | J. Hodges |
| Second Officer | R. K. Seaver |
| Navigation Officer | J. K. Brearley |
| Engineer Officer | D. R. Fairweather |
| Engineer Officer | W. A. M. Forbes |
| Flight Steward | F. Wilks |
| Flight Steward | F. Wilson |
| Flight Steward | R. J. Rowe |
| Flight Hostess | D. Aspinall |

At the very time we inaugurated our round-the-world service, our new Boeings were being built in Seattle, and preparations to operate this revolutionary type of civil aircraft were being undertaken. They were due for delivery in mid-1959.

As was usually the case the use of this revolutionary commercial type had been foreshadowed by its use by the military. The Australian and New Zealand public had followed with amazement the international air race from London to Christchurch, New Zealand, in celebration of the centenary of that city. Hume Christie, an old World War I pilot, was president of the Christchurch committee which worked hard to organize the race. The Duke of Gloucester flagged away the competitors from London airport on 8th October 1953, the great interest being in the speed section, for which five English Electric "Canberra" turbo jet bombers were entered. The winner was Flight Lieutenant R. L. Burton, RAF, who covered the distance in 23 hours 50 minutes 42 seconds, including only 1 hour 25 minutes on the ground at intermediate fuelling stops. Squadron Leader P. F. Law, RAAF, in an Australian built "Canberra" was placed second in 24 hours 32 minutes, and Flight Lieutenant R. M. Furze, RAF, third in 24 hours 41 minutes.

The "Canberras" were powered by trusty Rolls Royce Avon Turbo-jet engines, and such was their reliability that less than one hour separated the place getters. Such astonishing times and reliability attracted much attention, and propeller driven aircraft appeared to be outdated. The public was looking for civil air transport to provide the same times. By 1959, with the Comet IV, the Boeing 707s and DC8s taking shape, a revolution in international air transport was on its way.

With feelings of great anticipation my wife and I set out in May 1959 to attend the IATA executive committee meeting at Lac Quimet in Canada. At this wonderful hostelry run by Tom Wheeler, pioneer bush pilot and operator, the host and hostess were Gordon McGregor, a Battle of Britain pilot and president of Trans Canada Airlines, and his wife Mae.

When the meeting concluded, we proceeded to Seattle to pick up the first Boeing 707 for delivery flight to Australia. Out on the tarmac was the *City of Canberra*, the flagship of our new fleet looking most workman-like and attractive. We were shown the interior by Captain Bert Ritchie and Captain Ian Ralfe. The spacious interior of this aircraft, leading the world in size, speed and comfort, broke all conventions. It was like entering a new and up-to-date tastefully decorated restaurant. The *City of Canberra* was a magic carpet to waft its passengers at the speed of sound from continent to continent. A QEA report said:

> The comfortable reclining passenger chairs were covered with fabric manufactured from Australian wool and alternating in colour from tur-quoise to persimmon. The back of the chairs, and boxing, were in aqua or persimmon, with the centre panel in a herringbone gold-thread off-white. Australian hide was featured in the arm rests.
>
> The passenger cabin side-walls were made of aluminium alloy panels on which silk screened vinyl was laminated. On these removable and washable panels were imposed artistically painted and presented Australian wild flowers, sweet scented wattle, tall yellow-eye, dwarf apple, Sydney golden wattle, black wattle, flannel flower, and bottlebrush, all on a washed blue-background. The ceilings were of off white vinyl, with trims in a warm black.

Juan Trippe wrote of the new turbo jet transports:

> Mass travel by air—made possible in the jet age—may prove to be more significant to world destiny than the atom bomb. For there can be no atom bomb potentially more powerful than the air tourist, charged with curiosity, enthusiasm and goodwill, who can roam the four corners of the world, meet-ing in friendship and understanding the people of other nations and races.

In their discussions with Boeings our experts arranged for a variation of the standard 707-120. Our special 138s were faster than the 120 at some 595 m.p.h. and had better all-round performance, particularly in taking off from shorter runways. In this the 138 was aided by the water injection system incorporated into the Pratt and Whitney JT3C-6 engines which provided for the injection of approximately 250 gallons of de-mineralized water during take-off, adding 7% of power. The 138, with its lower capacity of 120 passengers, fitted perfectly into our medium density traffic pattern, and enabled us to maintain a high frequency of service. It was a pleasing aeroplane, appealing alike to the travelling public, our traffic and economic section and to flying staff and cabin crew.

Bill Allen, head of the Boeing Company, was to fly to Australia with us on the delivery flight of the *City of Canberra*. The acceptance papers were signed, the official handover took place in a hall in the city where Wellwood Beale, Boeing's top executive, presided. I must have felt that the Boeing, with its complexities and need for technical understanding, was bringing me beyond my times. I compared myself to an historical relic brought out to celebrate this historical occasion, and twitted my Boeing friends with the fact that in 1926 we were building at Long-reach four-passenger D.H.50 aeroplanes while Boeing's star turn in 1927 was the 40A which carried only two passengers.

The *City of Canberra* had cost £A2,185,000, and a token of its hand-over had to be made, so someone dug up a Woolworth's Yale key, attached it to a red QEA travel tag, and this was handed to me.

It is hard to believe that it is only nine years since we left Seattle on that memorable delivery flight of our special Boeing, the 138, and became the first operator outside U.S.A. airlines to fly this amazing new type. On the following day, Captains A. A. E. Yates and Ian Ralfe touched down at Honolulu, in the first commercial jet aircraft to reach that airport.

Turner, as chief executive, supported by efficient executives, and in association with the QEA board and Civil Aviation authorities, had been responsible for analysis and organization. It was a new and costly com-mitment, but behind it was the world acceptance that QEA service was dedicated to its passengers, whether on the ground, in the booking office, at the airport or in the air. The new Boeings brought us to a peak, which was the apex, not only of that one operation, but of thirty-nine years of experience, trial and error, and building up of confidence.

We had left Seattle on 30th June 1959 and plans for delivery were so exact that the inauguration of the first Boeing service from Sydney to San Francisco was set for 29th July. As we settled back in a new, gently wafting, vibrationless comfort, with a 550 m.p.h. singing hiss of air past our cabin windows, my wife said to me, "So Qantas is using me again as a guinea-pig. Remember when Lester Brain flew me from Longreach to Winton in a three-passenger D.H.9C, and you lost your hat in that willy-willy which came over the ground? That aeroplane did 80 m.p.h. and I sat under a lid closed over my head." And I reminded her of the time when she tested out with her high-heeled shoes the wet runway at Long-reach for Charles Scott.

The flight from San Francisco to Honolulu took 4 hours 55 minutes, smashing the commercial aircraft record between the two cities and pro-viding the press with banner headlines. A triumphant reception had been arranged by Alec Barlow, Ken Wetherell, our local manager, and the civic authorities. As we descended the passenger steps to proceed along

158

a red carpet to the official dais, we were greeted by Hawaiian hula belles who draped us with garlands. Governor Quinn and Mayor Blaisdell extended a welcome; the Royal Hawaiian band blared forth, and the Aloha Week Court, led by the King and Queen, said the islands were ours for the asking. Speeches followed, a great fifteen foot garland of orchids was draped over the nose of the *City of Canberra* by the Hawaiian King, and a myriad orchids showered down from helicopters, their sweet-smelling petals settling on and around us.

In the midst of the ceremonies the engines of a Pan American Airways DC7 parked nearby suddenly sprang into life. It was a test by their mechanics which drowned off the rest of the speeches. If the incident had got to the ears of Juan Trippe, I am sure there would have been trouble for someone. The incident brought to mind the remark of one of our people when he saw in Honolulu the advertisement: "Pan American Airways, the world's most experienced airline". As Qantas was founded in 1920 and Pan American not until 1928, he suggested a Qantas advertisement: "QEA, eight years' more experienced than the world's most experienced airline".

A feature of American thinking is that they are the best and the mightiest. It is of little use telling many Americans that the beautiful Californian eucalyptus first came from Australia or that the macadamia nut is the Queensland bush nut. Or to do as I did, stop a citizen in the street in New York when Britain was giving birth to the jet, and say, "Look at that British jet, isn't it wonderful?" only to be told with no uncertainty, "The British haven't got them. It's one of ours." But this pride and unquestioned belief in one's country, admitting no other, were counter-balanced by magnificent assistance to world recovery after the war.

In Fiji there was another impressive welcome, with the native Fijians playing an important part. Then came the welcome at Kingsford Smith airport where cars choked the entrance and a crowd gathered, reminiscent of the days when the pioneers arrived on their early record-breaking flights. The press said:

> When Qantas' new Boeing 707 jet liner streaked into Sydney, breaking all existing speed records for the trans-Pacific air route, it won for Australia the coveted Aerial Blue Riband of the Pacific.

The actual flying time between San Francisco and Sydney had been 16 hours 10 minutes, against the previous best of a Pan American Airways DC7C which had taken 27 hours 30 minutes. Our new Boeing service, which commenced on the 29th July, cut the time it took for a passenger flight from San Francisco to Sydney by just on half, and at no extra cost in fare.

The welcome in Sydney was spectacular, a red carpet flanked by a bodyguard of QEA employees from all sections of our services, the RAAF band playing a martial air, and cheers from the crowd as we stepped down the passenger ladder to be greeted by Athol Townley, the Minister for Defence. Then the Boeing 707 was hustled off to Avalon in Victoria on 5th July where was our crew training centre. The press and public watched the monster with particular interest because of the controversy as to whether the external noise level was acceptable.

We ourselves knew this was a critical issue. Boeings had been working feverishly to muffle the engine exhaust noises. The problem was not fully solved though much progress had been made. The aircraft could operate from normal stations in front of airport buildings, but residents near the take-off runways were inconvenienced until further noise reduction took place. Then there was the cloud of fumes which billowed out from the engines, as a result of the water injection system, and formed a miniature cloud during the take-off run. The press reported:

> A huge black cloud of fumes and dust blanketed Mascot runway and General Holmes Drive today, when the new Qantas Boeing jet took off. The dense cloud obscured the giant airliner as it screamed down the runway, and into the air.
> Botany Council representatives who watched the take-off said they were shocked and amazed at the noise, fumes and dust it created.

In the few months that followed it was a close call whether the Boeing Jets would be acceptable to the authorities; but the cloud of fumes did not prove as bad as anticipated, and with no take-offs during the night hours and the steep initial climb which soon took the Boeing high above the houses at the end of the runways, the opposition died down. Then came the cessation of water injections, and added silencing, and with familiarity, the big jets of today are more acceptable. They create a degree of public nuisance, as do some other forms of transport. There always seems to be some pay-off for progress, some countering sacrifice, and in the case of aircraft, it has been noise. This remains the big problem, and the major one associated with the introduction of supersonic aircraft, with their supersonic boom. As always, it will be solved.

On 29th July 1959 we inaugurated our Boeing 707 service from Kingsford Smith Airport, when the *City of Canberra* left Sydney, under the command of Captain Ian Ralfe, for San Francisco. The names of the crew were:

| | |
|---|---|
| Commander | I. D. V. Ralfe, Captain |
| First Officer | R. F. Uren, Captain |
| Second Officer | C. G. Fox, Captain |
| Navigation Officer | R. G. Goodwin |
| Engineer Officer | K. D. Stark |
| Flight Steward | H. Smith |
| Flight Steward | J. Brown |
| Flight Steward | B. Slater |
| Flight Steward | G. Sweeney |
| Flight Steward | E. Duker |
| Flight Hostess | E. Wright |
| Supernumerary First Officer | J. P. Theobald |
| Supernumerary Navigation Officer | R. R. Sherwin |
| Supernumerary Engineer Officer | D. S. Moorhouse |

The dispatch was a colourful ceremony with the Minister for Civil Aviation, the Hon. Shane Paltridge, and the Minister for Air, the Hon. F. M. Osborne, being in attendance. Mrs Paltridge christened the aircraft, cutting the ribbon which sent it on its way. The Postmaster-General, the Hon. C. W. Davidson, handed a special bag of mail to Captain Ian Ralfe. The contents were postmarked 29th July, and because of the crossing of the international date line, they arrived in San Francisco also on the 29th July. It was an indication of the complications which will arise with the introduction of supersonic aircraft when mails, on occasion, will arrive at their destination on a date before the date mark of their despatch.

My rather down-to-earth comment at the time of the inauguration of the Boeing service was:

> With the world airlines order of some 400 Boeing 707s and DC8s, the whole consideration is as simple as this: Either Australia had to be in it, or out of it; there was no middle course.

Before long our Boeings were regularly flying the full round-the-world service in 57 hours 15 minutes flying time, and 70 hours 15 minutes elapsed time. This compared with the Super Constellation times of 103 hours 30 minutes flying time and 127 hours 50 minutes elapsed time.

## ❧ 19 ❧

## *Changes and Progress*

I HAVE EXPLAINED in some detail the workings of IATA, that influential body responsible for international stability in air transport, not only in the rate fixing sphere but also in promoting friendship and understanding between the great international airlines of the world. I had served on the executive committee of IATA since its inception, and the position attained by Qantas caused me to feel that it was time we did something about holding an annual general meeting of IATA in Australia.

The international organization was, however, regarded by my board as, if I may say so, one of the intangibles, and there were objections as to whether the expense was justified. Could our young country stage the meeting creditably? Would we be able to get the support of the Minister and Department of Civil Aviation?

At the New Delhi annual general meeting of IATA I sought the support of the executive committee. Sir William Hildred and Laurence Young, secretary of IATA, came to Sydney and approved our accommodation and conference hall facilities, though these were barely suitable. It was proposed to use the Great Hall at the University of Sydney as the main place of assembly, and though this is fine architecture, it was scarcely designed to house an international conference.

In 1959, the next year, I went to the annual general meeting of IATA in Tokyo with an official invitation from Senator Paltridge for IATA to hold the annual general meeting in Sydney, opening on 23rd October 1961. The invitation was well received and accepted.

In 1960 the IATA full members numbered seventy-eight. There was a top five group of operators, led by Pan American Airways with 731,547,000 tonne kilometres flown for the year, this performance nearly doubling BOAC, the next on the list, and followed by KLM, Air France and SAS. Then there followed a group of eight operators, TWA, Qantas, Lufthansa, BEA, TCA, Sabena, Swissair, and Alitalia. After this group there was a big drop. Actually in 1960 Qantas stood seventh on the world list with 154,803 tonne kilometres flown and paying an annual due of $US39,600. Pan American Airways paid $US115,300.

QEA's position entitled us to take our turn in entertaining representatives of the world's international airlines. The organizational work was in the hands of Captain W. H. Crowther, an able organizer. At the Copenhagen annual general meeting in 1960 I was elected president of IATA for the year 1961-62, to take office in Sydney in October 1961. We were conscious that the older countries with their good hotels, conference halls, general culture and fine architecture, had far more to offer visitors than we had in Australia and we wondered, along with some in IATA, what sort of a job we could do.

For example, in Copenhagen the conference had been attended at its opening meeting by King Frederick and Queen Ingrid, and had been addressed by the Danish Prime Minister, Mr Viggo Kampmann. Then Piet Hein had dramatically delivered his long epic poem, beginning:

> *Welcome, well travelled travellers in air,*
> *To these cold homelands of the Vikings, where*
> *A thousand years ago our ships were blown*
> *Seaward to space a spacious world, now grown*
> *So small in terms of travel as this wee*
> *Old kingdom used to be—or not to be. . . .*

We were taken over the historic castle of Elsinore; we were entertained at a spectacular dinner presided over by Ake Rusck, the head of SAS and president of IATA.

I was sitting next to Mrs Rusck and at the height of all the magnificence I remarked, "What a wonderful dinner party. We will never be able to do anything like this at our A.G.M. in Australia."

Mrs Rusck turned to me and said, "Oh, but you have your kangaroos."

So we began to think of what Australia could provide in the way of outdoor entertainment—something that was to prove effective.

About this time QEA introduced the Lockheed Electras. The Boeing 707 fleet on the main trunk lines had taken the place of the Super Constellations which had about seen their service. The last of the successful piston-engined airlines, they were being phased out, and it was necessary to introduce a new supplementary type. Something smaller than the 707 in carrying capacity was needed, and adapted for more restricted runways. The choice lay between the Comet IV and the Lockheed Electra.

The Electra, with its four Allison D13 turbo prop engines, cost £A1,300,000. It carried a maximum (all tourist) capacity of 73 passengers at 400 m.p.h. for a full payload range of 2,000 miles. Its economics were excellent. We obtained four Electras and first introduced them on our service to Hong Kong and Japan on 18th December 1959, and then in the following year to Noumea and New Guinea. On 3rd October 1961 we opened our initial service with this type to Wellington, New Zealand. In April 1963 the Electra went on the South African run, replacing the Super Constellations and reducing time between Sydney and Johannesburg by 7 hours 40 minutes. The 8,504 miles journey was flown in 54 hours, the long Cocos Island-Mauritius stage being at somewhat restricted loads.

The Electras did a fine job on these services, but just as was the case with the early Constellations, they were grounded in America shortly after their introduction. This was because of two tragic crashes in the U.S.A. The safety of the aeroplane was questioned, and faults in the engine mounting and wing attachment were revealed. Our aircraft had to be flown back in rotation to the Lockheed factory for modification.

The two large Australian domestic airlines, TAA and Ansett-ANA, had also obtained Electras. TAA wanted the French Caravelle, a very good small to medium range twin-engine turbo jet aircraft, but Ansett-ANA wanted the Electra, which had the wider range if required. Ansett-ANA won the day, as the Government wanted uniformity, but TAA were disappointed. Competition in Australia between the Caravelle and the Electra would have been a colourful affair, and it is a pity it did not occur.

TEAL also became disappointed owners of Electras. The Australian Government had held a half-interest in TEAL for some time, and in 1959 the board consisted of the following, nominated by the New Zealand Government: Sir Leonard Isitt, chairman, G. N. Roberts and Dr A. M. Finlay; nominated by the Australian Government were Sir Hudson Fysh, vice chairman, W. C. Taylor and Air Marshal Sir Richard Williams; F. A. Reeves was general manager.

The DC6 fleet was now below a competitive par, even for a total monopoly operation, and was in need of replacement. The New Zealanders wanted the Comet IV or the Convair 880; the Australians, the Electra. It was the old argument about equipment, with each side wanting the type best suited to its ambitions. This problem after the war had broken up the original BOAC/QEA partnership until it was replaced by a new arrangement.

On the day of decision in favour of the Electra, it has been said with authority, the TEAL flag flew at half-mast over the Auckland office, but the tussle had other consequences. It hastened full ownership of TEAL by the New Zealand Government. An old photograph shows the signing of the agreement by the Rt Hon. Keith Holyoake, Prime Minister of New Zealand, the Hon. J. K. McAlpine, N.Z. Minister for Civil Aviation, and

164

Maori ceremony at Christchurch, New Zealand, on opening our Lockheed Electra service
(*Photo*: Photo News Ltd)

IATA annual general meeting in Sydney. Sir Hudson Fysh, president, Sir William Hildred, director general, J. F. Dempsey, president elect

Lady Fysh welcomes Mrs Paul Sampaio of Panair do Brazil

Ned Kelly's armour demonstrated at the Australian A.G.M. of IATA

the Australian Minister, Senator Paltridge. The old board held its last meeting; the new New Zealand board its first, the take-over being dated from 1st April 1961.

Soon after I received from John McAlpine a letter of appreciation which I greatly valued:

Dear Sir Hudson,
     . . . I wish to convey to you, on behalf of the New Zealand Government, our gratitude for your many years of service with the Company. You have helped it along its way from the very beginning and I know that TEAL means much to you. Indeed, New Zealand owes much to you, and to Australia, for these many years of collaboration when the country was not ready to shoulder the whole responsibility for its international airline. I also know that you will share my pleasure in the fact that TEAL now intends to take its place in the Commonwealth co-operative scheme of things and, as a part of this, will be co-operating closely with Qantas.

The new board of TEAL was made up of Sir Leonard Isitt, chairman, G. N. Roberts, deputy chairman, A. F. Gilkison, A. R. Guthrey, Sir Andrew McKee and G. A. Nicholls. In 1964, Sir Leonard, after a long and dedicated service to New Zealand aviation, was retired, and his place as chairman was taken by another distinguished old RNZAF Senior Officer, Sir Andrew McKee ("Square"). Then, in 1966, G. N. Roberts, the former successful general manager for so many years, came through to a well-deserved chairmanship of the board. Sir Andrew remained on the board and was also chairman of the N.Z. domestic government-owned operator, NZNAC.

In 1965, the old TEAL name was replaced in favour of Air New Zealand. The DC8s were introduced at the same time and carried the new name across the seas to Los Angeles in December 1965; to Hong Kong in March 1966; and to Singapore in April of the same year. Operations were in pool with QEA and BOAC and this was of great advantage to the new operator. New Zealand was happily launched with an overseas air service of its own.

The 1961 Australia-New Zealand agreement provided for TEAL and QEA trans-Tasman operations, the main source of revenue for the new TEAL. There was to be parallel and co-operative organization, but with a TEAL entitlement to considerably more than half the traffic until the new operator was firmly established. It had been a tough conference but the development which gave New Zealand its own international airline was as it should be. The Australian Director-General, D. G. Anderson, had been the dominant force in the negotiations, with Bruce Rae, N.Z. Air Secretary, as his opposite number.

The agreement ended my twenty-one years' association with TEAL

165

M

during which I was often a severe critic on the board, as was W. C. Taylor. On the other hand, on the QEA board, it was my lot ceaselessly to fight the battles for TEAL, to plead for understanding, and to moderate, as far as I could, that hostile QEA higher management which would have liked to see TEAL go out of business. Management could scarcely be blamed for this as TEAL was carrying trans-Tasman traffic, half of which, in a strict sense, should have been carried by QEA. On the other hand, QEA was carrying much of New Zealand's third and fourth freedom traffic to far places, and most of this would be lost when TEAL operated to its full strength. The circumstances caused a lack of trust in us by the New Zealanders. QEA and Australia were bounding ahead, and our more conservative kinsmen across the Tasman were perturbed.

All this was altered by the new agreement, and on 3rd October 1961 QEA flew its first service to New Zealand. On that day my wife and I landed in Wellington from Sydney in a Lockheed Electra, to be greeted by the Deputy Prime Minister, Mr Marshall, and our old friends Sir Leonard Isitt and his wife. A full scale traditional tribal welcome was impressively performed by Maori men and women. A new trans-Tasman era had begun, to be described by the *Wellington Evening Post* as "Winged Partners across the Tasman". The paper commented:

> When the Qantas Electra left Wellington Airport for Sydney last evening, it did more than inaugurate one of several new Trans-Tasman services. It put paid once and for all to TEAL's comfortable and long-enduring monopoly of the Tasman route.

We had shared in a monopoly; but it had been to assist New Zealand ride out a difficult initial period in the development of her overseas services. IAL and BOAC had helped QEA in our early years, and QEA had done the same by New Zealand and TEAL.

There had, however, been much criticism of the TEAL monopoly, from the U.S.A., Canada and Australian sources. The economy class fares charged from Sydney to Auckland, a journey of some 1,333 miles, was £A41.3s. as against the £A45.15s. fare charged by TAA and Ansett-ANA for the 2,030 mile journey between Sydney and Perth. Stanley Brogden had the last sensible word, however, when he wrote of the period:

> That the continued presence of TEAL is really uneconomic is undeniable, but if this argument was continued overseas, no small nation would have an airline—including Australia.

Through the years one of the most important events which marked the general acceptance of air transport was the use of air travel by British

Royalty, a practice that not so long ago would have been regarded as far too novel and risky. Over thirty-three years Qantas had carried many of the world's great people, including members of the British Royal Family, but the honour of carrying the Queen herself first came to us on 9th March 1954. On this, the first of a series of Australian journeys, we flew Her Majesty and His Royal Highness the Duke of Edinburgh from Melbourne to Brisbane. The aircraft was the Lockheed Constellation *Horace Brinsmead* which had been specially fitted out and was commanded by Captain D. F. MacMaster, one of our most experienced captains, who had first gone through for his wings with the Royal New South Wales Aero Club. He was decorated with the M.V.O. at the hands of Her Majesty in a small private ceremony on completion of the Royal Flight.

In March 1958 we were scheduled to take Her Majesty the Queen Mother on a flight from Australia to London, with Captain A. J. R. Duffield commanding our Super Constellation. We had been experiencing considerable engine trouble, and this, our first long international Royal Flight, became a nightmare for Captain Duffield and his crew, and for us back in Sydney. There was a three-day delay in Mauritius where an engine had to be changed, another eighteen-hour delay at Entebbe in Uganda, and finally a delay at Malta, where a BOAC Britannia came to the rescue and took the Royal party on to London. We, of course, all had red faces; but an outstanding feature was the gracious understanding of the Queen Mother who stood by our aircraft at Entebbe and refused to proceed in a waiting BOAC Britannia. As with all who came into contact with Her Majesty, the Queen Mother endeared herself to our suffering crew.

In 1959 we flew Princess Alexandra from Vancouver to Canberra, and then on to Bangkok. Their flights with that wonderful young lady will never be forgotten by our staff. In 1963 we again had the honour of flying the Queen and the Duke of Edinburgh, this time in a Boeing 707, from Christchurch to Canberra. In 1965 the Duke and Duchess of Gloucester flew as passengers with us from London to Sydney. These were old friends, for the Duke had declared open our original overseas service from Brisbane in 1934. In 1966 the Queen Mother again entrusted herself to our care; this time in trouble-free flights, we flew Her Majesty from London to Adelaide, and then from Canberra to Nadi.

Our Vice Regal patronage had a very long history, for it may be remembered that in 1926 we flew Lord Stonehaven, Governor-General of Australia, across Australia in our Longreach built D.H.50A *Iris*.

A most important event came early in 1960 when the new tripartite pool

167

agreement, which involved BOAC, Air India, and QEA, was finally agreed upon by the principals of the three airlines. The Kangaroo route partnership agreement, complicated as it was and entailing much annual discussion and review, had been working effectively for many years. It was to set the example for similar associations both within the British Commonwealth and with outside operators.

In 1958 Gerald d'Erlanger, chairman of BOAC, and Basil Smallpiece felt that it was desirable that Air India, a Commonwealth operator, should be included in the BOAC/QEA pooling arrangements. Competition to and through India was keen, and growing. Foreign rights were being eagerly sought, and India was increasingly conscious that she stood in a key position astride the route from Europe to Asia and Australia. Air India, led by the great Indian industrialist, J. R. D. Tata, had Boeing 707 aircraft on order and was anxious to expand, but needed the support of powerful interests abroad. QEA stood in much the same position as BOAC. Everything was set for a combination of forces, Air India holding the geographical advantage and also achieving important international connections through BOAC and QEA. India had talked of restricting BOAC and QEA in the lifting of Indian traffic.

The three chief executives, and their teams, met in conference in Bombay, November 1959. Basil Smallpiece, managing director, represented BOAC; B. R. Patel, vice chairman and general manager, led for Air India International, and C. O. Turner, general manager, for QEA. They were three academically brilliant executives, well equipped for the difficult discussions which followed. On 4th December they signed an agreement which was to be ratified by their respective boards and governments.

The agreement was concerned mainly with the Kangaroo route, but was later extended to other areas where the three partners operated.

The preamble to the agreement stated that one of the objects was:

> To attract more revenue than the total otherwise obtainable by the partners separately, and thus to achieve an improvement in the financial results of each partner.

Whether this objective was achieved for all three partners, and in what degree, would have been argued differently by each, but it soon became apparent that Air India were doing well out of it though there were some advantages for all.

The machinery for annual financial adjustment of the pool, and who got how much, was most complicated, and indeed difficult of comprehension by the ordinary man. The difficultly-worded agreement made by the three brilliant executives at Bombay led to the employment of quite a large expert staff to unravel and execute its mechanics, and examinations of some of the final interpretations led to some difficult and heated discussions in the board room at Qantas House. However, especially in the world of today, any agreement which promotes co-operation and friendship, if reasonably equitable financially, is a good one, and I wish it well for the future.

In working on this book I have given serious thought to what I should record regarding the series of strikes by QEA pilots, and have come to the decision that it would be injurious to both the present company and its pilots to delve fully into this unfortunate subject . . . in the full knowledge that whatever I put down would attract a measure of misunderstanding, and perhaps, disruption to the present harmonious relations which I hope exist. However, that the disastrous strikes should have been engendered by the direct action of those highly paid officers left the Australian public gasping in disbelief; and a new turn of industrial unrest was sensed, more usually associated with classes of unskilled and one-time "downtrodden" workers outside the aircraft industry. What was the reason, and where would it all end?

Not only in Australia, but the world over, pilots' unrest seemed to be growing up in the big airlines, and a series of disastrous strikes were to take place, Pan American Airways, Eastern Airlines, BOAC and others being involved. But QEA, with its tradition of solidarity and reasonableness, we thought in our false pride was different, and it just could not happen to us.

The first strike of QEA pilots took place on 12th April 1957, and lasted nine days. Navigators and flight engineers also went out in sympathy. Then followed years of unrest, years of failure to solve the problem, till the second pilots' strike which commenced on 14th February 1964, and which lasted three days. This was followed by a further strike which commenced on 25th November 1966 and lasted for twenty-eight days. This strike took place after my retirement, and resulted in a disastrous loss of revenue to the company, and also to its pilots.

These differences with the pilots caused me much anguish of mind, especially as I felt that I was one of a small group of us who understood the pilots' position; but I was frustrated and unable to do anything about it. I was accused of favouring the pilots in the critical early days of the first strike when I felt future trouble might have been avoided; but of course later on they lost my sympathy as the result of their refusal to settle by independent arbitration.

169

One of the mainsprings of misunderstanding was the fact that senior pilots received a higher remuneration than many hard-working senior executives. This of course was a tradition of the old Air Force days, and so also was the fact that an air pilot was a man of great independence, a man who could not be ordered about as others could. In fact they were damn' difficult, as I suppose I was.

Difficulties over the pilots, and attempts to put forward my views, whether right or wrong, led to much unhappiness and unpleasantness during my last days. Those most involved in the difficulties were the pilots, the pilots' leaders and their Association, the QEA executive management, the QEA board (where I personally failed), the Department of Labour and Industry at Canberra, and the Australian arbitration machinery. Nobody came out of it with the slightest bit of credit, but the time to write the full story, if anyone would then be interested, which I doubt, would be in fifteen years' time.

Let us remember that through it all the QEA air crews were true to their calling when in the air. They built up a magnificent record, with the strong participation of management, in organization, training, checking, discipline, and the like; a record which I feel is not excelled anywhere in the world. A captain of aircraft who is in real command, perhaps far from home half-way round the world, bears a great responsibility for the safety and well-being of his immense and costly ship of the air, and the passengers, mails and cargo in his care. This should be well recognized by Authority, as should his rather unique place in the community, a world community from his point of view. Then, finally, efforts should be continued to do all possible to bring these elusive people of the air more into a unified Company circle of "one for all", which is the well-being of QEA.

In *Qantas Rising*, I commented on aircraft insurance in the early days when from 10% to 12% per annum on the cost of each aircraft was paid to the underwriters. With greater reliability the world rate dropped until in the early 1950s we were paying only $3 \cdot 5\%$. Then, with the Comet and other catastrophies, the underwriters increased the rate in 1959 to over 5%. It was not until some years of operation by the big jets, when they had proved their reliability, that the rate dropped drastically.

For the year ending 31st December 1959 we paid out in aircraft insurance premiums £A495,225. This was a heavy item in the profit and loss account, and a drain on Australia's balance of overseas funds. We tried to insure in Australia but without result. The board then, with the support of the Australian Government, decided to become self-insurers. It was a big risk and I remember that I suggested we go only halfway, but the board, with managerial backing, decided on the full coverage.

Under the agreement premiums based on commercial rates were charged to an Insurance Reserve, and invested in Commonwealth Bonds. If we had a few years of accident-free operations, a good reserve would be built up. The catch was that our aircraft needs were increasing enormously and quickly, in number and value, and what was a good reserve today was not necessarily so for tomorrow.

Our gamble of 1959, however, paid off for by 31st March 1964 our aircraft accident reserve had grown to £A4,991,955. It was at this stage that the board decided to take advantage of the lower rates now being offered by underwriters. In November 1963 a new agreement provided that the company should continue to self-insure against losses up to an agreed limit, while any losses in excess of this limit were to be covered by the underwriters.

The full circle was then turned when, in 1965, self-insurance ceased, as the premium quoted by the underwriters was considered to be an acceptable commercial proposition. On 31st March 1966 our Insurance Reserve stood at $A12,496,582 and brought in a nice sum in annual interest. Our fleet of aircraft at this time stood at a cost value of $138,510,698.

The interesting experiment in self-insurance of aircraft was another QEA success story. The risk taken paid off; and we were well rewarded for our confidence in the new Boeing fleet, the excellent maintenance by engineers and the expert piloting by air crews.

# ⇛ 20 ⇚

## IATA in Australia

THE 17th annual general meeting of IATA, held in Sydney in October 1961, was a happy occasion for my wife and me. For years we had been guests in other great cities, and had made many firm friends among leaders of international air transport and their wives. Now was the opportunity to repay past kindnesses and to extend to them a warm welcome to Australia.

The world's weight of population lay to the north and Sydney was the second city south of the equator to hold an AGM of IATA, Rio being the first. Only in 1961 did sufficient international airline frequencies operate to Australia to permit accommodation of the incoming delegates without interference to normal traffic. Hotel accommodation was marginal, facilities for big conventions non-existent, tourist attractions but little developed. Many doubted whether we could hold a successful conference and provide the traditional entertainment for the 450 visitors.

We were put on our mettle. After all, we were vitally interested in the tourist and convention business and recognized its importance to Australia. My wife and I had many years' experience of IATA meetings and were able to assist Captain W. H. Crowther, the host airline's liaison officer, who with A. Mackay and a committee, organized the Sydney AGM of IATA.

We were helped by the completion of the Chevron Hilton Hotel just in time. The conference was held there, and most of the guests stayed either at the Chevron or at the old Wentworth. Our chief worry was the weather, for the main entertainment was to be staged in the Australian outdoors, and alternate arrangements had to be made to meet the possibility of a wet day at "Kangaroo Flat".

The first visitors to arrive were members of the executive committee and their wives. They were whisked away to Canberra to be entertained by the Governor-General, Lord De L'Isle, at Government House, and by Sir Robert Menzies and Dame Pattie. Visits were made to Canberra's War Memorial, golf was played; but the most interesting event was a day at Booroomba, the sheep station home of Mr and Mrs John Hyles. In the real Australian atmosphere, kangaroos crossed the road, two black snakes were killed and hung on the fence near where a demonstration of pasture fertilizing from the air was going on. Sheep shearing, buck jumping, boomerang throwing and cattle droving delighted our visitors.

After a very happy weekend we were taken back to Sydney on Monday morning by courtesy of TAA and Ansett-ANA, to enter the great pillared, sparkling conference room of the Chevron Hotel where Sir Robert Menzies was to make the principal address of welcome to the delegates. Normally, it would have been the duty of Ake Rusck, the past president, to hand over the office of president; but Scandinavian Airlines System, which he headed, had experienced a disastrous financial year and Ake had been one of the casualties. J. R. D. Tata, a past president of IATA, called the meeting to order and handed me the gavel of office.

The Prime Minister did not disappoint the delegates but gave a witty, meaningful talk. It was natural, as I was in the chair, that he should make some reference to my years in air transport, and these he concluded by saying:

> He saw, with an eye of imagination, all round the world and, what is more, he has, in my experience (and I do not want to say this to encourage any of the others of you), an unrivalled capacity for rifling the Treasury.

Sir Robert explained that, after reading all the welcoming speeches since IATA annual general meetings had begun, he had found himself asking the question, "What is it you are doing?"

> Well you are, I believe, primarily engaged in developing what, in effect, is a co-operative system, a system based on mutual understanding and mutual willingness to help and to eliminate absurd things. I believe that, if you can do this to perfection, the future of aviation is going to be much better than even its very remarkable past.

Senator Paltridge in his address of welcome sounded a well merited warning about the evils of airlines providing jet aircraft capacity in excess of the needs of traffic. This was, indeed, a current danger in the industry.

From my own presidential address, I quote one paragraph:

> In a restless, diversified world, whose peoples now hold ultimate powers for good or for evil—powers to prolong life or destroy it, the first thing for us is to continue our orderly progress. Everything depends on that. This thought should dominate the whole of our debates here.

I had a trouble-free week for there was no actual crisis during the Sydney conference, as there had been on a few other occasions. One of the most valuable reports presented was that of the Director-General, with his comments on the state of the industry which, at this time, was glutted with aircraft and trying to absorb the new jets.

In 1960 IATA members had carried 86·8% of the world's international air traffic, leaving out Russia. Passengers totalled 23,000,000 or 42,000,000,000 passenger kilometres. This was an increase of 23·5% over the previous year, and cargo and mail carriage had also prospered. The figures looked excellent, but, collectively, it had been a bad financial year for the airlines, profit being in the region of 1%.

Sir William Hildred and the airlines were worried about the unfavourable financial position. It was a case of acute aerial indigestion, resulting from the rapid absorption of the new jet fleets. The airlines had not been able to dispose without loss the old piston-engined equipment, some of which was being delivered along with the jets to certain operators. It was a horrifying situation which QEA had avoided by careful planning. In 1960 and 1961 QEA had still been able to pay small dividends of $3\frac{1}{2}$%, despite a revenue load factor which had declined to 53%, a low proportion for those years.

IATA members at the end of 1960 had 3,339 aircraft, comprising 382 jets, 480 turbo props, and 2,477 piston-engined aircraft. At the time of our Sydney meeting, the world's airlines had ordered 900 pure jet aircraft. Some 500 were flying, and there would be 620 flying by the end of the year. Each time a piston-engined aircraft was replaced by a jet, at least double the capacity was added, and all these new jets represented a speedy and massive increase to the operating fleet. Many of the old piston engined aircraft were not obsolescent and numbers were sold to small non-IATA operators to fly on a charter basis. All this extra capacity caused a crisis for some airlines from which they took years to recover. The Director-General summed up the position:

> We have thus, in this past year, come face to face with one of the most important results of the jet transition—a period of great excess capacity over demand.

The problem was freely debated, and so was the unhappy result that some operators, whose planes were flying about less than half full, were illegally cutting rates and resorting to all sorts of dodges to attract traffic. The IATA enforcement section had been kept busy so that $US245,000 had been paid in fines by the airlines during 1960. The rebates practice had caused losses to honest operators and resulted in a huge loss to the industry as a whole, South America had the worst record in respect to rebating, for there, by shopping around, a passenger could get up to 40% off the agreed IATA fare.

The conference turned to an interesting debate on the IATA Super-

174

sonic Symposium, which resulted in the IATA members as a whole informing governments and manufacturers what they required in this new controversial type and what operating pitfalls should be avoided. It was pointed out that this exciting new type for the 1970s, besides being fully airworthy and operable, and with all the new aids which would be necessary, must vie in economy of operation with the present day jets. What IATA members, or at least the enlightened ones, were most interested in was to see air fares progressively reduced so that air transport was brought within the reach of the ordinary people of the world.

There were debates on reports on technical matters, air traffic problems, rate fixing and enforcement, medical aspects of flight, legal and financial matters, and that most important subject, facilitation.

It was at the Sydney conference that Don Reynolds was appointed traffic director of IATA. He had an important role in arranging the traffic conferences, the IATA machinery for fixing rates and conditions of carriage. These would be agreed upon by the airlines and then ratified by their respective governments. The procedure was for an airline, before it went to the conference, to agree with its government upon the limit of rise or fall in rates. However, trouble was experienced at one time from the United States CAB which was not in a legal position to discuss these matters with its operators before a conference. The result was the humiliating position of the United States international operators agreeing upon rates at a conference, only to have them turned down later by the CAB.

T. E. Roff was our IATA expert, our representative on the traffic advisory committee, and attending all traffic conferences. He came to be much respected over the years, taking part in many difficult debates.

The following list of QEA men who served on IATA committees during the 1960s gives also an idea of the scope of the work carried out for the benefit of all:

| | |
|---|---|
| T. E. Roff | Traffic Advisory Committee |
| Dr R. R. Shaw | Technical Committee |
| N. H. Hay | Legal Committee |
| N. T. Quayle | Financial Committee |
| G. G. Badgery | Facilitation Advisory Committee |
| D. E. Morgan | Ground Handling Advisory Committee |
| R. Nelson | Clearing House and Revenue Accounting Sub-Committee |
| E. S. Burley | Data Processing Sub-Committee |
| Dr E. H. Anderson | Medical Committee |
| J. A. Ulm | Public Relations Conference Committee. |

At the Sydney AGM I had, with an eye to the future, arranged for Dr T. K. Glennan, president of the Case Institute of Technology, to address us on "Man in Flight. The next Ten Years". It was a most interesting address.

Our big day of entertainment had been organized months ahead to take place at Lane Cove National Park, where we had chosen as our venue a small, greenly swarded meadow set in gum-trees and wattles, with a stream meandering past on one side. In the city, yet a typical outback setting, we christened it for the occasion, "Kangaroo Flat".

The day was fine and we were able to show something of the Australian outdoor life. Sheep were shorn, the golden wool rolling off under the flashing blades of the shearers. Border collies showed their uncanny skill and patience in working and yarding sheep. There was stock-whip cracking, tree felling, wood chopping, and boomerang throwing by an expert. Aborigines demonstrated their bark painting art, and many Australian birds and reptiles were on show.

I had arranged for two Australian "swaggies" to stroll down to the river, throw down their swags, have a drink or two and proceed to make a fire and boil the billy. As this was going on, a recording of the kookaburra's laugh was played, but I gave instructions not to play it too long. The kookaburra chorus continued, and grew in volume. I suggested that the record should be stopped. However, what had happened was that the record had brought the local kookaburras into the trees around, and they treated us to a great chorus.

A sensation was caused when two uniformed policemen led into the crowd a man dressed up in armour. I had arranged with the Victorian police force that we should borrow Ned Kelly's armour beaten out of ploughshares in which the police had captured this notorious bushranger eighty years before.

The following night, New Zealand was brought into the entertainment by a group of Maoris who gave a great performance. It was the night of the Airlines Dinner, and the Australian theme was followed through with recitations of Australian bush ballads and "Banjo" Paterson's "The Man from Snowy River". A special feature of the dinner was the introduction to the assembly of two renowned Australian aviation pioneers. H. C. Miller, a contemporary of Harry Hawker and Tom Sopwith in England in 1911, was our oldest living aviation identity. Also with us was Sir Patrick Gordon Taylor, the great pioneer trans-ocean flyer who, with Sir Charles Kingsford Smith, had been one of the world's aerial trail blazers.

On the Friday came the final open session when the next year's president, J. F. Dempsey, general manager of Aer Lingus, was elected, and the 17th annual general meeting of IATA declared closed. John Leslie of PAA, W. Deswarte of Sabena, and G. A. Obregon of Avianca, thanked QEA, the host airline, with particular mention of Lady Fysh, W. H. Crowther and A. Mackay.

It had been a great event for me personally, something I had worked towards; but it also signified that QEA had taken its proper place in the support of IATA. I felt strongly about IATA's beneficial work, and said at the time:

> An assessment of the value of these IATA annual general meetings cannot be put through on an accounting machine, or mechanical computer. No, their value is much greater. It is the value of an increase in friendship and understanding; one of the great intangibles. Our aim in this Australian annual general meeting of IATA has been to add to this store of friendship and goodwill.

We felt it had been a satisfactory gathering, though the great distance from the homes of most members had caused a low attendance; twenty-three of the ninety-three member airlines were unrepresented, and six of the eighteen members of the executive were absent. But there had been a wonderful feeling of friendship, a genuine appreciation of the unusual entertainment provided. When I smacked down my gavel on the wooden block and declared the 17th annual general meeting of IATA closed, the members all rose and accorded me a standing ovation. It was a very moving experience. Wayne Parrish, the great U.S.A. aviation editor, reported, "It was generally agreed that Qantas had performed the best organization task in IATA history." I would not put it as high as that, but it was an effective and happy meeting.

A year later, at the end of my term of office as president, we met in Dublin, to be welcomed and feted in an Irish atmosphere by our new president, J. F. Dempsey, and his wife. One of the most interesting happenings, for me, was a private interview with the President of Ireland, Eamon de Valera, at his residence, Aras An Uachtarain. I found the President most interested in Australia which he had visited.

The main theme in the business of the AGM was the heavy airline operating losses, declining load factors which had become unprofitable, and the consequent cheating and fare rebating which threatened the very existence of IATA. The Director-General reported that in 1961 IATA members had collectively lost huge sums. The biggest losers were BOAC £A15 million, and Lufthansa £A13·4 million, before their governments kept them solvent with a subsidy. KLM had in the year 1961-2 lost $US27,514,000; SAS and TWA had also lost heavily. Qantas, PAA, Air

India, JAL, Swissair, PAL and Aer Lingus were the only airlines to show profits, although they were small ones. The Director-General estimated that fare rebating had taken $US400 million out of the pockets of the operators, turning a profit into a loss. A 10% handout to someone on a fare meant a 10% loss on that fare to the industry.

In my retiring presidential address, I reverted to the subject of blatant fare rebating which had blighted the 1961 operations of IATA:

> By the act of becoming members, we assume certain responsibilities one towards the other. . . . Mainly through a more or less world-wide over-provision of capacity, a certain state of anarchy has existed, which has brought loss and disruption to the industry through the illegal rate cutting. This has now reached the point where any continuance cannot be tolerated if IATA is to continue its work.

A very full debate on these matters took place, most members speaking. It reached an unusual point when members who would promise to observe IATA rates and regulations, which they themselves had approved, were asked to stand up. There was hesitation, especially from big operators on the European continent where the main trouble was coming from; but finally agreement was reached, and a pledge given.

It should be made clear that one of the main problems was competition from non-IATA airlines which could break up IATA. I campaigned for a more complete membership, but with little result, and, after all, the small non-IATA operators had only a nuisance value. The pledge to observe IATA rules was not fully observed, but the position gradually improved, largely, I felt, because of the intervention of governments, and the possibility of the winding up of IATA if we proved incapable of controlling our members. The Australian Government and Civil Aviation Department, for example, were not going to stand idly by and see their own conforming operator robbed, and their bilateral government agreement contravened in the rates and conditions clause through undercutting tactics.

The IATA enforcement section was strengthened, a concerted attack was made on infringements, and fines increased. But, despite the assurances given at Dublin, fines imposed on IATA members in 1962 reached $US659,150, and, in 1963, $US1,171,100. Total fines imposed by IATA from 1951 to 1967 reached the sum of $US5,347,150. During this time, in 1965, QEA received a reprimand for neglecting to charge a passenger for excess baggage, the passenger having failed to disclose the additional items. In 1966, we received our first fine, $US1,000, for charging a general cargo rate for a shipment of wild flowers, instead of assessing the charge by measurement, as required for low cargo density.

178

While being proud of the QEA record, I must mention the miti-gating circumstance that while in Australia it was just not customary to haggle over fares and cargo rates, in areas such as Hong Kong and the Middle East, bargaining for every kind of service was part of normal business practice. Fare cutting is also another way for an operator to become established in rivalry to the dug-in operators, and I have seen it practised on domestic lines in Australia, though never by Qantas, QEA or a major airline. As Dick Hildred was fond of saying, you can never totally eliminate sin, the thing to do is to keep it within reasonable bounds.

The guest speaker at the Dublin meeting was Lord Brabazon, that grand old man of British aviation and holder of the No. 1 British avia-tion pilot's certificate, issued in 1909. He was witty and, as ever, provoca-tive, but rather out of touch with the present and future developments of air transport.

Although I was by now the "dean" of the executive committee, I was one of the quieter members of IATA, and did not play a leading part when compared with some of the great Plesman-like figures. However, at Dublin, in addition to being deeply involved in the over-provision of capacity problem, I had something to say on "Airline Payability", though perhaps the paper would have been better entitled "How to avoid over provision of capacity, by Qantas". In a lighter vein, I read a short note on "The Time factor in Air Travel," a subject which always interested me, and the bad effects of which have not yet been overcome. Another "bug" of mine was the danger of flying large airliners unarmed but con-taining a hundred or more passengers. I read a short paper on "Arming of Aircraft". Because of international law it is a difficult issue. I advo-cated the development of some form of tranquillizer to control passen-gers, if necessary, which I called a "space gun", for any weapon such as a revolver which would hole the skin of the aircraft and let the pressure out, was dangerous. I pointed out:

> The present dangerous position does not bear thinking about, inasmuch as aircraft and their passengers today for their safety and survival in the air are subject to the whim of madmen, cranks, and aerial pirates. Shipping provides safeguards in its "brig" armoury and handcuffs.

My suggestion that there should be provision for a tranquillizing weapon which would receive the approval of governments for carriage on international airlines, was treated as something on the lighter side, but I am still of the belief that the time will come when consideration has to be given to my idea of a "space gun."

179

## ✤ 21 ✤

# *Valedictory in Vienna*

WHEN IATA held its annual general meeting in Rome, 1963, the financial troubles of the airlines had eased and so had the anarchy resulting from them. A crisis in the existence of IATA had passed. But at Rome, where Count Carandini was president, a new problem emerged when sixteen African members virtually boycotted South African Airways and Transportes Aereos Portuguese because of the racial troubles in South Africa. The African members endeavoured to exclude the two companies' representatives from all official positions in IATA.

The entrance of politics into IATA was unfortunate, as was the attempt to use that body to further a national and racial dispute. Feeling ran high at Rome, but the African members abstained from extreme action. The withdrawal of sixteen members would have greatly weakened it and withdrawal from IATA would have also affected the Africans adversely. The uncontrolled fares and rates, that would have resulted, would have removed the protection IATA gave to small operators against the powerful. Still, for a time in Rome it was touch and go.

In 1964 the IATA general meeting was at Bogota, the capital of Colombia, where Juan Pablo Ortega, chairman of Avianca, served as president of the gathering. Bogota lay on a mountain plateau between two Andean ranges, at an altitude of 8,355 feet. It was a quiet but effective meeting. The elderly delegates, noting their quickening rate of respiration in that altitude, took pains not to break into a run. However, no one suffered any ill effects.

The big event of 1964 was for QEA the opening of our new service between Sydney and London, by-passing the U.S.A. and touching Tahiti, Acapulco, Mexico City, Nassau and Bermuda. The opening flight from Sydney took place on 26th November, the Boeing 707 *City of Launceston* being dispatched by the Director-General of Civil Aviation, D. G. Anderson. It was appropriate, for he and his department had been responsible for negotiating the rights for this exciting new service.

The extraordinary progress made in a few years of air transport caused me to remark at the opening of the service:

> On our original service the longest stage flown was $132\frac{1}{2}$ miles from Winton to McKinlay in Western Queensland; but since then we always seemed to

180

Interlude in a balloon—Vienna, 1965 (*Photo*: Foto Schidola)

Playing for the Shane Paltridge Cup. Hudson Fysh, Shane Paltridge, and Don Anderson
(*Photo*: QEA)

At the Civil Aviation farewell dinner to Senator Henty, Minister for Civil Aviation. *Left to right*—Sir Giles Chippindall, chairman of TAA, Sir Reginald Ansett, chairman and managing director of Ansett-ANA, Senator Henty, Sir Donald Anderson, Director-General of Civil Aviation, and Sir Hudson Fysh, chairman of QEA (*Photo*: Dept. of Civil Aviation)

A last official act in 1966. The author and Lady Fysh seeing off Sir Robert and Dame Pattie Menzies (*Photo*: Qantas)

be reaching out, and in 1934 the 512 miles Timor Sea stage between Darwin and Koepang we felt to be quite a hop. Then came the 3,515 miles stage on our Perth-Ceylon wartime service—a terrific affair; but now on this fascinating new service we will operate a 4,150 miles stage between Tahiti and Acapulco.

The installation of the new service was a credit to C. O. Turner and his managerial staff.

At the annual general meeting of IATA in Vienna, October 1965, I was on the eve of relinquishing the active part I had played in aviation over forty-seven years. My story in these three books began with the establishment in 1919 with the first international services between England and the Continent. In that same year Paul McGinness and I were gaily "Fording it across Australia", surveying and establishing airways facilities between Longreach and Darwin, which led to the foundation of Qantas in 1920.

By 1965 most of the pioneers were either dead or out of office because of their age. Not one of the original directors of Qantas, except myself, or of the original management, was alive. It was so with the other airlines. H. J. Symington, the first president of IATA, had recently died, and John Cooper was gone. Vienna saw a final clean-up of the old hands. Dr H. J. Gorecki, the first treasurer of IATA, had died in 1964, and at Vienna, A. J. Quin-Harken, manager of the IATA clearing house which he had established in 1947, and one time chief accountant of Imperial Airways, announced his retirement. So did Stanislaw Krzyczkowski, technical director for many years, who gave way to Dr R. R. Shaw, the very alert QEA technical head.

On the executive committee we had lost Sholto Douglas, Lord Douglas of Kirtleside, one of the few remaining pioneers. At Vienna we lost Gregorio Obregon and Charles E. Beard. This was the last meeting of Sir William Hildred, the director-general, whose place was taken by Knut Hammarskjold. I had served on IATA since the beginning and this was my last general meeting. There were still some wise old hands on the executive, as well as the brilliant new ones, but the changes were so many that I think 1965 marked the ending of an era.

When we arrived in Vienna, the first duty for my wife and me was to act as host and hostess at a party in our new city office, to celebrate the inauguration of regular calls at Vienna on our Sydney-London service. It was to prove a most popular stopping off place.

Both because of the particular charm of Austria and because of the valedictory nature of the Vienna AGM, this gathering will always have a strong hold on my memory. To read the IATA record of proceedings at

Vienna brings back the great depth of feeling which prevailed as partings took place and international associations and friendships built up over the years were severed.

The marked inborn courtesy and friendliness of the people of Vienna made our visit very pleasant, and there were memorable occasions such as when we saw "Don Giovanni" excellently performed at the Opera House. There was music and singing in our ears during our whole stay, for in Austria music comes as naturally as sleeping and eating, and just about every member of a family plays some instrument.

We had a grand suite at the fabulous old Imperial Hotel, mellowed in exquisite, unobtrusive personal service, perhaps the best hotel in Europe. The Nazis had occupied it, and then the Russians, and who knows who else back in history.

Perhaps the most striking thing in Vienna is the unique Spanish Riding School where can be seen in fantastic action the famous horses of the Kras, as white as pure marble, descendants of the Imperial stud at Lipica in Yugoslavia, founded in 1580 by the Archduke Charles, brother of the Emperor Maximilian.

We wandered through numerous palaces and art galleries but always ended up in giving our greatest admiration to the autumnal wonder of the Vienna woods whose charm and blaze of colour have been immortalized in poetry and music.

The new IATA president, Dr Lambert Konschegg, managing director of Austrian Airlines, had thought up a unique event. Five lucky members of IATA, whose names had been drawn from a hat, were to make a balloon journey. I bought a number of tickets but was unlucky, then as the "Dean" of IATA, I was given a seat in the balloon basket which Sir William Hildred was unable to use because of pressure of business. No student of the air as a means of conveyance could fail to be interested in balloons and their history, for ballooning produced the world's first air pilots and marked the beginnings of a tradition of skilful and courageous airmanship.

When we arrived at the castle of Eisenstadt, in the pleasant countryside outside Vienna, there were two balloons in a small clearing in the woods, swaying gently in the light breeze, and tethered to the ground by a ring of ballast bags, with Austrian soldiers hanging on the ropes which would be later cast off. After a final topping up of hydrogen to give just the required degree of buoyancy, small meteorological pilot balloons were released to give the strength and direction of the wind. Our balloon pilot, Hans Bergmann of the Austrian Balloon Club, clambered aboard into the basket where he was joined by his passengers, Franz Grubhofer,

182

chairman of Austrian Airlines, Mme. Maurice Lemoine of Air France, and myself.

The ballast bags on the ground were detached, the soldiers with the ropes disappeared, and we gently bumped on and off the ground, held to earth only by two trained men of the Austrian Balloon Club. Hans Bergmann then threw over a bag of ballast, the helpers let go their ropes which were pulled in, and our free balloon, OE-UZB *Pro Juventute Austria* gently swayed off and we rode with the wind while the pilot dramatically took a double handful of ballast sand and let it trickle through his fingers over the side. Our sensitive balloon responded like an eager horse given its head. The ground receded. We stood in the balloon, gripping a parallel rail, as it floated gently, so very gently upward, and we peered down on the waving crowd below. The sensation was not so much one of adventure as of great tranquillity and detachment.

Ground and air were united, we groundlings in our little ship had surrendered ourselves to the air, and we proceeded at the whim of the breeze. There was no mechanical noise-making distraction, no mundane machinery, no wind whistling through rigging or roaring over rushing wing surfaces. The main impression in that balloon was one of complete and breathless silence, broken only by a few sharp creaks from our wicker basket as we moved round in it.

We were now at 300 metres and saw the other balloon ahead. Overcoats were discarded, our voices came sharp and clear to each other. A dog barked on the ground, a train whistled and its engine clanked; workers gathering grapes in a vineyard left their tasks and shouted up at us. We shouted back, and Herr Grubhofer let out a blood curdling yodel, which was answered in kind. The shadow of our balloon followed us faithfully below.

After an hour of this sort of enchantment our pilot valved off some hydrogen and we came floating in over a fence and then above a large field. In we came drifting along at about six miles an hour, and gently touched down. Gently, for such was our critical buoyancy that we promptly shot aloft again in a hundred foot bounce. Our attendants dashed across the field and, at our next descent, grabbed the trailing rope and brought us to earth. Our pilot gave us a last urgent instruction not to leave the balloon too soon or it would shoot skyward again.

Thus ended my one and only balloon journey. We had drifted about eight miles in an hour, the experience carrying our minds back to the romance of ballooning in the nineteenth century. Our experience on this lovely Austrian autumn day, over that castle and vineyard dotted country, fitted in with the old world courtly attitude of our Austrian hosts.

183

In the Conference Hall, after this pleasant outing, we faced the closing session of the 21st annual meeting of IATA and the valedictory addresses. The principal one was in farewell to the Director-General, Sir William Hildred, and Lady Hildred. It fell to me to make the address which was supported by John Leslie in English, and Gregorio Obregon in Spanish. My address, incidentally, contained my own brief swan song, my retirement from IATA being referred to by the other speakers. Amongst other things, I said:

> And now, today, in the person of Sir William Hildred, we are farewelling from our midst a very great man of air transport, the man who, far more than any other, is responsible for the success of our own association; the man who made it work through twenty years of high-strung tension at the wheel; a man who assumed office at the most critically developmental time of world transportation, when the drowsy movement of the ages had been blasted awake by a crescendo of jet-propelled progress, with attendant complications; a man who took over at this time having an understanding of the human problems inherent in the attempt to give peace, stability, and common loyalty to a great, new, but heterogeneous industry; a man damn' downright with High Authority, yet who wondrously lived to tell the tale; a man so conciliatory that he successfully mixed the oil and the water of the nations—by the apparent secret of constant agitation; a man whose singleness of purpose in service to the world's international airlines, to all of us here, has been crowned by success.
>
> And I now wish to conclude by quoting the great words of Sir William Hildred:
>
> "We, who serve mankind through air transport, must co-operate in that endeavour. We must do so voluntarily rather than by coercion. We constitute a community in which each member, large or small, has an equal right to live and an equal obligation to let live. We must co-operate through established constitutional processes, democratically fashioned and applied; and by marching together, we shall in the long run cover more ground than by marching alone."
>
> I think the greatest parting gift we can bestow on Dick and Connie Hildred is to strive to live up to those principles, so that their work will not have been in vain.

The womenfolk, the wives, were of course very much a part of these IATA meetings, and I said:

> Not only has the D.G. represented us and fought for us in the tangible things—the material things, but in the spiritual—the great intangibles. One cannot healthily live one without the other.
>
> The great intangibles—like having our wives with us here, and all that this means, though God forbid that I should allude to a woman as an intangible!

Then came the few words which I spoke in regard to my own retirement:

As you know, this is the last annual general meeting of IATA which my wife and I will attend. We are the last of the Mohicans, and it is with some rather deep feelings that we say goodbye to you, not only because of the sincere friendships which have been made, but because of the extraordinary opportunity that this association has presented to us in meeting, and getting to know and understand other peoples and their problems.

I am, personally, very gratified to have been associated with Qantas during its long history, principally, and above all, because the company has tried hard to stand for something in being a persistent seeker after truth— no matter to what degree we have been successful in the quest . . . after all these years of storm and trial, and in today's complexities . . . often seeing the beating up of right and wrong in the one bowl, and the grey mess which results.

I have also felt very proud to have belonged to IATA and to have served on the executive committee, even in a humble capacity, right through what, in the future, will be known as the W. P. Hildred years. I am gratified because IATA has also stood for something in striving for universal agreement for the common good in a fraternity of international air transport operators —this IATA, one of the only international bodies which, despite difficulties, really worked in doing visible good.

Other speeches were both moving and complimentary. Then there was a presentation to Dick and Connie Hildred; and my wife, Nell, who was on the dais with me, presented on behalf of the members a magnificent offering of flowers in a gift bowl to Connie Hildred. The emotional final scene was over, and we, whose day was over, bowed out at the end of this drama of the foundation era of world air transport.

The younger ones were there to carry on with Knut Hammarskjold on the executive committee. Sir Roland Wilson took over the unexpired portion of my term. Fine and gifted people such as Gilbert Perier, Walter Berchtold, Gordon McGregor, and the other committee members, were there to grapple with the new problems.

Although never prominent nor a gifted leader in the twenty-one years I had served in IATA, I found my association a tremendous education and help, and I shall always be grateful to Ronald McCrindle of the old Imperial Airways and a prominent figure on the executive committee, for his support and encouragement.

## ☙ 22 ❧

# I Fold My Wings

I NOW COME to my retirement on 30th June 1966 and there ends my story and this history of forty-six years of Qantas and QEA.

During my years of service and leadership, a privileged way of life had been built up, and to have this suddenly swept aside naturally meant a difficult stage of adjustment for my wife and myself. This is no doubt the experience of many retired people who, like myself, feel fit and well but are over seventy. We go out with the conviction that the accumulated knowledge of the business we are leaving should enable us to be of more service.

If, however, I had been given the usual three years' renewal of office as chairman of QEA, I would have been 74½ on retirement, a heavy strain on a chairman wishing to remain efficient. There would have been the inevitable tough stuff to handle on the board, the constant demands of public appearances and entertainment. My Minister, the Hon. N. H. D. Henty, realized that I had reached the retiring age for Government appointed heads of instrumentalities. For some political subtlety, unfathomed by me, I was pressed to resign, but declined to do so. It was agreed that my resignation should be by mutual consent, and honour was resolved by this compromise, which did not mean anything anyhow.

When the 30th June 1966 came along, the Hon. R. W. C. Swartz was Minister for Civil Aviation, and Harold Holt was Prime Minister. I can only say that I have no criticism of my treatment by the Federal Government, for my position as a whole-time chairman was unusual and special consideration had to be given for the provision of a pension. I had been so closely identified with the old and new Wentworth Hotels, and had so many ideas for the efficient operation and development of QEA hotel interests, that I let the board know I wished to continue to serve on the hotel board, though not as chairman. The issue was cleared with the Minister, but it was a decision for the Qantas board, and I was not appointed. No doubt it is now a more tranquil board without me, and it was better to make a clean break.

The QEA board briefly appointed me "consultant". I was accorded the courtesy of an office and secretarial assistance for which I was very grateful, and which greatly assisted me with my writings. However, with the present break in these amenities my severance with the old company is now complete.

A witty Vickers friend, "Wick" Wickens, once said to me, "So you have been either managing director or chairman since the 1920s. Do you mean to tell me you have never been bossed for forty years?" And, on being told that Bob Menzies and I were the same age within a few weeks, and it was a good vintage year, "Wick" said with a twinkle in his eyes, "You might be, but old vintages go off, you know."

This reminds me that as my wife and I were seeing Sir Robert and Dame Pattie off at Mascot, after his retirement, he told me he was writing, and I said I planned to continue with my writings. He must have been feeling the enormous break with a lifetime of political leadership, for he turned and said, "Hudson, who would have thought you and I would have ended up as journalists?"

The round of farewell functions began on 20th June 1966 when the Minister, the Hon. R. W. C. Swartz, gave a luncheon in Canberra attended by the Minister and the Civil Service heads. The QEA board then gave my wife and me a farewell dinner at the Australian Club, and on 25th July the QEA staff gave a send-off, Sir Roland Wilson, the new chairman presiding. There was always a warm and close association between myself and the staff, led by Jack Avery, Bill Bennett, Bennett-Bremner, and Mrs Margery Strang. They had thrown in for a presentation. The result was that my wife and I purchased in London a beautiful antique grandfather clock which will always remind us, as it ticks away, of our beloved friends in the ranks of Qantas.

Then the old-hand engineers gave me a lunch at Mascot. Our motor transport section in Sydney had always been an extraordinarily close knit group, and I had a high regard for them. At a pleasant little gathering at the transport centre, George Irvine, on behalf of the drivers, presented me with a suitably inscribed axe for use at Dural. At the same gathering my wife and I presented our old chauffeur friend, George West, and his wife, with a suitably inscribed entrée dish.

As I had now lost my marble as deputy chairman of the Australian National Travel Association, the chairman, my friend John Bates (later Sir John) and his directors, put on a farewell luncheon in Canberra which was attended by a number of Ministers and the Leader of the Opposition, Arthur Calwell, who, I remember, made a very witty speech. The president of the Royal Aero Club of New South Wales, Peter Lloyd Jnr, and his committee, gave a dinner at Bankstown where old and pleasant associations were revived, and the splendid work done by the club over the years recalled.

187

In Auckland, Geoff Roberts, chairman of TEAL, and his board, held a farewell dinner for myself and my wife. It was a warm and friendly occasion which we will always remember.

In London, there were two events, the IATA executive committee's presentation to my wife and myself, and then a farewell dinner on 26th April 1967 at the Dorchester Hotel given by Sir Giles Guthrie and his BOAC board. It was a moving event, attended by many of my old friends and associates over past years and by the present-day leaders of British air transport. Sir Giles made a very kind speech, and in my reply I stressed my ever firm support and loyalty to the BOAC/QEA partnership. I said:

> Particularly do we in Australia realize the value of the service which the Lion and the Kangaroo partnership has given us, and which in thirty-three years, has reduced the travel times between our two countries to little over thirty hours, thus lifting our former isolation and enabling us to take our part in world affairs.
>
> In looking over important events in Australian history of modern times, great dates were the opening of our first railway in 1854, and then Federation of the Australian States in 1900. But, in more recent times, with the possible exception of the inauguration of Australia's immigration scheme in 1945, which brought two and a half million people out in twenty-one years, I know of no more significant date than the day of 10th December 1934, when Imperial Airways and Qantas commenced their through air service between our two countries.
>
> Our art is air transport. We are dealers in time and space, and we know it to be a great human endeavour—one of the greatest of our times.
>
> My old friends here, and I, have lived in a stirring period and a changing one, and we have tried to maintain values which we felt essential. Now a new era in air transport and, indeed, all human affairs, is gaining impetus, and in dealing with the exciting challenge of the future, we the old-timers, wish the new generation good luck and a large measure of success, "as the old era ends and a new one begins".

A pleasant little final function had been the granting to me of the Freedom of the City of Launceston, Tasmania, my home town and the first freedom to be granted. Launceston had always been most kind to me.

Much has been written about the problem of retirement and how to prepare for it. It is an issue which must face ever increasing numbers of people as medical science achieves a longer life span. There are those who have nothing to fall back on, and they are soon in trouble. I have always felt the most fortunate are those who are deeply interested in music, art or literature, though to have an absorbing hobby is a great stand-by. In one of my twenty-four Christmas messages to QEA staff, I wrote:

It seems to me that everybody should have a hobby, or other personal interest to which he or she can look forward in the evening, at weekends, or during holidays.

The people of Great Britain are strong on hobbies and rarely does one go into a home there without being aware of the owner's hobby, be it book collecting, stamps, ships' bells, old door knockers, or breeding dogs. In the case of my friend, J. A. Boyd-Carpenter, British Minister for Civil Aviation, it was walking sticks.

Churchill, besides his writing, found solace in painting and brick laying; King George VI and President Roosevelt in stamps.

I know of one Qantas man who recently found much happiness in building a brick wall; we also have an expert on miniature railways, and our Cocos Island Fiji shell collectors.

Great joy can be had from a garden, however small, where nature rules, and in the working of which the mind, over-sharpened from the week's business conflicts, takes rest in the untroubled contemplation of a carefully cultured rose and its exquisite scent, or the beautiful colour of a rare orchid.

In my own case, literature, reading and the constant challenge to keep trying to express myself, and to record history, has been almost a life-long absorption, with which I hope to continue to the end of the road. Since I retired, I have written three books, totalling some 350,000 words. Love of trout fishing I turned into a literary experience. Book collecting, and first airmail covers, have been two of my many other interests.

As an antidote to the tough days of the 1950s and the constant, ever-demanding entertainment, I bought a small twenty acre property twenty-two miles north-west from Sydney, at Dural Heights. On the first day we saw the area, the beautiful Sydney golden wattle was out in profusion on the 700 ft high ridge with its magnificent sweeping view over the long valley of the Nepean to the Blue Mountains. My wife and I fell in love with the place at once; we named it "Golden Ridge".

I fenced the land, erected a small cottage, and all my family had great fun, felling trees, burning out stumps and clearing. Rabbit shoots were staged, quail and plover visited, eagles soared in the far atmosphere; and small bird life was profuse, shrike thrushes, southern yellow robins, tree-creepers, honeyeaters, whipbirds, kookaburras and butcher-birds, fairy wrens and firetail finches. Diamond sparrows nested under the house alongside the welcome swallows. Even the shy bronze-wing pigeons nested in the bottom paddock. Of reptile life there was the rare snake, but frilled and blue-tongued lizards abounded, and an odd three foot long old man goanna. Nearly all the bird and reptile life has since been swept away as the city moved out and made suburbia; but Golden Ridge is still a place of delight where I grow figs, oranges, grapefruit, lemons, peaches, plums, grapes, persimmons and apples, hear the butcher-birds call, and where, at night, the clear stars look down.

But now no longer can I do a grand day's manual labour at Golden Ridge, so what are my contemplations?

First of all, I am intensely interested in the concepts of God, of religion and Christianity, in the light of the theological crisis which has been brought about by the advancing scientific knowledge of man. If religion is a developing concept, like all else, then Man's *interpretation*, though based on the words of Christ, the great prophets and teachers, must alter in the light of that scientific knowledge. Galileo was once thrown into prison for denying the Church's teaching that the sun and planets moved around the earth. It was long before Charles Darwin's theory of evolution was generally accepted, and many deny it applies to the human race. But new knowledge is continually crowding in on us and must profoundly affect theology.

It seems to me that the human mind, in its desperate search for the hidden truth of life and the hereafter, and in seeking consolation from the world's harsh realities, has been prone to enmesh itself in many religious misconceptions, teachings and interpretations. So much is unacceptable to our scientifically "enlightened" generation. A new *affirmation* is needed to carry forward the historical progress of man in his search for God.

For many of us, the great central fact in religious belief is the coming of Christ. But where stood man before Christ? And what will happen as the result of the "new inquiry" now in every thinking mind? Early man certainly had religious beliefs and his spiritual world. Then, after many centuries of evolution and development, man advanced in intelligence to be ready to receive the new message Christ gave to the world. But what of those who lived and died and never heard his word? We can trace the development of man after the advent of Christ, but now it appears that the great increase in the knowledge of man has ripened him for a new theological acceptance. It seems more than evident that man is ready, and indeed crying out for, a new revelation carrying upward and forward his association with his God—a new vision.

I cannot reconcile myself to the atheist position. The mystery of the universe, our lack of knowledge as to where it all started, and will end, is too great. I know of nothing to take the place of the Divine moral and ethical teachings of Christ. From the life of Christ must be our starting point. Each night of my life, as I pray to the unknown God, I ponder these matters and on many more: the divinity or the futility of human life as in the present day it seems to be balanced.

Christianity has come a long way since my ancestor, John Frith, was burned at the stake at Sevenoaks in the reign of Henry VIII for his part in distributing William Tynedale's Bible in England; but now we are found wanting in faith and resolve. A new revelation of interpretation must come to help us all, but particularly the rising generation.

Another contemplation is that of time and space and the universe, but more particularly our own solar system, and the development of space flight within its bounds. What are the possibilities of flight within its bounds? I write "within its bounds" because the more distant planets seem unreachable. Though very ignorant on the subject of modern space flight, I once read a paper on the subject and was, surprisingly, elected a Fellow of the British Interplanetary Society. To me, mechanical and human exploration of our solar system by space flight is one of the most thrilling undertakings of our day. In my address, "World Peace through Rotary", I once said:

> The project of space flight holds out epic possibilities for the human race, and will bring out all those great qualities of courage, endeavour and comradeship, which hitherto have been produced only by war.

Still, space flight is for our younger generation, and I recall with amusement the San Francisco newspaper which reported:

> Sir Hudson gave us an interesting chat on air transport, but the only thing we were disappointed with was that he said he did not want to go to the moon.

The disappointing result of space probes, so far, is that they tend to convey the impression that prospects are not bright for either Mars or Venus being able to sustain intelligent life akin to our own. But these things are not yet conclusive. Perhaps, in the long course of time, some form of human colonization from the earth will take place in other parts of the solar system.

The next thought I would like to mention is: What is the future of the human race, now that we have the means of world suicide in our hands? Could it happen, as in that fanciful story of total world war, that nothing might be left except a small party of men and women, deep in Antarctica, who survive to form a small colony, reverted to savagery, from which a new human world is built up? The maintenance of world peace is now so essential, that I have ventured to add my voice to those who have written on the subject. In 1962 at the Los Angeles Rotary International Convention, as one of a world panel under the moderation of Luther M. Hodges, United States Secretary of Commerce, I spoke on "Developing World Understanding through Trade". I stressed that nations must never again allow trade conditions to deteriorate as they did before the world wars, and that nations in difficulties must be helped by the stronger. In my own field, I pointed out:

> Air tourism in the volume we hope for presents the one great opportunity for people effectively to get to know one another. It teaches us all the saving graces of courtesy, welcome and service.

The Convention was held in the great Los Angeles covered Sports arena, where I addressed 23,000 Rotarians and their wives and families. It was an experience never to be forgotten. When I saw the great sea of faces before me, and realized the sense of power and the opportunities accorded to the great speakers, I understood how incumbent it is on them to use their talents for the furtherance of good.

I have often pondered whether the world would survive or experience some catastrophe that would end all in futility. I have speculated as to how we shall solve the excess population problem. The outlook at present is so fantastically difficult and so little is being done. Advanced nations might legislate so as to limit the growth of population to the amount of food available and the living room, but is this likely in lands such as China, India and South America where the need is greatest?

Man's natural desire is to know how things turn out in the years after he has gone. Is there consciousness after death? In my lifetime, I found myself out of tune with so much of the old forms of beliefs, repeating in the Church mouthing of Divine Service many things in which I did not believe at all. I felt that without a great change in revelation, an up-dating of interpretation *such as had occurred right through the ages of man's seeking for his God,* I was religiously sunk, so was Christianity, and who would help the generation coming on? At night I sought help for a new revelation.

It came when in a shop one day I found a book by Pierre Teilhard De Chardin, a Jesuit priest with whose new outlook his Church could not altogether agree. I went on to read all the works of this great modern thinker I could lay my hands on, and found that he expressed in words many things that were in my mind. He has given me, and others including many scientists, new faith and hope.

Here are a few quotations which may cause some to consider his thinking:

> . . . above and beyond ourselves there exists some superior force, and that, since it is superior to ourselves, must possess some superior form of our own intelligence and our will.
>
> Evolution, which offers a passage to something that escapes total death, is the hand of God drawing us to himself.

The greater our power of manipulating inertia and living matter, the greater proportionately must be our anxiety not to falsify or outrage any part of the reflective conscience that surrounds us.

What a neo-humanism that looks to the future must have is nothing less than a more profound Christianity, re-thought to fit the new dimensions of the world.

Everywhere I find the birth, or at least the expectation, of the new creed of man in a spiritual evolution of the world.

Of death, Teilhard De Chardin wrote in *Le Milieu Divin*, in the form of a fervent prayer:

Vouchsafe, therefore, something more precious still than the grace for which all the faithful pray. It is not enough that I should die while communicating. *Teach me to treat my death as an act of communion.*

The great religious and revolutionary thinker does not provide the answers, but points the way like a strong star of the future. As he said, "I am a pilgrim of the future."


Qantas Airways Limited (the "Empire" was dropped in 1967) and air transport in general must always occupy my mind; but that now is the only thing left for me, except for my good wishes. In 1970 will come the 50th anniversary of that day in August 1920 when Fergus McMaster, Ainslie Templeton, Paul McGinness, Alan Campbell and I sat around a little glass-topped table in the Gresham Hotel lounge in Brisbane, and the final decision was made to form the Queensland and Northern Territory Aerial Services Limited—"Qantas."

We started operations at Longreach with a staff of three, Paul McGinness, Arthur Baird and myself, with Frank Cory as part-time secretary. Our paid-up capital was £A6,037 and we owned two rather rickety aeroplanes of the "cap and goggle" era as our stock-in-trade. In mid-1966, when I end my story, Qantas Empire Airways had 8,873 persons on its payroll and nineteen Boeing 707 jet airliners were being operated on 72,220 miles of globe-encircling routes.

In my last year of office the net profit of QEA was $A4,030,183, matching the record profit of the previous year. A $7\frac{1}{2}\%$ dividend was paid, and forty-three years of unbroken annual profits by Qantas and QEA was a farewell gesture from the board, management and myself as I left the scene. At this time, issued share capital of QEA amounted to $A35,400,000. Shareholders' funds amounted to $A42,229,752, and loans for the purchase of aircraft and on account of buildings amounted to $A64,170,362.

We were at a new peak, at the top of the curve in the golden years of the big jets. We were successful, prosperous, and had emerged as a key

Australian national business, with enormous expansion ahead, and with a name for dependability and service second to none in the world.

The one dark cloud on the immediate horizon, partly the result of rapid expansion, was continued pilots' unrest, which blew up after I left in the disastrous strike of December 1966. The strike was the direct cause of the company's 1967 Profit and Loss account showing a loss of $A1,510,130. The real loss to the company, in view of a budgeted profit for the year of some four million Australian dollars, would have been not far short of six million dollars.

This strike, I felt, should never have happened. However, other large world airlines had their pilots' strikes. It was a situation that had to be faced, and now both company management and the pilots themselves and their management are wiser in their knowledge of each other.

This book is part of a history, and I have no comment on the future except to say that the part to be played by Qantas Airways in the development of Australian and, indeed, world air transport, will be in keeping with the forward surge of Australia as a nation. In the immediate future, Qantas is headed into a period of intense competition, and has been obliged to order the so-called Jumbo jets. There will soon be an awful lot of capacity flying around which can be supported only by spectacular advances in the amount of air travel and air carriage. It is possible that we are headed for another situation such as existed in 1960 and 1961, when the world's airlines had over-bought and almost went bankrupt. If such a situation does occur again, it would be of temporary duration. The key factor, while current world trade, customs, migratory and finance conditions exist, is the first protection of Australia's basic overseas rights. That is to say, Australia equally owns the air traffic to and from any country, with that country. We should employ an economic volume of equipment to cater for that traffic, and form a correct estimate of other types of traffic.

It is obvious that in all human activities we have to think and act more as one world body, if any future exists for the human race. Those of us who have worked in international air transport have had the opportunity to realize this more than has the average person. I, myself, believe firmly that the trade of the air, the enormous capital investment and its employment in the near future, the millions of air travellers intermingling the peoples of the earth, and the inter-dependence between nations that world air traffic creates, will go a long way towards binding together the nations.

At the time of my retirement, Harold Holt, who was then Prime Minister, sent me this letter I trust I will be excused for including here, to counteract the criticisms I have included in this Qantas trilogy:

Dear Sir Hudson,

Before leaving Australia, I feel I should write to you in formal terms how much I have in mind that this is your last week in the position you have filled so admirably. It is in fact the culmination of the great public service which you have rendered to this country for what truly constitutes a great many years in the life of any man.

On behalf of my Cabinet colleagues and myself, I say, "Thank you for all you have done." I know that Cabinets and Governments of the past, of whatever complexion, would wish to be associated with me in expressing our gratitude and our admiration for what you have done for us all.

We thank you, and we extend our very best wishes for the future.

In more homely style, Bob Menzies, our very great Prime Minister, wrote:

As I have so often told you, when I am overseas, and step on to a Qantas plane, it seems like home again, and I can close my eyes and relax.

Finally, I have written this Qantas trilogy with an earnest desire to leave a record of the truth, omitting nothing which I have felt to be important in the portrayal of history as it unfolded. I trust that the Qantas trilogy, together with my voluminous correspondence, memoranda, pamphlets, articles and addresses, extending as they do over forty-seven years of air transport, will be preserved not only as a lasting and accurate account of the rise of Qantas, but of the times and conditions of air transport in its early international phase.

The Qantas story, above all, is typical of the emergence of Australia from its former geographical isolation, and world insignificance, to what she is today; a superb transformation, which could never have been achieved except for the coming of international air transport initiated and pioneered in Australia by Qantas and Imperial Airways in 1934.

APPENDIX 1

## "ETHICS AND OTHER THINGS"

I first wrote and distributed *Ethics and Other Things* to senior staff towards the end of 1938 when, after eight years in Brisbane and nine at Longreach, we moved our head office to Sydney. In new conditions, there were extra demands on staff and organization. Then, in 1948, the first roneo issue was revised, and in 1955, the year in which I relinquished the managing directorship of QEA, the code of behaviour and ideals was issued in booklet form.

I felt that what was expressed in *Ethics and Other Things* was private and personal, and I saw that the booklet was distributed only to a select Qantas circle. Looking at it today, I believe that it contains in primitive language something of the innermost personality of a group of people banded together in service in Qantas.

We were fortunate in having as our foundation chairman, Sir Fergus McMaster, a man of integrity and great singleness of purpose. In my long association with him, and after his death, I attempted to carry out his personal philosophy and aim to build up an organization which would inspire trust and confidence.

Air transport services today were built and proven in those earyl formative years from what was considered a dangerous and uneconomic novelty. In the early and middle years we were laying a solid business and ethical foundation. The extracts here given should be read in the light of conditions of thirty years ago.

When we came to Sydney in September 1938 to start the new flying boat service, we were a staff of less than three hundred, and it was a thrilling new adventure. Ten years later, in 1948, staff had grown to 3,000. We had passed through the war when the problem of the very existence of QEA had been solved by the historic Indian Ocean service, New Guinea charter, and other operations. Then the company passed into Commonwealth Government ownership in conformity with the policy put into effect in the other Empire units.

When the booklet was issued in 1955 I noted in the foreword that the company then had a staff of 5,195 and owned a fleet of modern aircraft valued at £8,050,000, with an unduplicated route mileage of 62,579.

> This simple little booklet [I wrote] is a souvenir of my and your stewardship while working for Qantas and is somewhat of an historical oddity of simple beliefs and hopes in which we all have shared.

196

With Mr George West, our driver for many years (*Photo*: Qantas)

The QEA board on my retirement. *Left to right*—R. J. Ritchie, deputy C.E. and deputy G.M., C. O. Turner, chief executive and general manager, J. M. Fotheringham, director, R. R. Law-Smith, deputy chairman, Sir Hudson Fysh, chairman, Sir Norman Nock, director, Sir Roland Wilson, director, Sir James Kirby, director, F. Derham, secretary and finance manager (*Photo*: Qantas)

The Hotel Wentworth board on my retirement. *Left to right*—W. J. Lyons, secretary, Sir Hudson Fysh, chairman, S. McNeill, managing director, Sir Norman Nock, director, R. R. Law-Smith, director (*Photo*: Qantas)

Frank Clune gets it across to Bert Ritchie, who as the new chief executive of Qantas Airways surveys his parish, the world (*Photo*: Qantas)

The views were not the official views of QEA, I pointed out, but personal observations. "The first and paramount object of the company is to give a worthy service." Without realization of the basic principle of "service" to other members of the community, we are a failure.

It may be maintained that duty towards our shareholders (now the Commonwealth of Australia) comes before our duty to the public. I maintain that duty to the public comes first, in that, if we are unable to provide that "worthy service", it is doubtful if we should be in business. Now that the Government of Australia owns QEA, our duty towards the public is increased through our being their instrumentality.

Under 21 sub-headings the pamphlet dealt with a very wide variety of topics which I thought essential to the ethical structure of the company. The following is a very brief summary:

The company has a duty to the Government to record a *profit* on operations if this is reasonably possible. *Integrity* is the greatest asset a company or an individual can possess. *Fair charges* should always be adhered to. This is actually the best business in the long run. The acceptance of *bribes*, or near bribes, is a matter against which every member of QEA has set his hand. *Complimentary remarks* come only as the result of a service which is giving satisfaction. *Complaints* form a golden opportunity to increase the value of our service, and to right wrongs. Each complaint should be taken up immediately and investigated, and the complainant written to in a friendly manner. All misleading or untrue *advertising* should be avoided. The public appears often to tolerate a type of aircraft advertising which is extravagant, and which they would condemn as untrue if applied to older services.

*Compromise* consists in unifying two points of view, with both sides taking less than they wished, for the good of both.

*Loyalty* has been often exemplified in the company in a marked manner. True loyalty will forgive a good deal, does not condemn hastily and is always constructive and never destructive.

*Staff and staff relations.* In the same way as employees' efficiency and acceptance of reasonable conditions react to their own benefit and that of the company, so does the reasonable treatment of the staff by the company. Men and women are human beings, not machines, but the larger an organization becomes, the more difficult it is to avoid over-regimentation, and in place of the easy personal contact of the small organization must come organized social activity.

*Diplomacy* is a word which almost links in with compromise. They both lubricate the machinery of the company; but over-lubrication is not a good thing. Diplomacy should be used in personal contact whenever possible, but should always be used to the full in correspondence. Over-diplomacy results in a weak neutral attitude; but too great a lack of diplomacy to harmful disagreement. In letter writing, don't be tersely abrupt, either to a client, business associate, or a fellow member of the company. The test of a letter is how the writer would react himself, if he were the recipient.

o

According to his *character*, so does a man react under the imposition of the various conditions. Real character is often brought out under the stress of great pressure. The manner in which an individual accepts success or praise provides an index to character. An exaggerated sense of importance or overbearing manner are signs of weakness, and the test of a man is how he "stands corn".

The planning ahead or *vision* is the first essential of successful management. The practical use of vision can be exercised through the responsible staff of an organization and demands recognition.

*Initiative and enterprise*, which resulted in the original Qantas coming into being in 1920, are just as important today. It is usually some necessity which brings these qualities into play. I think that today our urge should spring from competition. It is necessary to fight complacency, to fight "it is good enough", to fight "it can't be done."

QEA has a good record of *discipline* and quiet *self* respect. Our clear duty is now to the Commonwealth of Australia.

*Co-operative Individuality.* An organization is first based on the written word. It depends on the executives to see that the routine is carried out, to add to it, to alter it when necessary. Routine only establishes the basis; co-operative individuality then comes into play. Individuality of effort counts first in leadership, but it must be co-operative.

One of the greatest sources of human *satisfaction* still remaining to us is in the job of work well and truly done. H. Veenendaal, one of the outstanding, hard-working and sound-thinking personalities in air transport, drew for me the following diagram which, he said, illustrated what it took to be successful.

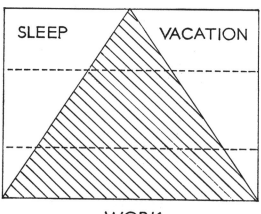

A fair balance must be struck between sleep, work and vacation. The man who is represented by the top section will not get anywhere, nor can he achieve satisfaction. On the other hand, the hard-worker represented by the middle section is doing the job which makes for success.

198

Thomas A. Edison, who used to go almost without any sleep, is represented by the bottom section.

How can a policy of moderate *expenses* be reconciled with the principle of "nothing but the best"?

All provisions should be limited by being kept within "the fitness of things". The expenditure of the most money does not necessarily produce the best results. The essential requirement is to obtain the best value for money expended.

## A SIMPLE CREED

He said: "Who then are the true philosophers?"
"Those," I said, "who are lovers of the vision of truth."

PLATO

# CHAIRMEN, DIRECTORS, CHIEF EXECUTIVES, AND SECRETARIES
## QANTAS EMPIRE AIRWAYS LTD
### 1946–66

#### CHAIRMEN

| | |
|---|---|
| Sir Fergus McMaster | 22/1/34–30/6/47 |
| Sir Hudson Fysh | |
| chairman and | |
| managing director  1/7/47–30/6/55 ⎫ | 1/7/47–30/6/66 |
| chairman  1/7/55–30/6/66 ⎭ | |
| Sir Roland Wilson | 1/7/66– |

#### DIRECTORS

| | |
|---|---|
| Sir Hudson Fysh | 22/1/34–30/6/55 |
| (managing director) | |
| F. E. Loxton | 22/1/34–30/6/47 |
| A. E. Rudder | 22/1/34–21/3/47 |
| (vice chairman) | |
| F. J. Smith | 22/1/34–23/11/47 |
| Sir Keith Smith | 24/8/45–19/12/55 |
| W. C. Taylor | 21/3/47–2/8/61 |
| (vice chairman) | |
| G. P. N. Watt | 21/3/47–30/6/62 |
| A. R. McComb | 16/8/47–30/12/47 |
| Sir Daniel McVey | 2/9/47–15/6/61 |
| Sir Roland Wilson | 1/7/54–30/6/66 |
| R. R. Law-Smith | 21/5/56– |
| (vice chairman from 3/8/61) | |
| Sir Norman Nock | 16/6/61–30/6/66 |
| Sir James Kirby | 3/8/61– |
| A. M. C. Buttfield | 1/7/62–30/6/65 |
| J. M. Fotheringham | 1/7/65– |
| T. J. N. Foley | 1/7/66– |
| K. C. Wilkinson | 1/7/66– |

#### CHIEF EXECUTIVES AND GENERAL MANAGERS

| | |
|---|---|
| Sir Hudson Fysh | 21/1/34–30/6/55 |
| (managing director) | |
| H. H. Harman | 1/9/45–30/6/51 |
| (general manager) | |
| C. O. Turner | |
| (general manager) | 1/7/51–30/6/55 |
| (chief executive and general manager) | 1/7/55–30/6/67 |

#### SECRETARIES TO THE BOARD

| | |
|---|---|
| I. O. G. Lawson | 24/8/45–31/7/46 |
| I. G. Esplin | 1/8/46–23/5/47 |
| R. E. Fulford | 24/5/47–31/8/51 |
| N. H. Hay | 1/9/51–1/3/52 |
| F. C. Derham | 2/3/52–31/10/69 |

# AUSTRALIAN PRIME MINISTERS, MINISTERS IN CHARGE OF CIVIL AVIATION, AND HEADS OF CIVIL AVIATION ORGANIZATION
## 1946-66

PRIME MINISTERS

| | |
|---|---|
| Joseph Benedict Chifley | 13/7/45–19/12/49 |
| Robert Gordon Menzies | 19/12/49–26/1/66 |
| Harold Edward Holt | 26/1/66–19/12/67 |

MINISTERS IN CHARGE OF CIVIL AVIATION

| | |
|---|---|
| A. S. Drakeford | 7/10/41–19/12/49 |
| T. W. White | 19/12/49–11/5/51 |
| H. L. Anthony | 11/5/51–9/7/54 |
| A. G. Townley | 9/7/54–24/10/56 |
| S. D. Paltridge | 24/10/56–10/6/64 |
| N. H. D. Henty | 10/6/64–26/1/66 |
| R. W. C. Swartz | 26/1/66–12/11/69 |

HEADS OF CIVIL AVIATION ORGANIZATION

| | | | |
|---|---|---|---|
| Daniel McVey | Director-General | | 17/2/44–10/6/46 |
| Air Marshal Sir Richard Williams, K.B.E., C.B., C.B.E., D.S.O. | ,, | ,, | 11/6/46–31/12/55 |
| Donald George Anderson, C.B.E. | ,, | ,, | 1/1/56– |

# BRITISH PRIME MINISTERS, CIVIL AVIATION HEADS, AND BOAC HEADS
## 1946–66

### PRIME MINISTERS

| | | |
|---|---|---|
| Winston Leonard Spencer Churchill, K.G. 1953 | | 26th October 1951 |
| Sir Robert Anthony Eden, K.G. 1954 | | 6th April 1955 |
| Maurice Harold Macmillan | | 10th January 1957 |
| Sir Alex Douglas-Home | | 19th October 1963 |
| Harold Wilson | | 16th October 1964 |

### MINISTERS

#### MINISTRY OF CIVIL AVIATION

| | |
|---|---|
| Lord Winster | August 1945–October 1946 |
| Lord Nathan | October 1946–June 1948 |
| Lord Pakenham | June 1948–May 1951 |
| Lord Ogmore | June 1951–October 1951 |

#### MINISTRY OF TRANSPORT AND CIVIL AVIATION

| | |
|---|---|
| J. S. Maclay | November 1951–May 1952 |
| A. Lennox-Boyd | May 1952–August 1954 |
| J. A. Boyd-Carpenter | August 1954–December 1955 |
| H. A. Watkinson | December 1955–October 1959 |

#### MINISTRY OF AVIATION

| | |
|---|---|
| D. Sandys | October 1959–July 1960 |
| C. E. P. Thorneycroft | July 1960–July 1962 |
| J. Amery | July 1962–October 1964 |
| R. H. Jenkins | October 1964–December 1965 |
| F. W. Mulley | December 1965–January 1967 |

### HEADS OF BRITISH CIVIL AVIATION

W. P. Hildred, C.B., O.B.E.    Director-General of Civil Aviation    October 1941–6

#### PERMANENT SECRETARIES—MINISTRY OF CIVIL AVIATION

| | |
|---|---|
| Sir Henry Self, K.C.B., K.C.M.G., K.B.E. | 1946–7 |
| Sir Arnold Overton, K.C.B., K.C.M.G., M.C. | 1947–53 |

#### PERMANENT SECRETARY—MINISTRY OF TRANSPORT AND CIVIL AVIATION

| | |
|---|---|
| Sir Gilmour Jenkins, K.C.B., K.B.E., M.C. | 1953–9 |

#### PERMANENT SECRETARIES—MINISTRY OF AVIATION

| | |
|---|---|
| Sir Henry Hardman | 1959–63 |
| Sir Richard Way | 1963–6 |

# APPENDIX 4

BRITISH OVERSEAS AIRWAYS CORPORATION

### CHAIRMEN

| | |
|---|---|
| Lord Knollys, K.C.M.G., M.B.E., D.F.C. | 26/5/43–30/6/47 |
| Sir Harold Hartley, K.C.V.O., C.B.E., M.C., F.R.S. | 1/7/47–30/6/49 |
| Sir Miles Thomas, D.F.C., M.I.Mech.E. | 1/7/49–30/4/56 |
| (chairman and chief executive) | |
| Sir Gerard d'Erlanger, C.B.E. | 1/5/56–28/7/60 |
| Sir Matthew Slattery, K.B.E., C.B., D.Sc., F.R.Ae.S. | 29/7/60–31/12/63 |
| Sir Giles Guthrie Bt., O.B.E., D.S.C., J.P. | 1/1/64–31/12/68 |
| (chairman and chief executive) | |

### CHIEF EXECUTIVES

| | |
|---|---|
| Hon. W. L. Runciman, O.B.E., A.F.C. | 24/11/39–24/3/43 |
| Brig. Gen. A. C. Critchley, C.M.G., C.B.E., D.S.O. | 26/5/43–31/3/46 |
| (director-general) | |
| Whitney W. Straight, C.B.E., M.C., D.F.C. | 1/7/47–1/7/49 |
| (chief executive) | |
| Sir Miles Thomas, D.F.C., M.I.Mech.E. | 1/7/49–30/4/56 |
| (chairman and chief executive) | |
| Basil Smallpiece | 1/5/56–31/12/63 |
| (managing director) (knighted 1961) | |
| Sir Giles Guthrie Bt., O.B.E., D.S.C., J.P. | 1/1/64–31/12/68 |
| (chairman and chief executive) | |

# QANTAS EMPIRE AIRWAYS "FIRSTS"
## 1948–65

| | |
|---|---|
| First survey flight Australia to South Africa | 14/11/48 |
| First regular air service to South Africa | 1/9/52 |
| First round world service through the U.S.A. | 14/1/58 |
| First regular service from Australia with civil jet aircraft, the Boeing 707 | 29/7/59 |

## QEA FINANCIAL STATISTICS
### 1945/6–1965/6

| Year | Paid up Capital £ | Net profit after tax £ | Dividend Rate % | Dividend £ | Net profit earned on capital per cent |
|---|---|---|---|---|---|
| (31 March) 1945-6 | 523,000 | 54,061 | 7 | 36,610 | 10.34 |
| 1946–47 | 523,000 | 65,705 | 7 | 36,610 | 12.56 |
| 1947–48 | 523,000 | 79,900 | 5 | 26,150 | 15.28 |
| April/Dec. 1948 | 2,523,000 | 104,384 | 5 | 71,757 | 7.27 |
| (31 Dec.) 1949 | 3,623,000 | 213,185 | 5½ | 156,779 | 7.46 |
| 1950 | 4,000,000 | 197,024 | 3½ | 127,492 | 5.41 |
| 1951 | 4,000,000 | 222,666 |  | — | 5.57 |
| 1952 | 4,000,000 | 211,932 | 3½ | 140,000 | 5.28 |
| 1953 | 5,000,000 | 551,466 | 3½ | 157,980 | 12.26 |
| 1954 | 5,000,000 | 328,277 | 5½ | 275,000 | 6.57 |
| 1955 | 6,500,000 | 401,329 | 5½ | 317,644 | 6.48 |
| 1956 | 7,200,000 | 484,477 | 5½ | 378,068 | 7.05 |
| 1957 | 8,700,000 | 344,039 | 4½ | 340,233 | 4.30 |
| 1958 | 9,950,000 | 419,097 | 4½ | 400,170 | 4.71 |
| 1959 | 13,700,000 | 853,963 | 5 | 596,130 | 7.16 |
| (15 months) 1960–1 | 14,800,000 | 671,892 | 3½ | 633,108 | 3.71 |
| (31 March) 1961–2 | 16,200,000 | 408,817 | 3 | 477,690 | 2.57 |
| 1962–3 | 17,700,000 | 1,406,246 | 5½ | 952,931 | 8.12 |
| 1963–4 | 17,700,000 | 1,797,508 | 5½ | 973,500 | 10.16 |
| 1964–5 | 17,700,000 | 2,050,506 | 6½ | 1,150,500 | 11.58 |
| 1965–6 | $35,400,000 | $4,030,183 | 7½ | $2,655,000 | 11.38 |

# AIRCRAFT OWNED OR OPERATED BY QEA
## 1946–66

| Aircraft | Engines | Registration | Capacity | Approx. cruising speed m.p.h. | Disposal |
|---|---|---|---|---|---|
| Short S23 Empire Flying Boat | 4 × 920 h.p. Bristol Pegasus XC | VH-ABG *Coriolanus* | 5 crew 15 pass. | 165 | Broken up Rose Bay 1948 |
| Liberator LB30 | 4 × 1200 h.p. Pratt & Whitney R1830-92 | VH-EAI | 5 crew 16 pass. | 200 | Broken up Mascot 1950 |
| ,, | ,, | VH-EAJ | ,, | ,, | ,, |
| Avro 691 Lancastrian | 4 × 1635 h.p. Rolls Royce Merlin T24/2 | G-AGLS | 5 crew 9 pass. (seats, day) 6 pass. (bunks, night) | 230 | — |
| ,, | ,, | G-AGLT | ,, | ,, | — |
| ,, | ,, | G-AGLV | ,, | ,, | — |
| ,, | ,, | G-AGLW | ,, | ,, | — |
| ,, | ,, | G-AGLX | ,, | ,, | Lost at sea 23/3/46—Indian Ocean |
| ,, | ,, | G-AGLY | ,, | ,, | — |
| ,, | ,, | G-AGLZ | ,, | ,, | — |
| ,, | ,, | G-AGMA | ,, | ,, | — |
| ,, | ,, | G-AGMB | ,, | ,, | — |
| ,, | ,, | G-AGMC | ,, | ,, | — |
| ,, | ,, | G-AGMD | ,, | ,, | — |
| ,, | ,, | G-AGME | ,, | ,, | — |
| ,, | ,, | G-AGMF | ,, | ,, | — |
| ,, | ,, | G-AGMG | ,, | ,, | — |
| ,, | ,, | G-AGMH | ,, | ,, | — |
| ,, | ,, | G-AGMJ | ,, | ,, | — |
| ,, | ,, | G-AGMK | ,, | ,, | — |
| ,, | ,, | G-AGML | ,, | ,, | — |
| ,, | ,, | G-AGMM | ,, | ,, | — |

Lancastrians were withdrawn from passenger services on the Kangaroo route in 1947. Qantas purchased four of these aircraft for use on other services.

| | | | | | |
|---|---|---|---|---|---|
| ,, | ,, | VH-EAS | ,, | ,, | Crashed 7/4/49, Dubbo, N.S.W. |
| ,, | ,, | VH-EAT | ,, | ,, | Broken up Mascot, 1952 |
| ,, | ,, | VH-EAU | ,, | ,, | ,, |
| ,, | ,, | VH-EAV | ,, | ,, | Crashed 17/11/51, Mascot. |

| Aircraft | Engines | Registration | Capacity | Approx. cruising speed m.p.h. | Disposal |
|---|---|---|---|---|---|
| Short S25 "Hythe" Class Flying Boat | 4 × 1030 h.p. Bristol Pegasus 38 or 48 | G-AGER | 7 crew 16-24 pass. | 170 | — |
| ,, | ,, | G-AGEU | ,, | ,, | — |
| ,, | ,, | G-AGEW | ,, | ,, | Sank at Sourabaya, 5/9/48 |
| ,, | ,, | G-AGHW | ,, | ,, | — |
| ,, | ,, | G-AGHX | ,, | ,, | — |
| ,, | ,, | G-AGHZ | ,, | ,, | — |
| ,, | ,, | G-AGIA | ,, | ,, | — |
| ,, | ,, | G-AGJJ | ,, | ,, | — |
| ,, | ,, | G-AGJK | ,, | ,, | — |
| ,, | ,, | G-AGJL | ,, | ,, | — |
| ,, | ,, | G-AGJM | ,, | ,, | — |
| ,, | ,, | G-AGJN | ,, | ,, | — |
| ,, | ,, | G-AGJO | ,, | ,, | — |
| ,, | ,, | G-AGKV | ,, | ,, | — |
| ,, | ,, | G-AGKW | ,, | ,, | — |
| ,, | ,, | G-AGKY | ,, | ,, | — |
| ,, | ,, | G-AGKZ | ,, | ,, | — |
| ,, | ,, | G-AGLA | ,, | ,, | — |
| Douglas C53 | 2 × 1050 h.p. Pratt & Whitney R1830 | VH-CCB | 2 crew | 170 | Returned to U.S.A.A.F. 20/4/46 |
| ,, | ,, | VH-CCC | ,, | ,, | ,, |
| ,, | ,, | VH-CWA | ,, | ,, | ,, |
| Douglas C47 Converted to DC-3 | ,, | VH-AEY | ,, | ,, | Returned to Australian National Airlines Comm. April 1947 |
| ,, | ,, | VH-AEZ | ,, | ,, | ,, |
| ,, | ,, | VH-AFA | ,, | ,, | Returned to Australian National Airlines Comm. Sept. 1946 |

QEA purchased its own DC-3s after the war and fourteen of them were in service by early 1950. Only eight remained by 1955 and all of these were sold when the company withdrew from New Guinea in 1960. There were eleven changes in individual registrations of DC-3s between 1949 and 1958. In the table below, each aircraft's Constructor's Number is shown first, followed by its registrations in the order they were carried. The date when a registration was changed is shown in parentheses.

| Aircraft | Engines | Registration | Capacity | Approx. cruising speed m.p.h. | Disposal |
|---|---|---|---|---|---|
| Douglas DC3 | 2 × 1200 h.p. Pratt & Whitney R1830-92 | C/N25491 VH-AIH VH-EBH (2/50) | 3 crew 21 pass. | 170 | Sold—Royal Thai Air Force 11/53 |
| ,, | ,, | C/N13622 VH-AII; VH-EBI (9/49) | ,, | ,, | Sold—Trans-Aust. Airlines 11/50 |

| Aircraft | Engines | Registration | Capacity | Approx. cruising speed m.p.h. | Disposal |
|---|---|---|---|---|---|
| Douglas DC3 | 2 × 1200 h.p. Pratt & Whitney R1830-92 | C/N12667 VH-AIJ; VH-EBJ (9/49) | 3 crew 21 pass. | 170 | Sold—Royal Thai Air Force 11/53 |
| ,, | ,, | C/N12872 VH-EAK | ,, | ,, | ,, |
| ,, | ,, | C/N13084 VH-EAL; VH-EBH (8/54) VH-EBW (3/58) | ,, | ,, | Sold—Brown & Bain |
| ,, | ,, | C/N9286 VH-EAM | ,, | ,, | Sold—East-West Airlines 7/53 |
| ,, | ,, | C/N12187 VH-EAN; VH-EBF (5/56) VH-EBU (1/58) | ,, | ,, | Sold—TAA 1960 |
| ,, | ,, | C/N25367 VH-EAO; VH-EBX (8/57) | ,, | ,, | Sold—TAA 1960 |
| ,, | ,, | C/N12873 VH-EAP; VH-EBY (1/57) | ,, | ,, | ,, |
| ,, | ,, | C/N11870 VH-EAQ | ,, | ,, | ,, |
| ,, | ,, | C/N12035 VH-EAR | ,, | ,, | Sold—W. R. Carpenter 1960 |
| ,, | ,, | C/N10000 VH-EBE; VH-EBT (2/58) | ,, | ,, | Sold—TAA 1960 |
| ,, | ,, | C/N12248 VH-EBF | ,, | ,, | Sold—Royal Thai Air Force 11/53 |
| ,, | ,, | C/N12541 VH-EBG; VH-EBV (9/57) | ,, | ,, | Sold—TAA 1960 |

Three DC-3s were chartered by QEA in 1948. These were VH-BHD and VH-BHE owned by the Zinc Corporation, used as freighters, and VH-AEO, owned by Trans-Australia Airlines.

| Aircraft | Engines | Registration | Capacity | Approx. cruising speed m.p.h. | Disposal |
|---|---|---|---|---|---|
| Douglas DC3 | 2 × 1200 h.p. Pratt & Whitney R1830-92 | VH-EDC | 3 crew 21 pass. | 170 | Still in Qantas service |
| ,, | ,, | VH-EDD | ,, | ,, | ,, |

| Aircraft | Engines | Registration | Capacity | Approx. cruising speed m.p.h. | Disposal |
|---|---|---|---|---|---|
| Catalina PB2B-2 | 2 × 1200 h.p. Pratt & Whitney R1830 Twin Wasp | VH-EAW | 4 crew 14 pass. (Pacific Is. services) 22-31 pass. (New Guinea services) | 105 | Destroyed by explosion Rose Bay 27/8/49 |
| ,, | ,, | VH-EAX | ,, | ,, | Mooring broken—washed onto rocks, Lord Howe Island 23/6/49 |
| ,, | ,, | VH-EBA | ,, | ,, | Reduced to spares March 1954 |
| ,, | ,, | VH-EBC *Island Chieftain* | ,, | ,, | Reduced to spares November 1958 |
| ,, | ,, | VH-EBD *Island Patrol* | ,, | ,, | ,, |
| ,, | ,, | VH-EBU *Island Warrior* | ,, | ,, | Reduced to spares March 1954 |
| Lockheed Constellation L749 | 4 × 2500 h.p. Wright Cyclone R3350-C18BD1 | VH-EAA *Ross Smith* | 10 crew 38 pass. | 300 | Sold to BOAC February 1955 |
| ,, | ,, | VH-EAB *Lawrence Hargrave* | ,, | ,, | ,, |
| ,, | ,, | VH-EAC *Harry Hawker* | ,, | ,, | Sold to Aerovias Guest, Mexico, October 1955 |
| ,, | ,, | VH-EAD *Charles Kingsford-Smith* | ,, | ,, | ,, |
| ,, | ,, | VH-EAE *Bert Hinkler* | ,, | ,, | Sold to BOAC August 1954 |
| ,, | ,, | VH-EAF *Horace Brinsmead* | ,, | ,, | Sold to BOAC July 1954 |
| ,, | ,, | G-ALAN *Beaufort* | ,, | ,, | On charter from BOAC. Operated by QEA from July 1948 to April 1950 |
| Douglas DC4 Skymaster | 4 × 1450 h.p. Pratt & Whitney R2000-D5 | VH-EBK *Malayan Trader* | 7 crew 44-50 pass. | 210 | Still in service with Qantas, now VH-EDA *Norfolk Trader* |
| ,, | ,, | VH-EBL *Hong Kong Trader* | ,, | ,, | Sold to Ansett-ANA Jan. 1961 |
| ,, | ,, | VH-EBM *Philippine Trader* | ,, | ,, | Sold to Zantop Air Transport October 1959 |

209

| Aircraft | Engines | Registration | Capacity | Approx. cruising speed m.p.h. | Disposal |
|---|---|---|---|---|---|
| Douglas DC4 Skymaster | 4 × 1450 h.p. Pratt & Whitney R2000-D5 | VH-EBN *New Guinea Trader* | 7 crew 44:50 pass. | ,, | Still in service with Qantas. Now VH-EDB *Pacific Trader* |
| ,, | ,, | VH-EBO *Pacific Trader* | ,, | ,, | Sold to Air Carrier Service Corp. U.S.A. May 1956 |
| ,, | ,, | VH-EBP *Australian Trader* | ,, | ,, | Sold—to Zantop Air Transport October 1959 |
| Short S25 Sandring-ham | 4 × 1200 h.p. Pratt & Whitney R1830 Twin Wasp | VH-EBV *Pacific Warrior* | 7 crew 30 pass. | 145 | Reduced to spares at Rose Bay June 1955 |
| ,, | ,, | VH-EBW | ,, | ,, | Holed and sunk Vila 10/6/51. Total loss |
| ,, | ,, | VH-EBX *Pacific Chieftain* | ,, | ,, | Sold to Ansett Airways December 1954 |
| ,, | ,, | VH-EBY *Pacific Voyager* | ,, | ,, | Reduced to spares at Rose Bay July 1955 |
| ,, | ,, | VH-EBZ *Pacific Explorer* | ,, | ,, | Reduced to spares at Rose Bay June 1955 |
| Lockheed Super Constellation L.1049 | 4 × 3250 h.p. Wright Turbo Compound R3350-TC18-DA3 | VH-EAA *Southern Sea* | 10-12 crew 39 pass. In all First Class config. or 27 Deluxe 30 Tourist or 60 all Tourist | 335 | Sold to Eagle Aircraft, U.S.A. Departed Sydney January 1963 |
| ,, | ,, | VH-EAB *Southern Horizon* | ,, | ,, | Sold West Coast Airmotive Corp. Departed Sydney March 1963 |
| ,, | ,, | VH-EAC *Southern Wave* | ,, | ,, | Crashed at Mauritius 25/8/60 |
| ,, | ,, | VH-EAD *Southern Dawn* | ,, | ,, | Sold to Lockheed March 1960 |
| ,, | ,, | VH-EAE *Southern Moon* | ,, | ,, | ,, |
| ,, | ,, | VH-EAF *Southern Wind* | ,, | ,, | Reduced to spares in U.S.A. Departed Sydney April 1963 |
| ,, | ,, | VH-EAG *Southern Constellation* | ,, | ,, | Reduced to spares in U.S.A. Departed Sydney May 1963 |
| ,, | ,, | VH-EAH *Southern Sky* | ,, | ,, | Sold to Lockheed November 1959 |
| ,, | ,, | VH-EAI* *Southern Sun* | ,, | ,, | Sold to Lockheed December 1959 |

* (VH-EAI, renamed *Southern Boomerang* was leased from Lockheed in November 1960, while QEA's four L.188 Electras were returned to Lockheed for wing modifications. VH-EAI was returned April 1961 to Lockheed.)

| Aircraft | Engines | Registration | Capacity | Approx. cruising speed m.p.h. | Disposal |
|---|---|---|---|---|---|
| Lockheed Super Constellation L.1049 | 4 × 3250 h.p. Wright Turbo Compound R3350-TC18-DA3 | VH-EAJ *Southern Star* | 10-12 crew 39 pass. In all First Class config. or 27 Deluxe 30 Tourist or 60 all Tourist | 335 | Sold to Lockheed January 1960 |
| ,, | ,, | VH-EAK *Southern Mist* | ,, | ,, | Reduced to spares in U.S.A. Departed Sydney February 1963 |
| ,, | ,, | VH-EAL *Southern Breeze* | ,, | ,, | Sold to Lockheed November 1959 |
| ,, | ,, | VH-EAM *Southern Spray* | ,, | ,, | Sold to Air Newmex U.S.A. Departed Sydney July 1962 |
| ,, | ,, | VH-EAN *Southern Tide* | ,, | ,, | ,, |
| ,, | ,, | VH-EAO† *Southern Aurora* | ,, | ,, | Sold to Lockheed October 1959 |
| ,, | ,, | VH-EAP *Southern Zephyr* | ,, | ,, | ,, |

† (VH-EAO, renamed *Southern Prodigal*, was repurchased in August 1960 and departed Sydney in March 1963, sold to California Airmotive Corporation.)

| Aircraft | Engines | Registration | Capacity | Approx. cruising speed m.p.h. | Disposal |
|---|---|---|---|---|---|
| Boeing 707-138 | 4 × 13,000 lb.st. Pratt & Whitney JT3C-6 Turbo Jet | VH-EBA *City of Melbourne* | 10 crew 36 First Class pass. & 54 Economy or 120 all Economy | 550 | |
| ,, | ,, | VH-EBB *City of Sydney* | ,, | ,, | — |
| ,, | ,, | VH-EBC *City of Canberra* | ,, | ,, | — |
| ,, | ,, | VH-EBD *City of Brisbane* | ,, | ,, | |
| ,, | ,, | VH-EBE *City of Perth* | ,, | ,, | — |
| ,, | ,, | VH-EBF *City of Adelaide* | ,, | ,, | |
| ,, | ,, | VH-EBG *City of Hobart* | ,, | ,, | — |

All seven Boeing 707-138 aircraft were returned to the Boeing factory between July 1961 and January 1962 for modification to Boeing 707-138B specifications, i.e., fitting of turbo-fan engines and alterations to wings and tail surfaces.

211

| Aircraft | Engines | Registration | Capacity | Approx. cruising speed m.p.h. | Disposal |
|---|---|---|---|---|---|
| Lockheed Electra L188C | 4 × 3750 h.p. Allison 501-D13 Turbo Prop | VH-ECA *Pacific Electra* | 9 crew 16 First Class pass. 47 Economy | 400 | — |
| ,, | ,, | VH-ECB *Pacific Explorer* | ,, | ,, | — |
| ,, | ,, | VH-ECC *Pacific Endeavour* | ,, | ,, | Sold to Air New Zealand April 1965 |
| ,, | ,, | VH-ECD *Pacific Enterprise* | ,, | ,, | |
| Boeing 707-138B | 4 × 18,000 lbs. Pratt & Whitney JT3D-1 Turbo Fan | VH-EBH *City of Darwin* | 10 crew 20 First Class pass. & 84 Economy or 120 all Economy | 580 | — |
| ,, | ,, | VH-EBI *Winton* | ,, | ,, | — |
| ,, | ,, | VH-EBJ *Longreach* | ,, | ,, | — |
| ,, | ,, | VH-EBK *City of Newcastle* | ,, | ,, | — |
| ,, | ,, | VH-EBL *City of Geelong* | ,, | ,, | — |
| ,, | ,, | VH-EBM *City of Launceston* | ,, | ,, | — |
| Boeing 707-338C | 4 × 18,500 lb. Pratt &. Whitney JT3D-3B Turbo Fan | VH-EBN *City of Parramatta* | 10 crew 20 First Class pass. 84 Economy & 630 cu. ft. cargo space on upper deck or 165 pass. all Economy | 550 | — |
| ,, | ,, | VH-EBO *City of Townsville* | ,, | ,, | — |
| ,, | ,, | VH-EBP *Alice Springs* | ,, | ,, | — |
| ,, | ,, | VH-EBQ *City of Ballarat* | ,, | ,, | — |
| ,, | ,, | VH-EBR *City of Wollongong* | ,, | ,, | — |
| ,, | ,, | VH-EBS *Kalgoorlie* | ,, | ,, | — |

In addition to the preceding mainline aircraft, Qantas operated:

| | |
|---|---|
| 17 DH84 Dragons | 4 DHC.2 Beavers |
| 2 C.A.C. Wackett Trainers | 1 Avro Anson |
| 5 DHA.3 Drovers | 2 Vickers Supermarine Sea Otters |
| 4 DHC.3 Otters | 1 Grumman G44A Widgeon |

APPENDIX 8

## ACCIDENTS TO QEA AIRCRAFT
### 1946–66

Excluding Accidents to Light Aircraft

| Date | Aircraft | Captain | Location | Nature of Accident | Damage to Aircraft | Injuries Sustained |
|---|---|---|---|---|---|---|
| 23/3/46 | Lancastrian G-AGLY | O. F. Y. Thomas | Probably vicinity Cocos Is. | Aircraft disappeared in flight between Colombo and Cocos Island. | No wreckage located | Crew: 5 killed Pass.: 5 killed |
| 2/5/46 | Lancastrian G-AGMC | J. J. Griffith | Mascot | During landing attempt aircraft struck sandbank 60 yards from end of runway, collapsing undercarriage. | Starboard mainplane, engines, undercarriage and tailplane extensively damaged. Fuselage slightly damaged | Nil |
| 22/1/47 | Lockheed 14 VH-ADT | K. G. Jackson | Schofields | During take-off the aircraft swung slightly to port and then violently to starboard. Aircraft left the runway, and port undercarriage collapsed after striking small log. Fire broke out immediately. | Damaged beyond repair by impact and fire | Nil |
| 31/1/47 | Lancastrian G-AGMB | A. R. H. Morris | Mascot | After landing, the aircraft swung to port violently and the undercarriage was torn off when it sank into soft sand. | Undercarriage destroyed, starboard engine badly damaged, lower portion of fuselage extensively damaged; all propellers bent. Nose portion of aircraft dented and twisted | Nil |
| 10/4/47 | DH84 VH-AON | F. S. Furniss | Kainantu | After landing, the aircraft overshot the runway and fell into a deep ditch. | Both undercarriage legs collapsed. Mainplane slightly damaged. Nose of aircraft damaged. Port propeller broken | Nil |
| 14/7/47 | DH84 VH-BHF | R. K. Crabbe | Wampit River | Owing to low cloud aircraft entered valley which was unknown to pilot, with insufficient height to clear rising ground and continued on until crashing into trees. | Aircraft damaged beyond repair | Crew: 1 slightly hurt Pass.: 1 seriously hurt |

| Date | Aircraft | Captain | Location | Remarks | Damage | Injuries |
|---|---|---|---|---|---|---|
| | Widgeon VH-AZO | | | third and final impact with the water the port wing dropped and aircraft swung violently to port. | ...bent, starboard tailplane fractured and fabric on port wing damaged | *Crew:* 1 slightly hurt *Pass.:* Nil |
| 12/2/48 | Lockheed 10A VH-AEC | D. A. Tennent | Condamine | Aircraft crashed 3 miles south of Condamine while making a forced landing after failure of starboard engines. | Aircraft damaged beyond repair | |
| 19/8/48 | Douglas DC3 VH-EAM | D. A. Tennent | Archerfield | The aircraft crashed during take-off on a test flight for renewal of C of A. | Aircraft extensively damaged requiring complete rebuilding | *Pass.:* 2 injured |
| 27/8/48 | Lancastrian G-AGMB | Garside | Tengah | One hour after departure the aircraft returned to Tengah with No. 4 propeller feathered. During landing the aircraft swung to port and collided with an embankment. | Total loss | |
| 5/9/48 | Hythe Flying Boat G-AGEW | I. C. Peirce | Sourabaya | Flying boat suffered damage to port float while attempting to take-off and subsequently capsized and sank. | Total loss | Nil |
| 21/11/48 | DH84 VH-AMN | G. F. Macrae | Cloncurry | Whilst parked, aircraft was caught in high wind and blown distance of 100 yards. | Both undercarriage assemblies broken; both lower mainplanes and ailerons extensively damaged | Nil |
| 24/11/48 | DH84 VH-AYM | P. R. C. Buchanan | Canobie | During engine starting, fire that could not be controlled started in the starboard engine. | Aircraft destroyed by fire | Nil |
| 22/3/49 | DH84 | J. R. Rose | Kerowagi to Goroka | In bad weather Rose flew along a road which was under construction, at a low altitude; he had just completed a turn to the left and was commencing a right hand turn when he became aware of a rending noise. He immediately throttled back and continued flight to Garoka at a reduced speed. | Wing damage | Nil |
| 7/4/49 | Lancastrian VH-EAS | J. G. Morton | Dubbo | After landing aircraft could not be brought to a stop within the limits of the runway. The undercarriage collapsed during deliberate ground loop and fire broke out. | Aircraft destroyed by impact and fire | Nil |

| Date | Aircraft | Captain | Location | Nature of Accident | Damage to Aircraft | Injuries Sustained |
|---|---|---|---|---|---|---|
| 10/5/49 | Anson VH-BBZ | D. N. Mitchell | Kerowagi | During take-off aircraft swung off runway and was extensively damaged when port undercarriage collapsed on striking a small drain. | Mainplane front and rear spars fractured; tailplane rear spar fractured and port undercarriage torn away | *Crew:* 1 slightly hurt |
| 15/9/49 | Lancastrian VH-EAV | J. H. Cole | Mascot | During landing a deliberate ground loop to port was carried out but during this manoeuvre the starboard and then the port undercarriage struts collapsed. | Aircraft extensively damaged | Nil |
| 30/10/49 | L1049 VH-EAA | J. P. Shields | Darwin | Flap panels extensively damaged during retraction by coming into contact with a loading rostrum. | Extensive | Nil |
| 10/12/49 | DH84 VH-AOR | R. E. Biddolph | Chimbu | The undercarriage was extensively damaged when landing at Chimbu. | Extensive | Nil |
| 17/2/50 | DH84 VH-AXL | L. W. Purkiss | Banz | After landing, the aircraft swung to starboard; an attempt to prevent this was of no avail as the rudder was jammed. | Extensive wing and fuselage damage | Nil |
| 9/3/50 | DC3 VH-EAR | Twenblow | Hayfields | When landing it became apparent that the surface of the strip was greasy and the brakes were ineffective and with no wind there was insufficient space to stop. | Wing damage | Nil |
| 24/11/50 | DH83 VH-URI | W. H. Carter | Boana | After the take-off was abandoned the aircraft entered kunai grass at the end of the strip and nosed over. | Extensive | *Pass.:* 1 seriously hurt |
| 4/4/51 | Sandringham VH-EBW | H. M. Birch | Rose Bay | During a landing run the starboard float carried away and the wing entered the water but the aircraft was saved by crew members and passengers on the port wing tip. | Extensive wing and float damage | Nil |
| 13/4/51 | Lancastrian VH-EAV | G. Jakimov | Singapore | Towards the end of the landing run a ground loop resulted in undercarriage collapse. | Aircraft extensively damaged | Nil |
| 10/6/51 | Sandringham VH-EBW | P. J. R. Shields | Vila, New Hebrides | Whilst being taxied prior to take-off, VH-EBW struck a coral niggerhead. | The flying boat was holed below the water line at several places between the keel and | Nil |

216

| Date | Aircraft | Pilot | Location | Description | Damage | Casualties |
|---|---|---|---|---|---|---|
| | VH-EAO | | | being taxied to the take-off position; it was not until the aircraft had moved another 150 yards that they became aware of it. The fire was extinguished by the ground staff. | head damage | Nil |
| 16/7/51 | DHA3 Drover VH-EBQ | J. W. Speire | Lae | The aircraft crashed into the sea approx. 4½ miles south of the mouth of the Markham River, and approx. one mile off shore. | Total loss | Crew: 1 killed Pass.: 6 killed |
| 3/9/51 | Sandringham VH-EBX | L. W. Clarke | Rose Bay | The port wing was severely damaged when landing at Rose Bay was being carried out and a collision occured with the D.C.A. control launch. | Port wing extensively damaged | Nil |
| 21/9/51 | DH84 Dragon VH-AXI | F. G. Barlogie | Karanka | During flight the aircraft crashed near Kamvaira Village approx. half a mile from the eastern end of Karanka Airstrip, New Guinea. | Total loss | Crew: 1 killed |
| 8/11/51 | Douglas DC4 VH-EBM | G. A. Condell | Mascot | Nose wheel retracted at the end of the landing run on the 04 runway at Mascot | Front fuselage extensively damaged | Pass.: 1 minor abrasion |
| 17/11/51 | Lancastrian VH-EAV | R. M. Mullins | Mascot | Crashed during take-off | Damaged beyond repair | Nil |
| 13/12/51 | Dragon DH84 VH-URV | S. W. Peebles | Yaramanda, N.G. | The aircraft after having flown over Yaramanda airstrip at a low altitude flew into rising ground and was forced to enter the Minyemba River gorge until it could no longer clear rising terrain. | Total loss | Crew: 1 killed Pass.: 2 killed |
| 24/12/51 | DH84 VH-URD | R. J. Davis | Menyamya, N.G. | The aircraft when flying into Menyamya airstrip, was unable to maintain height and crashed. The pilot failed to appreciate the descending air after having observed that there was a wind at sufficient strength at ground level to prohibit landing. | Damage to the aircraft was extensive and economical repair was not possible | Crew: 1 slight abrasion |
| 31/1/52 | Sandringham VH-EBY | J. W. Solly | Rose Bay | Shortly after commencing take-off run the flying boat swung to port and in attempting to correct the swing the pilot inadvertently closed No. 3 throttle in mistake. | Extensively damaged | Nil |
| 23/7/52 | D.C.3 VH-EAL | L. Purkiss | Kavieng | During landing with flaps fully down the aircraft entered a water area on the strip resulting in extensive damage to the flap system. | Extensive | Nil |

| Date | Aircraft | Captain | Location | Nature of Accident | Damage to Aircraft | Injuries Sustained |
|---|---|---|---|---|---|---|
| 11/9/52 | DHA3 Drover VH-EBS | R. S. Cuthbertson | Mackay | The centre propeller of DHA3 aircraft failed during take-off at Mackay. | The centre engine installation and engine cowlings were extensively damaged as a result of blade failure | Nil |
| 8/12/53 | D.C.3 VH-EAO | J. C. Johnson | Yandina | The aircraft swung off the runway and the port wing collided with a palm which was growing alongside the strip. | The port wing tip suffered severe damage | Nil |
| 9/12/56 | D.C.4 VH-EBN | C. G. Fox | Norfolk Island | The landing approach was normal until flareout commenced and during this process the aircraft touched down heavily short of the runway. | Extensive fuselage damage | Nil |
| 28/3/58 | DC4 VH-EBN | J. A. Bird | Nadzab, N.G. | The aircraft touched down 1,320 ft. beyond the threshold during which the brakes and nose wheel steering ceased to function. Emergency airbrakes were applied. | All tyres destroyed | Nil |
| 3/8/58 | Otter VH-EAY | K. A. Montagu | Tapini, N.G. | During landing the aircraft swung off the runway and struck an open drain. | Substantial airframe and engine damage | Nil |
| 18/10/58 | DC3 VH-EAQ | I. S. Simpler | Wau, N.G. | The aircraft overran the runway, finally coming to a stop at an angle of 90° to the runway. | Substantial airframe damage | Nil |
| 14/11/58 | L1049 VH-EAP | J. N. Murray | Nadi | On arrival Nadi the aircraft was landed heavily 29 ft short of the runway. | Structural damage to wing | Nil |
| 24/8/60 | L1049 VH-EAC | T. Ditton | Mauritius | Soon after take-off had commenced an engine failure emergency was declared by the F/E and the Captain aborted the take-off. The aircraft did not stop within the overrun limits and was destroyed by impact and fire at the end of the runway. | Total loss by fire | Crew: 2 Pass.: 19 Minor injuries and shock |
| 23/12/64 | B.707-138B VH-EBK | R. C. Houghton | Singapore | Following an error of judgement by both pilots at the point of initial touchdown which caused the aircraft to bounce, incorrect technique was used by captain in the attempts to reland the aircraft, which placed it in such nose-down attitude that the nose wheel struck the runway before | Extensive structural damage in the nose landing gear area | Nil |

218

# SELECTED SPEECHES AND WRITINGS BY THE AUTHOR
## 1947–67

| | |
|---|---|
| 28th August 1947 | The History of Qantas, and Service.<br>Memorandum to QEA staff |
| 2nd November 1947 | 25 Years of Air Transport.<br>A.B.C. talk and pamphlet |
| 14th November 1947 | The QEA Political Tradition and Loyalty.<br>Memorandum to QEA staff |
| December 1947 | Future Operations on the Australia-England Air Route.<br>Pamphlet |
| 26th February 1948 | Air Force Veterans' annual reunion.<br>Address |
| 17th June 1948 | Sir Charles Kingsford Smith.<br>Address to the Australian-American Society |
| 31st July 1949 | Impressions in New Guinea.<br>A.B.C. Broadcast |
| 20th April 1950 | QEA Traditional and Historical Background.<br>Memorandum |
| 1st August 1950 | IATA and Friendship.<br>Pamphlet |
| 1st September 1952 | Opening of QEA Service to South Africa.<br>Speech |
| 3rd August 1952 | Guest of Honour, A.B.C.<br>Talk |
| 1952 | Thirty Years of Air Transport.<br>Pamphlet |
| 28th May 1953 | International Society of Australia.<br>Address |
| 28th July 1953 | Qantas dinner in honour of Knighthood.<br>Speech |
| 7th June 1954 | First Sydney-Vancouver Service operated by QEA.<br>Speech |
| 29th March 1955 | Ethics and other Things. Third edition.<br>Senior staff pamphlet |
| 8th December 1955 | Commemoration dinner in London. 21st anniversary of BOAC-QEA partnership.<br>Speech and pamphlet |
| 9th December 1957 | Tourism as a Business and Human Need.<br>Speech and pamphlet |
| 28th October 1957 | Official opening of Qantas House.<br>Speech |
| 14th January 1958 | Inauguration of QEA Round-the-World Service.<br>Speech |

| | |
|---|---|
| 17th February 1958 | Opening of Sydney Rotary Club Convention.<br>Address |
| 28th April 1958 | "10th December 1919"—Inaugural Sir Ross and Sir Keith Smith Memorial Lecture, Royal Aeronautical Society, Adelaide.<br>Address |
| November 1958 | Visit to Moscow.<br>Pamphlet |
| 11th August 1959 | Entrance of the Jet Age.<br>Sydney Rotary Club address |
| 9th August 1961 | Third Sir Charles Kingsford Smith Memorial Lecture, Royal Aeronautical Society, Sydney.<br>Address |
| 23rd October 1961 | IATA annual general meeting in Sydney.<br>Presidential opening address |
| 13th December 1961 | Launceston Grammar School Prizegiving.<br>Speech |
| 4th June 1962 | World Understanding through Trade. Los Angeles Rotary International Convention.<br>Panelist's address |
| 28th November 1962 | The Engineer in Transport. Cooma Branch of Institute of Engineers.<br>Address |
| 23rd February 1963 | World Peace through Rotary. Rotary conference at Katoomba.<br>Address |
| 12th July 1963 | Some Early Days. Royal Victorian Aero Club.<br>Address |
| 12th November 1964 | The Soldier and Service. Legacy Club of Sydney.<br>Address |
| 10th April 1965 | Opening of Brisbane-Christchurch Boeing 707 Service.<br>Speech |
| 14th June 1965 | Geelong Grammar School Founders Day.<br>Address |
| 10th July 1965 | Unveiling of Qantas Memorial at Winton.<br>Address |
| 14th July 1965 | The Increasing Success of International Airlines.<br>Article in *Airlanes* |
| 29th October 1965 | IATA annual general meeting at Vienna.<br>Valedictory Address for Sir William Hildred |
| 7th August 1966 | A.B.C. Guest of Honour talk.<br>Broadcast |
| 26th April 1967 | Farewell Dinner in London tendered by BOAC.<br>Speech |

## CHRISTMAS MESSAGES TO THE STAFF

| | |
|---|---|
| 1930 | Service and Loyalty |
| 1938 | Qantas, Worth Working For |
| 1939 | We Are at War |
| 1940 | The British Are Unconquerable |
| 1941 | Guns Crash over England |
| 1942 | Our War Job |
| 1948 | Satisfaction through Achievement |
| 1949 | You Lucky People |
| 1950 | Ich Dien, I Serve |
| 1951 | Kookaburra Pie |
| 1952 | Qantas, Bricklayers |
| 1953 | On the Washing of Shirts |
| 1954 | The Shortage of Reindeer in Lapland |
| 1955 | We All Work for Qantas |
| 1956 | On Hobbies |
| 1957 | A Christmas Thought |
| 1958 | Chairman Says Thanks |
| 1959 | Faith and Hope for the Future |
| 1960 | Looking Ahead to 2000 A.D. |
| 1961 | On Loyalty |
| 1962 | Pride in Our Achievements |
| 1963 | My Christmas 60 Years Ago |
| 1964 | Church Chaplains for Industry |
| 1965 | May You Prosper and Advance |

Q

# Index

231